Dogland

A Journey to the Heart of America's Dog Problem

Jacki Skole

Ashland
Creek
Press

Dogland: A Journey to the Heart of America's Dog Problem
By Jacki Skole

Published by Ashland Creek Press
Ashland, Oregon
www.ashlandcreekpress.com

ISBN 978-1-61822-038-7
Library of Congress Control Number: 2014957938

Printed in the United States of America on acid-free paper. All paper products used
to create this book are Sustainable Forestry Initiative (SFI) Certified Sourcing.

Cover design by Matt Smith (www.lilroundhouse.com).
Cover photograph by Shannon Johnstone.

DOGLAND

A Journey to the Heart of America's Dog Problem

JACKI SKOLE

For Kevin, Lindsey, Dhani, Galen, and Gryffin

"Some of our greatest historical and artistic treasures we place with curators in museums; others we take for walks."

— Roger Caras, author and former ASPCA president

Author's Note

While some names and identifying details of people and places in this book have been changed in the interest of privacy, all events are accurate, based on extensive research and firsthand interviews conducted during the reporting and writing of this book. In addition, in the parts of this book that are memoir, certain memories and incidents are portrayed through my own subjective lens; while these conversations and events are accurate to the best of my knowledge, they are based on my own interpretations. Finally, some people quoted in this book may have left the organizations they were associated with during the course of the reporting, writing, and publication of *Dogland*.

Table of Contents

Preface

I PULLED UP TO A HOUSE, not sure I was where I wanted to be. None of the homes in this rural North Carolina neighborhood were numbered, at least not that I could see.

I got out of the car and stepped onto the edge of the property. Glass and plastic bottles, metal canisters, cigarette boxes, and household trash littered the yard, which was a tangle of knee-high grass and overgrown weeds. There was no sidewalk, no pathway to the front door, just a dirt driveway leading to the side of the house. Five very large cats sat on wooden stairs just outside the front door; others slinked through the deep grass—perhaps at one time feral, they now looked well fed.

I wasn't sure I could do this.

The entire drive here my mind had been racing. Would I find the house? Would anyone be home? What would I say, showing up as I was about to do, completely unannounced? I didn't want to be accusatory. I just wanted to find out how Galen and her litter ended up in Gaston County's animal shelter.

The air was thick and hot, as it often is in North Carolina in late August. The house's windows were open, and I could hear muffled talking. I could even make out a man sitting at a table smoking.

Standing there, absorbing my surroundings—the trashed lawn, the run-down mobile home—I found myself hoping I was at the wrong house. I took a few steps onto the property, my eyes focused on the cats. They stared back but didn't relinquish their posts. I have an irrational fear of cats, stemming, I think, from being scratched when I was about five years old. So rather than knock on the door, I stood my ground and called out, "Excuse me!"

Moments later, a man, fiftyish perhaps, in jeans and an untucked, rumpled yellow button-down came to the door, cigarette in hand. He gave me a quick once-over before stepping outside, onto the landing.

I spoke first. "Hi. I know this may sound like an odd question, but did you, by chance, turn a litter of puppies over to Gaston County's animal shelter about two years ago?"

He shook his head. "Don't got a dog."

"I'm looking for house number three-fourteen. Would you know which property it might be?"

He shook his head again.

Silence.

Then he pointed over his shoulder and gestured behind him. "I think a house over that way has dogs."

I thanked him, and a moment later I was back in the car, bumping along the unpaved road. The houses were small but stretched apart, each on about two acres.

Again, those nagging questions. Did I really need to know how Galen came to be in the Gaston County shelter? It would change nothing about our relationship or my love for her. At the same time, I really did want to know, to understand. After all, I was more than 600 miles from home, and, at this point, I felt like my journey—inspired by Galen—was about so much more than one quirky, not-so-little canine. The more people I spoke with, the more research I did, the more I was beginning to grasp the complexity of the crisis—in the South, certainly, but throughout much of the rest of the country, too:

America has a dog problem. It's somewhat hard to believe, as nearly sixty million U.S. households have at least one dog and Americans spend tens of billions of dollars annually satisfying our dogs' needs and our wants. (After all, Fido isn't the one who asked for that rhinestone collar, cashmere sweater, or organic pet food.)

I knew Galen was unwanted—she was surrendered to the shelter by her owner, and the odds were good that Galen was part of an accidental litter, as so many shelter dogs are. Her story, as I was beginning to understand, is one that unfolds daily all across the country. Yet Galen's story, unlike the stories of hundreds of thousands of other dogs, would have a happy ending.

I pulled in front of another house—gray, with several cars crowding the driveway—and looked through the passenger window, into the yard, for any sign of canine inhabitants.

That's when I saw them—two dogs—one tied to a tree several hundred yards to the left of the house and one tied to a shed at the rear of the property.

I took a deep breath and stepped out of the car.

Ready or Not ... Here She Comes

My family was absolutely not ready for a new dog. It was the fall of 2010, and my husband, Kevin, suggested we wait until at least spring—after all, he kept saying, who wants to take a puppy out to pee in the middle of the night ... in the middle of winter? I certainly didn't want to, our daughters were too young to, and Kevin made clear he wouldn't. We would wait.

Yes, we would wait.

Then, sometime in late October, I started browsing through Petfinder, the online database that connects homeless animals with people looking for a new pet. I told myself I was just getting a sense of how the site worked so that, come spring, I'd be all set to start a serious search.

Looking back, I'm not sure what sent me to Petfinder, or how I even knew the site existed. I had never engaged in the kind of months-long dog searches many people conduct before adopting a dog. Gryffin had come along sort of like an unplanned pregnancy, with no forethought, no prior discussion. Later, I'd learn that spontaneous adoptions aren't uncommon. A 2011 PetSmart Charities survey found that just over 40 percent of pet owners said they'd done nothing before acquiring their pet—no search online or in pet stores or shelters, no discussion with breeders or even friends.

During one of my daily browsing sessions, I stumbled on a picture of Sherman, a handsome five-month-old black Labrador retriever who, his post read, liked carrots, was almost fully house-trained, and was living in a shelter in West Windsor, New Jersey, just a few towns south of us. For a few days, I couldn't shake Sherman from my mind: good-looking guy, right age, geographically desirable …

Ultimately I showed his picture to my daughters—Lindsey, who was then eight, and Dhani, then six. They asked the inevitable question: Are we adopting him?

"No," I said. "I'm just looking. But he's cute, isn't he?"

Later that evening, Kevin and I were in our bedroom getting ready for bed and prompting the girls to do the same. Lindsey, our queen of nighttime procrastination, lay on her stomach at the foot of our bed, feet swinging back and forth, head cupped in her hands. Suddenly she pronounced, "Lindsey is not Lindsey without a dog."

Kevin and I exchanged glances. We knew exactly how she felt.

We were still trying to come to terms with Gryffin's sudden death. Lindsey and Dhani were handling the situation far better than we were, but kids have a way of moving on more quickly than adults, and Kevin and I considered Gryffin our first child. For us, Gryffin's death, out of the blue as it was, had come too soon.

I had adopted Gryffin on September 7, 2000, from the DeKalb County Humane Society in Georgia. The decision made no sense, but in a rare moment of spontaneity—I am, perhaps, the least spontaneous person you'll ever meet—I did it anyway.

Back then, Kevin and I were engaged and living in Philadelphia, but as a producer with CNN, I would commute to Atlanta a couple of times a month. On one trip, a girlfriend introduced me to Caleb, a ten-week-old puppy she had just adopted. I'm not sure whether it was her powers of persuasion—she was determined to find homes for his siblings—or the few minutes I spent playing with the puppy, but the following day I found myself at the shelter staring at Caleb's littermates, particularly smitten by one guy in particular. He was a blend of bronze and black fur, and as friendly and clumsy as his siblings, but he seemed the calmest and least affected by the hubbub of the shelter. I took the little guy's picture and e-mailed it to Kevin. Despite my having no intelligent answer to his most obvious question—"Couldn't we just adopt a dog in Philadelphia?"—Kevin humored me, and our conversation turned to potential names. On Kevin's recommendation, I had just finished several books in the Harry Potter series, so talk turned to all things Potter. We immediately nixed the name "Harry," thinking it too obvious a reference to the series, which was nearing its height of popularity. But Gryffindor—Gryffin for short—resounded in our ears; it was restrained, subtle, yet the connection would be evident to anyone who'd read even one of the books.

The next day I called Delta Air Lines to make sure Gryffin could fly coach with me to Philadelphia—I wasn't going to adopt him if he had to fly cargo—filled out the Humane Society's application, paid the mandatory $80 "donation" fee, and became a mother.

Gryffin's papers from the Humane Society identified him as a "retriever-chow" mix. From the moment I saw him I was never sure whether "retriever" referred to a Labrador or a golden, because he looked like a mix of the two. As he matured, he developed a Labrador's shape but a golden's dark gold coloring; his fur was longer than a Lab's but shorter and thicker than a golden's. His chow lineage was evident in the dense fur that surrounded his neck, the purple spots that dotted his tongue, and the regal way he carried himself. He was a gorgeous dog, and when I would take him for walks around Philadelphia, people would stop me to inquire about his breed. "Pure mutt," I would tell them with pride, as if I had something to do with his good looks.

Gryffin's personality also reflected his mixed-breed heritage, with the chow in him most strongly defining his character. The American Kennel Club describes the chow's personality as catlike and uses words like "independent" and "aloof" to describe the breed's temperament. Gryffin was all that, and remarkably gentle. No dog has ever taken a treat from my hand as tenderly as he did.

After Lindsey was born, I started referring to Gryffin as our Secret Service agent because he was always around but never underfoot. He would position himself in whatever room of the house we were in but at a distance. He wasn't the type of dog who nudged his head under your hand while you were sitting on the couch to demand that you pet him; he was the type who tolerated you when you lay on the floor beside him to stroke his soft fur because he understood that allowing you this time benefitted you more than it did him.

Gryffin was my son, my teacher, and my protector. As my first child, he brought out maternal instincts I didn't even know I had, and he prepared me to be a mother to my two daughters. When we lived in Philadelphia and Kevin was spending long days and overnights in the hospital training to become a gastroenterologist, we never installed an alarm system because we had Gryffin. When we moved to New Jersey, Kevin and I joked that we bought our home especially for the dog because our city boy now had two acres of yard to patrol—no squirrel, groundhog, bird, or bunny was safe when Gryffin was around. I loved to watch him and my daughters romp in the backyard, especially during the winter, when the frozen ground was thick with snow. Only once in their lives together do I recall my girls getting angry at their brother, and that was after he tackled a snowman they had worked so hard to build.

Almost ten years to the day after I adopted Gryffin, Kevin decided to take him hiking in the Sourland Mountains, a not-so-rugged but picturesque preserve just minutes from our home. Lindsey joined them, and the trio set out a little after ten o'clock. It was Rosh Hashanah—the Jewish New Year—the day, the Jewish people believe, that God decides the fate of all living things. It was a beautiful morning—blue sky, bright sun—and we would be going to synagogue that afternoon.

Kevin thought a hike in the mountains would tire Gryffin sufficiently enough that he would sleep while we attended services.

Not long after the three left, Kevin called my cell phone. Gryffin, he told me, wouldn't jump out of the car. They were coming home.

Back in the driveway, Kevin opened the Prius's hatch; Gryffin lay on his side, completely still, except for the slow and rhythmic rise and fall of his broad chest. I gently stroked his fur and asked him what was wrong. As I did, he slowly lifted his head and looked at me, as though he wanted to tell me something. I could see pain in his eyes. I kissed his forehead and whispered, "I love you."

That was the last time I saw him.

The vet at the emergency animal hospital told Kevin that a tumor tucked behind Gryffin's ribcage had burst and that his stomach was filled with blood. We hadn't seen this coming, and I don't think Gryffin had either, because the previous night he had played ball like a puppy, and that morning he had eagerly jumped into Kevin's car to go hiking. Now Kevin, who loved that dog from the moment he laid eyes on him, and who affectionately referred to him as "my son," could do no more than comfort him as the vet delivered a life-ending medicinal cocktail.

At home, I cried. Then I called the girls into my bedroom, got down on my knees to see into their eyes, and kept crying as I told them that Gryffin wasn't coming home. I think they started crying and hugging me before I got all the words out, and I recall wondering what effect, if any, Gryffin's passing would have on them—they were still so young.

As for Kevin and me, Gryffin's death left us numb. In the days immediately following, when Lindsey or Dhani would ask if we were getting another dog, our answer was always, "Yes. But not yet." We needed to grieve; we needed to process the suddenness and unexpectedness of our loss. I agreed with Kevin that putting winter— and time—behind us made sense; perhaps by spring, the thinking went, our heartache—now so raw—would have begun to heal.

In the 1980s psychologists began studying—and taking seriously—the grief people report feeling after a pet dies. Their findings may not surprise those who've lost their best canine or feline friends, but researchers discovered that the grief triggered by the loss of a beloved companion animal can surpass the grief associated with the death of a human companion, even a family member. The day-to-day interactions and interdependence that ground the human-pet relationship lay the foundation for what can become a profound and anguished bereavement.

All I know is that there I was, weeks after Gryffin died, looking at dogs on Petfinder. Not just any dogs: dogs in Central New Jersey who were less than one year old. After seeing Sherman's picture and showing it to Lindsey and Dhani, I even called the rescue group to inquire about him, but I was quickly shot down by a woman who told me she wouldn't give Sherman to a family that didn't have a fenced-in yard. We have an invisible fence—most of my dog-owning neighbors have invisible fences—but the woman wouldn't negotiate. I was taken aback by how quickly she brushed me off—Sherman needed a home, and we could offer him a great one. (I've since learned that invisible fences are quite controversial within the animal welfare community and that many rescues refuse to adopt their dogs to homes that have them. Among the reasons: Invisible fences don't keep out animals or people who might do harm or be harmed, and once dogs cross the fence, they will often not return onto the property for fear of inviting another electric shock.)

Several weeks later, still surfing Petfinder, I came across pictures of six puppies being offered for adoption by a Flemington, New Jersey, rescue group. They were adorable, as all puppies are, but what caught my eye—in addition to their proximity to my home—was their breed mix. The postings said the dogs were Australian shepherd and Labrador retriever, two breeds with reputations for being good with children, smart, and easy to train.

The rescue organization had a curious name: It was listed on Petfinder as Catnip Friends Cat Rescue, but all I was concerned about at the time was whether this rescue would let us adopt a dog even though we didn't have—and weren't getting—a fenced-in yard. The woman I spoke with on the telephone asked me a few questions about whether I had ever owned a dog, and I told her about Gryffin—how I'd adopted him a decade ago and how we'd lost him suddenly and recently. Then I asked if she had any issues adopting dogs to families whose yards are enclosed by invisible fences. She told me she cared more about the quality of the people adopting her dogs than what kind of fences they had. And, by the way, if we wanted to see the puppies, they would be in Raritan, a town neighboring ours, that Saturday.

I kept returning to my computer to look at the puppies. Kevin was still adamant about waiting to adopt a new dog—I think he felt guilty that we would even consider replacing Gryffin so soon. I felt that guilt, too, but I also felt an emptiness that needed to be filled. No matter how much I loved Kevin and the girls and they loved me, they just couldn't fill that space, which is funny because I didn't even know that space existed until Gryffin came into my life. Now I knew I couldn't let it remain empty.

To my great relief, Kevin humored me—just as he'd done when I'd called from Atlanta wanting to adopt a dog—and agreed to go with me to see the puppies. We left the girls home with a sitter because I needed Kevin's full attention to persuade him we were ready to let a dog back into our lives; he wanted my full attention to persuade me we were not.

THE LOCAL AGWAY, A HYBRID GARDEN AND PET STORE, may have been less than ten minutes from our home, but we had never shopped there before. The rectangular store was small, its aisles to the left of the entrance packed with lawn and garden products, its aisles to the right crammed with pet products. We turned right, and as we neared the back I saw cats in cages stacked three high, a reddish-brown dog that resembled a fox splayed out on the floor eating a bully stick (a popular and not inexpensive chew toy made from the penises of bulls), and a dog pen crowded with puppies climbing over each other, hustling for human attention. Five of the dogs were black with a random white spot here or there; one was a speckled gray-black mix.

The woman in charge told me her name was Linda, that the puppies had arrived that morning from North Carolina, and that before being transported north they had been in what she called "a high-kill shelter." None of that information registered with me at the time. I just wanted to hold a squiggly little puppy, run my hands over its soft fur, and stare into its innocent eyes.

Kevin and I picked up each puppy one at a time to get a sense of each dog's individual personality. Even when puppies are about eight weeks old, you can get a sense of which guy is more rambunctious, which gal is more skittish, and which pup seems mellower than the others. I was committed to adopting a dark-haired dog for no other reason than our home has dark hardwood floors, and I had spent too many minutes of every day vacuuming up Gryffin's golden locks, which seemed to taunt me with their ubiquitous presence. I also presumed we would adopt a male because Kevin repeatedly joked about Gryffin being his ally in a house full of women.

But as I tested the temperaments of the black-furred boys, Julia, the petite gray puppy with eyes lined black like Cleopatra's, was squirming her way into Kevin's broken heart. I thought the puppy was a little funny looking; to me, she shared an uncanny resemblance with Stitch, the blue doglike alien from the Disney series *Lilo & Stitch,* but Kevin liked her unique look. The next thing I knew, Kevin was telling me that if I was truly ready to deal with all the work—and potential headaches—that come with adopting a puppy, he would support me, but he was sorta, kinda leaning toward Julia. I interpreted that to mean we could adopt a dog as long as we adopted this one.

For $250 in cash and a promise to spay her, Julia was ours. On the car ride home, I broke out my BlackBerry to look up girls' names. In the Jewish religion it is customary to name a baby after a relative who has passed away. It is said this keeps the person's memory alive and, in a metaphysical way, forms a bond between the soul of the newborn and of the deceased family member. For me and Kevin, it was a given that our new pup would be named after Gryffin, so I started down the list: "Gabby, Gable, Gabriela ... " When I got to "Galen," Kevin stopped me. The name held no significance to me, but he'd learned in medical school that Galen was the name of an Ancient Greek physician who today is considered one of the most influential physicians of all time. As if to confirm we'd hit on the right name, a quick web search informed us Galen meant "calm," which is, of course, the canine temperament we were hoping for in our new dog. In a nod to her Southern roots, we chose "Belle" as her middle name: Galen Belle.

When we arrived home, we called Lindsey and Dhani to the family room and let loose their pint-sized sibling. "Galen's a Southerner, like Gryffin," I told them. "Only she's from North Carolina." I don't think they heard me, and in truth, they probably didn't care where she was from. They just wanted to hear that she was theirs to keep, and they wanted to pet her and to hold her. And so, in true sisterly fashion, they proceeded to argue over who would get to do so first.

GALEN AND I GOT ACQUAINTED on my kitchen floor, where I was immediately taken by how emotionally needy she was, far needier than I recalled Gryffin ever being. When Gryffin was a puppy, he just wanted to be in the room Kevin and I were in, and then he would happily settle down and entertain himself with a chew toy. Not Galen;

being in the same room with us wasn't enough. She wanted to be on our laps—mine, Kevin's, Lindsey's, or Dhani's—and she'd whine if she wasn't. So, over the course of a good many weeks, I spent a good many hours sitting on one of Gryffin's two-inch-thick brown dog beds, my back flush against a cabinet door, with Galen curled up on my lap chewing a bone or her stuffed hedgehog, or nibbling my fingers with her tiny, razor-sharp teeth. Not knowing how much, if any, time she'd had with her mother, I turned pop–veterinary psychologist and wondered if the neediness I perceived stemmed from a broken maternal bond or reflected feelings of abandonment.

At night, so Galen didn't feel alone, and so I could hear her cry when she needed to go outside, she slept in our bedroom in a toddler's pack-and-play. We were crate training her, but neither Kevin nor I wanted to schlep the crate to and from its perch in the family room every morning and every night, so we decided the pack-and-play was a perfectly acceptable substitute.

Getting up with Galen in the middle of the night brought back memories of being a new mom and waking with my girls for their nighttime breast feedings. But I have to say, Galen treated me far more kindly than my newborn daughters ever had. Unlike them, she did her business quickly—by that I mean she peed in the yard—and after I returned her to the pack-and-play, she went right to sleep. In no time, this baby girl was sleeping through the night.

During the day, because I teach at our local community college, my schedule was flexible enough for me to drop in to spend a little time with Galen. We would go on mini-excursions around our backyard, and I noticed that the closeness Galen craved inside the house extended to the outdoors; she would explore her surroundings only if I explored with her, step by step. Of course, the benefit of this behavior was that I had no fear she would run away, but I did wonder about her apparent lack of curiosity.

Then I discovered Galen didn't even want to leave our property for a walk. I would leash her up and start down the driveway, and she would sit down. At first, I thought she simply didn't know how to walk on a leash. My vet—to whom I was making regular trips since Galen had come to us with an intestinal parasite common in shelter dogs—told me dogs need to be taught to walk on a leash (I don't remember teaching Gryffin) and that I needed to take the reins of our relationship. I became the alpha, but I felt bad yanking Galen's twelve-pound body along when she really seemed opposed to walking; treats of any kind provided little motivation.

But I kept the pressure on, week after week, and ultimately I got her taking regular walks with me around the small, horseshoe-shaped development across from our house. The route is about a mile, too short for a workout but long enough to notice another quirk of our canine: She never peed on these walks; she's still never peed on a walk. She's like a person who won't use public restrooms. So Galen and I would take our walk—such as it was—and then I would send her into the backyard to do her business.

I wish this had been her only urinary issue, but she had what veterinarians call "submissive pee," a condition not uncommon in puppies and rescue dogs but a common gripe of dog owners who don't appreciate their otherwise potty-trained dogs urinating on their hardwoods and rugs. Most dogs with submissive pee lose their bladder control when greeting people—even people they know well. The urination—combined with a cowering posture, tucked tail, and flattened ears—is the dog's way of saying, "Hey, I'm not a threat; don't hurt me." Galen cowered so low she would turn her head sideways and scrape her right ear across the ground while whining and whinnying like a horse.

It got to the point where no one—not me, Kevin, or our daughters—would say hello to her anywhere but outside. When I would return home from teaching or running errands, I would enter the house; rush to Galen's crate, which sits alongside the family room's sliding glass door; open the door, then the crate; and make a mad dash onto our deck, down the stairs, and onto the grass before saying a single word to her. When I was lucky, not one dribble would land in the house or on the deck.

On one of our visits to the vet—after Galen peed in the waiting room when a vet tech greeted her, and then again, in the examining room—the doctor told me dogs often outgrow this condition by the time they turn one. I hoped Galen was listening.

Then one day Galen gave me something else to ponder: She stopped walking on our hardwood floors and started slinking around the house spy-like, moving from room to room along circuitous routes determined by the layout of our area rugs, all the while hanging her head and looking like a child who knows she's done something wrong. She even refused to enter the kitchen for meals—we have hardwoods there—or for American cheese, her favorite treat, so I started feeding her outside. To this day—no matter the weather—she takes her meals on our deck and refuses to enter the kitchen. And she continues to slink, head low, about the house. "She looks guilty," Dhani has said on more than one occasion. I've often wondered what, if anything, she might have done or what it is she might fear.

All this is not to say that Galen wasn't also displaying typical puppy behavior and getting into typical puppy trouble. She ate my favorite brown slippers, chewed the wicker off a basket that stored some of my daughters' books, left teeth marks on the wooden leg of an end table in the family room, and nipped at Lindsey's and Dhani's ankles—herding them to nowhere. As for my ankles, she preferred to nip at them whenever I took the stairs from the second floor down to the first. She never nipped at them on the way up.

When the herding started, Galen was about four months old. She had a lot of energy, and I was having a hard time getting her to release it. Long walks were still not happening; neither was playing fetch in the yard because there didn't seem to be any type of toy or ball that she liked enough to chase, let alone retrieve and chase again.

Kevin was beginning to get frustrated with my inability to tire her out by day because she was starting to harass our daughters at night, and the problem was growing worse as Galen grew bigger. It got to where the girls couldn't take the few steps from their bedrooms to their bathroom without the dog charging them and nipping at their ankles with her sharp teeth. Commands such as *No!* or *Stop!*—whether issued by me, Kevin, or the girls—went unheeded; if anything, they would make Galen's harassing more frenzied. If the girls tried to push Galen away, she would bite at their hands and fingers. They were starting to fear her, and Kevin was afraid Galen was going to hurt one of them. He even started making subtle asides about returning Galen to the rescue if I didn't control her behavior. At first I didn't take him seriously, and fortunately the girls—despite being the victims of Galen's repeated attacks—didn't want to see her go. But as the herding continued, I could see in Kevin's face and hear in his voice that his threats weren't empty.

He knew all too well what a dog could do to a young child in a moment of unexpected aggression.

It was July 4, 2003, Lindsey's first birthday, and we were celebrating at my father's house on the Jersey shore. I was sitting on the living room floor next to my dad's golden retriever, Isaac, and Lindsey was crawling about, as she had yet to master walking. When she crawled over to pet Isaac, he swiftly and unexpectedly grabbed her by the ear, picked her up, and threw her to the ground. Kevin, Lindsey, and I spent much of the afternoon in Shore Memorial Hospital's emergency room, where a doctor stitched together the very top of Lindsey's ear, where Isaac's teeth had torn the cartilage.

Kevin hadn't been in the living room at the time of Isaac's attack, and even if he had been, there was no way he could have prevented it. But he could prevent Galen from hurting his girls, and if protecting them meant getting rid of our dog, I believe his thought was: "So be it."

Puppy socialization classes expose puppies to other young dogs in the hope that when a dog comes into contact with another—which it inevitably will—it will be less likely to respond with fear or, worse, with aggression. I viewed the classes as a twofer—they would acclimate Galen to other dogs, as well as give her an opportunity to release some of that pent-up energy that was leading Kevin to view her as a threat to our daughters.

The classes—more like a puppy free-for-all—were held on Wednesday nights at my vet's office, in the large waiting area. The trainer would ring the exterior of the room with chairs and benches for the dogs' human parents and siblings, and the puppies would play in the circle's center. I watched many dogs play, but not Galen. On our first excursion, she hid under a bench and wouldn't come out—not to play, not to eat the treats the trainer sprinkled all over the floor, not to drink from the bowls of water she set out. And of course, when it was time for the dogs to go outside to pee, Galen simply sniffed the grass surrounding the parking lot. We went to four sessions, and only once did she venture out from under the bench to play with other dogs; never did she pee—she always held it in until we returned home. All that stimulation did take the edge off her nighttime rambunctiousness, but by morning she was back to her unruly self.

The best advice I got for sapping Galen of some of her energy came from a trainer with an affinity for border collies, which, like Australian shepherds, are high-energy herding dogs. By the time I reached the trainer, frigid temperatures and a snow-filled yard were making spending long periods of time outside unappealing to me, if not to Galen, and the nighttime ankle nipping was increasing, as was Kevin's frustration. Fortunately, one suggestion—to have Galen run up and down the basement steps retrieving treats—did slow her down, but only for short periods because she would tire of the exercise before the exercise fully tired her. The herding continued.

Then, one February evening, Kevin snapped. About eight inches of snow had turned the backyard—which stretches two acres to the South Branch of the Raritan River—a luminous swath of white, and he, the girls, and Galen were outside: the girls making angels and poorly packed snowballs, Galen sniffing the snow and bunny-hopping through it, and Kevin drinking in the whole scene. It's this ruralesque nature of our property that initially drew Kevin to it, and at that moment, with the grass and trees blanketed by freshly fallen snow, his girls playing, he was having what he affectionately calls "a Hillsborough moment," when all is right in our little world.

And then it wasn't.

Out of the corner of his eye, Kevin saw Dhani fall to the ground and Galen jump on top of her.

"She was nipping at my boots," Dhani would later tell me. "So I started walking, and she followed me. I thought she wanted to play, so I ran."

Galen, who by now weighed more than Dhani, tackled her.

"I got up, and she tackled me again."

This time Dhani couldn't get up. She had fallen face-first into the snow. Galen climbed onto her back and started wrestling with the faux fur lining the hood of her winter coat.

From where he was standing several yards away, all Kevin could see was Dhani struggling to get up. He ran toward them, fearful that Galen would bite Dhani's face, the only part of her that wasn't covered in cold-weather wear. He grabbed the dog with two hands, lifted her off of Dhani's back, and threw her into the snow.

Not until that moment—and never since—had I seen Kevin so angry. He grumbled under his breath something about giving Galen back and being serious this time. But I wasn't ready to let her go, and neither, still, were our daughters.

I gave Kevin his space for the rest of the night, and neither he nor I brought up the incident the following day. I hoped he would simply put it behind him and give Galen another chance, or two.

WE USHERED IN SPRING as we do each year, hosting our family's Passover Seder. This year our gathering numbered twenty-two. With the main course complete, the adults remained at the table talking, while my daughters and five of their cousins ransacked my living room looking for the Afikomen—pieces of matzo I'd wrapped in tin foil and hidden. Galen, I thought, was napping in her crate.

Somehow, through adult talk and kid ruckus, a steady growl caught my attention.

Galen was under the table growling at my father. For so many reasons this struck me as odd, but primarily because prior to dinner I'd seen my dad petting Galen in our backyard. But now she was glaring at him, releasing a low-grade rumble. Rather than try to engage her, my dad simply ignored her and laughed it off; he wasn't much for confrontation with people, let alone dogs. Galen didn't let up until he left our house.

Galen had previously signaled she was no fan of strange men— strange as in the plumber, electrician, or contractor who would come to fix the routine problems associated with home ownership. She would bark angrily at the man before he entered the house, but as soon as he came in, she would rush into her crate. She seemed to have no problem with women she didn't know; with them, she would wag her tail wildly and whine, begging for attention.

This fear of men, Galen's severely submissive nature, and her idiosyncratic habits left me filled with questions. We adopted her when she was just eight weeks old—what could possibly have happened in such a short time to have so impacted her?

As I wondered about Galen, I remembered that in Gryffin's early years I would question some of his peculiarities, like his outsized fear of large black garbage bags and his hatred for boxers; he had an uncanny ability to identify dogs of that breed, and once he saw one, he would become uncharacteristically aggressive. I used to speculate about what experiences he might have had before I adopted him, but all those years ago, it had never occurred to me to look into his past.

But there was something about Galen, something I saw every time I looked into her big brown eyes and at her sweet gray face, that seemed to be telling me not to leave it at guesses. If I'm honest with myself, I saw something else when I looked into her eyes—I saw a woman who had traded career for family, journalism for motherhood, and who, while not regretting a single decision, still struggled with her identity.

This may sound a tad crazy—or maybe a lot crazy—but I believe that in the early spring of 2012, Galen inspired me to dust off my journalistic mantle to find out all I could about how an eight-week-old puppy from a North Carolina shelter ended up at a New Jersey garden-supply store available for adoption—and why there are so many dogs like her making an exodus from the South to live out their lives in the North.

At the time, I had no sense of the enormity and the complexity of the situation.

Back then, I knew only that I needed to dig out Galen's adoption papers. They had Linda Wilferth's contact information, and, as the woman responsible for bringing Galen to New Jersey, she would have some, if not all, of the answers to my many questions.

South Paws in the North

LINDA WILFERTH'S PATIENCE WITH PEOPLE RUNS THIN. Too often they let her down, but—far worse—they let down their dogs and cats. And when that happens, she says, she and rescuers like her are often all that stand between an animal's life or its death in an overcrowded shelter. What Linda finds most frustrating is that for all the lives she saves, she can't save more.

Linda and I are talking in Pet Valu, a pet store in Flemington, New Jersey, that doubles as an adoption center for her cats and dogs on Saturday afternoons and some Sundays, too. Linda, fifty-something and slender, with light brown, shoulder-length frizzy hair, has one eye on me, the other on her dogs and the people interacting with them.

This day, Linda's cats—there are only six of them—are in metal crates stacked on a table to the left of the entranceway. The cats are large, multicolored; there are no kittens. The cats gaze at people who walk past, but few people pause to look at them. I don't see anyone hold one. "No one wants cats," Linda will tell me months later.

Instead, the action is over by the puppies. Tucked behind tables of treats and dog bowls, beside piles of stain-resistant welcome mats, and in front of a wall loaded floor to ceiling with toys, are two pens and two crates holding nineteen puppies, all mixed breeds, all from the South. Today's puppies hail from the Carolinas and Georgia.

Adults and children crowd the pens, jostling to get a better look. Some stoop down and stick their fingers through the metal to pet a puppy or have one lick a finger or two. Several puppies see the fingers as toys to be swatted away with their little paws or nipped at with their diminutive teeth. In one of the crates, the puppies pounce on each other, biting one another's ears and necks, and tearing apart the newspaper that lines the floor. In the other, eight puppies sleep huddled in a mound of beige fur, their small, plump bellies rising with each breath; one puppy near the bottom of the heap is twitching—a bad dream, perhaps.

A young man, probably in his early twenties, leans toward his friend and says, "They are genetically designed to make you go *goo-goo ga-ga*." Amen. I am enamored with one of the black Lab mixes, the one named Sausage, whose legs are short, whose body is fat, and whose black fur is so fluffy he must be part chow. When he sits on his haunches he looks more like a stuffed animal than a live one. By the cash register, a teenage girl cradles a six-week-old dachshund mix; her younger brother is speaking to their father on a cell phone. "We sent you three pictures," he says. I notice their mother is filling out adoption papers.

Pet Valu is at the north end of a heavily trafficked strip mall next to, and across from, several other strip malls that crowd a one-mile stretch of Route 202. When the Agway chain of stores went out of business, Linda moved her operation to Pet Valu, and now, most Saturdays and some Sundays, from noon to four, she is here with her rescued but homeless dogs and cats. Most people find Linda like I did, on Petfinder, as the website has revolutionized the way people adopt pets, and it has spawned similar sites like Adopt-a-pet.com and RescueMe.org.

Petfinder was founded in 1996 by a computer-savvy New Jersey couple who made it their New Year's resolution to improve animal welfare. The site—a labor of love, they've called it—was first limited to residents of the Garden State, but its popularity prompted its expansion across the United States and into Canada and Mexico. Fast forward ten years, and Discovery Communications buys what's become the Internet's largest database of adoptable pets for $35 million. Then, in 2013, Petfinder changed corporate parents once again, when Nestlé Purina PetCare Company bought the for-profit company for an undisclosed sum.

On a recent afternoon, Petfinder was showcasing upwards of 315,000 animals, including dogs, cats, rabbits, horses, and even pigs, from nearly 14,000 shelters and rescues. What makes Petfinder—and those it spawned—a boon to people looking for pets is that they can search for Fido or Felix by breed, age, gender, location, or any combination of characteristics.

While in the pet store, I meet a woman who drove all the way from Massachusetts to adopt a boxer mix. Her family, already owners of two purebreds, wanted a third dog. It had to be at least part boxer, the woman told me, and it had to be a rescue. When she found the ideal dog on Petfinder, she made the five-hour drive to Jersey.

As for me, I'd been stalking Linda by telephone and e-mail for several weeks to learn everything she knew about Galen. I also wanted to find out why Linda—and so many rescues like hers—was bringing Southern dogs north. The anecdotes I was hearing from friends, friends of friends, and acquaintances who owned dogs from the South were piling up too high to discount. Did nobody own a New Jersey rescue?

But Linda never returned my phone calls. And my e-mails, filled with questions about Galen's past, went unanswered. Finally, I received an e-mail suggesting I show up at an adoption event. "Best way to get me," it read.

So on a Saturday afternoon in June, nineteen months after adopting Galen and more than two months after making my first phone call to her, I stood face-to-face with Linda. I was finally going to get some answers about Galen's past and, perhaps, some insight into her idiosyncrasies.

LINDA WILFERTH GREW UP IN Rochester, New York, in a house bursting with four-legged creatures. There were cats and dogs, turtles and rabbits, and two mice named Fatty and Skinny. There was also a revolving door of stray cats. Linda's mother says her daughter was constantly finding strays, bringing them home, wanting to keep them. "Some stayed," her mother recalls. "Some didn't."

A little girl's love of animals, even a commitment to their welfare, doesn't necessarily foreshadow a life in animal rescue, but it can certainly provide a solid foundation for one. Linda never intended for rescue to become her life's work; like so many who get involved, one thing led to another and she just fell into it, in part because of a deep-seated love of animals but also because of a deeply held belief that animals are the innocent victims of man's ignorance, maliciousness, and sometimes downright sadism. Because people harm animals, the rescuer's thinking goes, people must save them. "If not me, who?" is a common refrain, or, as Linda said to me, "Someone has to do something."

In the mid-1990s, no one was doing anything to help a man Linda calls Old Mr. Popkins. A widower in his nineties, he had no children and lived alone. What he had were stray cats—lots of them—who relied on him for food. Linda says the strays weren't spayed or neutered, so they had litter upon litter, and Mr. Popkins would simply increase the amount of food he put out to feed their growing numbers. The situation grew dire as Mr. Popkins grew older and frail. When he died, Linda wondered, who would take care of his cats?

As an adult, Linda had only dabbled in animal welfare work. Before moving to Flemington, she had volunteered at a regional animal shelter taking dogs for walks and turning over to the shelter the stray cats whose paths continued to cross her own. But now she was confronted with what to do about Mr. Popkins's cats. She could take them to a veterinarian to be spayed and neutered—and she did, paying for the surgeries out of her own pocket. But then what? That's when she came upon a fact that startled her: Unlike the town she had moved from, Flemington didn't have an animal shelter. "The police would hold the cats for seven days and then euthanize them," she told me. "I thought, there has to be a better way." Today, things in Flemington have improved: When animal control officers round up stray cats, the cats are quarantined for seven days at a local veterinary clinic, then offered up to rescue groups to be adopted out.

The vet who spayed and neutered Mr. Popkins's cats introduced Linda to Buff Barr, the woman who would become Linda's rescue partner. Like Linda, Buff is a cat lover, and, like Linda, the mid-1990s found Buff traveling down the path of the reluctant rescuer. Buff was working at the Hunterdon County Library when she couldn't help but notice several employees feeding a feral cat colony. "I tried to ignore it," Buff told me, "because I knew if I got involved, I'm really going to get involved."

But as the cats reproduced, and still others joined the colony, Buff found the situation too difficult to ignore. So she bought raccoon traps, captured the cats, and paid for their sterilization. Then she turned them loose. This method, Trap-Neuter-Return, or TNR, is considered by many in animal welfare to be the most humane means of reducing feral cat populations.

A decade later, Buff says, employees still feed the cats, but only four remain. Sixty have been fixed and have moved on. "Over time, these four will disappear and a new feral cat or two will come by. We'll try to trap it and fix it. It's the only way to help cats that will never be socialized."

Soon after Buff started trapping the feral cats at the library, she started noticing feral colonies all around the Flemington area. She would trap the cats, and on her own dime and with money donated by colleagues at the library, she would have the cats sterilized. She also started taking in strays—she and her husband live on an eight-acre farm with a large barn, so space wasn't an issue. Today the barn is home to one horse and thirty-odd cats.

"I end up with cats that are not adoptable," Buff told me. "Because of the barn, they have shelter, and they get fed two times a day. Most importantly, no kitten has ever been born here."

Linda and Buff began their joint rescue work doing TNR and volunteering with a nonprofit that sought permanent homes for unwanted, abused, and stray cats. It seemed a perfect fit for the women, but for reasons they don't talk about, it wasn't. The animal welfare community is notorious for its infighting, even backstabbing; for groups breaking apart; for factions splintering off; for people starting new nonprofits, new rescues, new shelters all the time. One longtime animal advocate told me, "New groups pop up every day because they think they can do it better. There's too much bickering, too much infighting at the expense of the animals."

Whatever their reasons for leaving the nonprofit, Linda and Buff decided that they could, in fact, do cat rescue better, so they launched Catnip Friends Cat Rescue in the early 2000s, and in 2007, they incorporated as a federal nonprofit. In doing so, they joined a large and quickly growing movement—according to the Humane Society of the United States, there are some 10,000 animal rescue groups at work across the country. Despite their numbers, many rescuers, like Linda, fear they are losing the battle to save lives.

That's because up to four million abandoned and unwanted dogs and cats are euthanized in shelters across the United States each year, according to animal welfare groups. That's more than 10,000 every day, about half the population that enters the shelters. In fact, shelter killing is the leading cause of canine and feline deaths in this country.

Strikingly, animal welfare groups say a vast majority of those killed—up to 90 percent—are healthy and adoptable and would make great pets. But because not enough Americans adopt dogs and cats from shelters, because people relinquish pets for reasons ranging from financial hardship and relocation to "the dog sheds too much" or "grew bigger than expected," and because too many Americans don't spay or neuter their pets, some shelters are so overcrowded that animals are euthanized just to create cage space.

In the fall of 2012, following a summer that saw record numbers of homeless dogs enter a north Georgia shelter, the director put into words the predicament many public shelter directors, like herself, face: "We're open admission, so when one comes in, we have to get rid of one that's already here," she told the *White County News*. "We evaluate all the dogs for how adoptable they are, looking at things like their behavior and their size. We only keep the best of the best."

The numbers—whether they reflect how many animals enter shelters each year or how many are euthanized—are only the best educated guesses researchers can come up with because there is no federal institution or animal welfare organization monitoring the country's shelters—some of which are private, some of which are taxpayer-funded, and some of which are private-public partnerships. It's even unclear just how many shelters there are. The Humane Society of the United States (HSUS) puts the number at 3,500, while the American Society for the Prevention of Cruelty to Animals (ASPCA) puts it at nearly four times that, at 13,600.

Another reason why getting an accurate count is so difficult is that animal control has traditionally been the purview of local governments, so there is no federal law mandating that shelters keep records of how many animals are adopted out and how many are euthanized. Some states require that shelters collect this data; some don't. Some states don't even require shelters. For all these reasons, some in animal welfare think the number four million may be low.

What is clear is that most Americans have no idea just how bad the situation is. According to a 2011 study by PetSmart Charities, nearly nine in ten Americans grossly underestimate the number of animals euthanized in shelters each year, putting it under one million. I admit I never really thought about it. I knew shelters euthanized dogs and cats, but I hadn't considered to what extent, and I'd assumed that the majority of animals killed were sick or too aggressive to be safely adopted out. I had assumed wrong.

Into this abyss come rescue organizations of all sizes and all preferences. Some rescues are breed-specific, while others accept all breeds; some have facilities that house homeless animals, while others rely on a network of foster families; some run sanctuaries where animals can live out their lives, and others focus solely on animal transport, i.e., moving animals by car, van, even airplane, from shelters directly to their new owners or to rescue organizations that handle adoptions. Some are large and corporate; some are tiny, run by just one or two animal lovers.

Catnip Friends falls into this last "mom-and-pop"—or, in this case, "mom-and-mom"—model. The rescue doesn't own a facility to house its dogs and cats, so Linda and Buff take as many animals as they can into their own homes and rely on a number of foster families to take in the rest. Theirs is a round-the-clock, year-round enterprise, fueled by compassion and infinite dedication.

"We're always stressed," Linda tells me one busy Saturday afternoon. "It's insane what we do to not see these guys end up in a landfill." Once, Linda says, she went Dumpster diving in a brand-new navy business suit to rescue a kitten trapped under a heap of trash—Linda had somehow heard its meows emanating from the large metal structure. When she found the kitten, she saw that it had gotten its tiny head stuck inside a tin can.

In addition to running the rescue, the women hold full-time jobs—Linda, the face of the organization, is a recruiter for technology and financial services companies, and Buff, mild-mannered and soft-spoken, works as a library assistant. That's why I presume Linda didn't return my phone calls or have time to answer my e-mails. That's why all the information I would learn from Linda about Galen and the rescue world would come over a span of weeks and months during short conversations in Pet Valu, as aspiring cat and dog owners ogled the animals and questioned Linda about an animal's breed or age or temperament, and as she sized up potential owners, as she once must have sized me up.

"I go by my gut, and I'm usually right," Linda says. Her long career as a recruiter has honed her instincts about people, she says, so she often makes judgments on the spot. "I watch people with the dogs, with each other, listening to what they say to me, going over their application, and making sure everything adds up."

One afternoon Linda points out a mother and daughter bonding with a petite black border collie mix and tells me she doesn't think she's going to permit the family to adopt the dog. She tells me the husband rubbed her the wrong way the moment he entered the store and plopped himself down on a stack of dog beds near the store's entrance. When I see him he is practically horizontal and has begun peppering Linda with questions about the rescue—where the dogs come from, how they are transported to New Jersey, whether the dogs are seen by vets in the South or here, in Hunterdon County. When Linda inquires whether the family has pets, he answers that they do not, although he says a stray cat had made their garage its home for several months before disappearing as suddenly as it had appeared. Linda asks if he or his wife had taken the cat to be spayed or neutered during the period the cat lived under their roof, and he gave an answer that ensured the family would not be leaving with a dog. "No," he said. "Why would we?"

Later, I ask Linda how often she turns away a potential adopter. She scans the store, resting her eyes on two young dogs—dark brown pit bull mixes, sisters, who still hadn't fully grown into their paws. "Not often, but it happens. The dogs have been through so much," she tells me. "I won't put them through more."

Before Facebook became the social media site favored by the rescue community to facilitate interstate rescues and adoptions, Linda and her fellow rescuers relied on Petfinder's message boards and urgent lists. Linda read the message boards like many people read the newspaper—daily—and it was on one such message board that she happened upon a municipal shelter in Gaston County, North Carolina. Numerous postings said the shelter was euthanizing large numbers of cats and losing others to outbreaks of feline parvovirus, a contagious virus that weakens a cat's immune system.

"Gaston kept coming up on the message board," Linda says, "and I would read about all the cats that would be killed if they weren't pulled from the shelter." For six months Linda read about Gaston's cats, wanting to do something but convinced she and Buff were just too busy with their own county's cats to take in more, especially those from as far away as North Carolina. Then Linda saw a posting out of Gaston for Siamese cats—cats she knew she could find homes for in New Jersey. "I said, 'I'll take them.'"

"Even though there are cats here, I never faulted Linda for pulling from the South," Buff told me. "A cat's life saved is a cat's life saved. Linda has a big heart and doesn't want anything to die."

This likely won't come as a surprise to those in rescue, but it came as a surprise to me: Linda has never been inside Gaston County's shelter—she's never even been to Gaston County. All the coordination, from deciding which animals to pull from the shelter to how they will be transported north, is done online and through e-mail via a network of dedicated volunteers. Over the years, Linda's developed close friendships with women with whom she's in contact daily but whom she's never met in person. "I'd love to move down there," she told me one afternoon when she was sounding more frustrated than usual with humankind. "I've met some great women."

After rescuing the Siamese cats, Linda started bringing more cats north, but she encountered a problem—many showed up with distemper, which, like parvovirus, is a contagious and deadly virus. Several of the kittens died. "Kittens are more fragile than many people realize," Buff told me. The deaths only made Linda more determined to get as many cats out of the shelter—and into New Jersey—as she could.

With the transport of Gaston County's cats to Flemington, Catnip Friends entered the burgeoning business of South-North rescue, a business that picked up sharply in the fall of 2005, after Hurricane Katrina slammed into the Gulf Coast. Northern rescue groups that flocked to Louisiana and Mississippi saw that throughout the South, shelters were already so crowded that there was little to no space for the estimated 600,000 animals displaced by the hurricane. As a result, many of the rescues brought the cats and dogs north to stay in private shelters and foster homes until they could be returned to their owners or adopted out.

There was a lesson in all this: While there weren't enough homes in the South for the South's cats and dogs—an assessment that, to this day, has the consensus of shelter directors, rescuers, and the country's two largest animal welfare organizations, HSUS and the ASPCA—there were homes in the North. Thus began what some rescuers have dubbed the "overground railroad," the transport of cats and dogs from the South up the Eastern Seaboard to the Mid-Atlantic and New England states. In the last several years, Southern dogs have also begun finding homes in the Upper Midwest—in Michigan, Wisconsin, and Minnesota. It's difficult, if not impossible, to know just how many dogs and cats have been relocated, as no federal institution is charged with regulating animal rescues or interstate transports, nor are animal welfare agencies able to monitor all the disparate activity. Still, a 2008 article in the *Christian Science Monitor* reported that a phenomenal 90 percent of dogs adopted in the Northeast are Southern-born.

Some of those canines, and many felines, too, were brought north by Wanda Bohannon, who got into the transport business in the wake of Katrina. Every two weeks for the past eight years—with a bit of time off here and there—Bohannon has left her Savannah, Georgia, home to transport dogs and cats rescued from shelters in Georgia and the Carolinas to rescue groups and adoptive parents in New Jersey and Pennsylvania. Some weeks she travels on to New York and as far north as Massachusetts. It was Bohannon who, in 2010, was fulfilling the bulk of Linda's transport needs.

When Wanda Bohannon and I spoke by telephone one Monday afternoon, she was recuperating from a weekend on the road. The rest is imperative—Bohannon doesn't sleep until after she's unloaded all of her traveling companions, which, on a typical weekend, is fifteen to twenty animals. "I leave at nine-thirty Friday morning and start drinking sweet tea and coffee after two p.m.," she said. "Then it's double and triple espressos, and I'm wired." She grabs a few minutes of shut-eye in rest stops on the return to Savannah and always stops at one in South Carolina to feed a colony of feral cats. Thus, in Wanda Bohannon, as in Buff, Linda found a fellow cat lover. "Cats suffer the most," Bohannon told me. "I'm always grieving for them."

For Linda and Buff, adding transport costs to the costs of running the rescue put additional strain on already strained finances. Running an animal rescue is an expensive enterprise, and a cat rescue especially so. Donations to save cats just don't roll in at the same dollar amounts or frequency that donations to save dogs do, Buff says, and people aren't willing to pay very much for cats. Catnip Friends was adopting out its cats for $100 each, while it cost about $140 each for food, litter, transportation north, and veterinary care, which, depending on the cat, could include de-worming, flea medicine, vaccinations, and spay/ neuter surgery. The women were spending their own money to keep the rescue solvent—a common practice and lament among people running private rescue organizations. "You inevitably dip into your own pocket to keep it going," Linda told me.

The change in the rescue's financial fortunes came unexpectedly sometime in 2009. Neither woman recalls the month or the day, but Linda vividly remembers the event that changed everything. The women were running a joint adoption day with New Jersey Puppy Rescue, and Linda spent more of the day with its puppies than with her cats. "Every time someone wanted to talk about a cat they had to come find me, because I was over with the dogs." What Linda learned that afternoon was that people in Central New Jersey were eager to adopt dogs, especially puppies. By expanding into dog rescue, Linda realized she could save more animals—her priority—while keeping the cat rescue viable.

"I don't think we ever discussed it," Buff said. "Linda just started transporting dogs north."

Linda learned that she could adopt out her dogs relatively quickly because Hunterdon and its surrounding counties are quite well off— Hunterdon is the sixth-richest county in the country, according to *Forbes* magazine, and neighboring Somerset County is ninth—so people can afford the cost of a new dog. And at $250 for a puppy that hasn't been fixed or $325 for one that has, Linda's puppies are significantly less than the price of a purebred purchased from a breeder. The living in the region is also diverse, as it is home to everything from horse farms and suburban subdivisions to townhomes and apartment buildings, making dogs of every breed and size welcome and—perhaps even more important—wanted.

While some rescues are choosy about what breeds they bring north, Linda is not. "I will take hound mixes. Lab mixes go quickly. I like fluffy dogs like collies and shepherds, so I take them. I also take pit mixes. With a little effort I can adopt them out." One other factor often influences whether or not she takes a dog. "I take dogs that when I look at their picture I just feel sorry for them."

Linda's first puppies came from two shelters in Georgia, then from Gaston County, picked not so much because of their breeds—most are mixes—but because of their "release" date, a euphemism for the day the dog can legally be euthanized. Every shelter has its own rules about how long it will hold a dog or cat. In the case of publicly funded shelters, those rules are often set by the state, county, or municipality. Usually strays are held longer than animals surrendered by their owners. The thinking is that a stray may simply be someone's lost dog or cat; thus holding a stray for several days gives the owner time to retrieve his or her pet. In some shelters, owner-surrendered dogs and cats can be euthanized the day they enter the shelter.

To publicize their animals, more and more shelters are putting animals' pictures online, along with their release dates, so prospective adopters know how quickly they need to act. This is especially important for rescue groups that use the dates to prioritize; a dog or cat set to be killed will be given priority over one that still has three days left to live. In the latter case, there's always the hope that a local resident will adopt the animal.

Some shelters are trying to improve the quality of the photographs now that so many people start their search for a pet online. This is especially the case at shelters where dogs may spend weeks, even months, waiting for that forever home—a "luxury" not afforded to dogs in shelters so crowded that they are euthanized as soon as the law allows.

In North Carolina, photographer Mary Shannon Johnstone has focused her lens on dogs that have been in the Wake County shelter for at least fourteen days and for whom time is literally running out. I came across Johnstone's photography in late 2012. That year she'd completed *Shelter Life* and *Discarded Property,* two series chronicling life and death in North Carolina animal shelters.

The photos in the *Discarded Property* series are graphic—close-ups of dogs and cats being anesthetized, dead dogs splayed on a shelter floor beside their feces, a freezer piled with cat carcasses, a large black garbage bag filled with dead kittens. (The photos can be viewed on Johnstone's website, www.shannonjohnstone.com.)

"Those pictures are hard to look at," Johnstone acknowledged when we spoke by phone. "They ended up repelling people as much as they attracted them." And they did little to drive people into shelters to adopt pets. Rather, they perpetuated the stereotype of the shelter as a squalid place where animals go to die.

Johnstone followed up *Discarded Property* with *Landfill Dogs* (landfilldogs.info), which takes a radically different approach to telling the story of the state's overcrowded shelters. Each week she springs a dog from the shelter and takes the animal to a landfill-turned-county-park to be photographed for the shelter's website. Most of the dogs are pit bulls and pit mixes. All are large, as the shelter's large dogs don't get adopted as quickly as their smaller counterparts. "Each dog receives a car ride, a walk, treats, and about two hours of much needed individual attention," Johnstone writes on her website. The resulting photographs capture the unique personality of each dog. Some are action shots—dogs running, jumping, or catching a ball; some are portraits showcasing that powerful combination of strength and kindness characteristic of so many large breeds. The goal, Johnstone says, "is to offer an individual face to the souls that are lost because of animal overpopulation, and give these animals one last chance."

Award-winning photographer Seth Casteel has already shown that photographs that reflect a dog's personality can save lives. Casteel, best known for a series of groundbreaking photos of dogs swimming underwater, began taking pictures of shelter dogs in 2007. The results: Every shelter he visited reported that his photos drove up adoption rates.

Linda didn't remember whether she saw pictures of Galen's litter online—by 2010 she had rescued so many litters that they blurred together—but she did recall that the puppies came out of Gaston County's shelter. It's quite possible, she said, that one of her colleagues in North Carolina saw the pictures, or perhaps came upon the litter while in the shelter pulling out other dogs. That happened quite often. What Linda did remember is that when she learned about the puppies, she knew she'd bring them to New Jersey. She would never let an entire litter be killed—not when she had the means to save it.

GALEN ROLLED ONTO HER BACK as I entered my bedroom, tail thumping the floor, belly stretching toward the ceiling. She loved having her belly rubbed. Many mornings—having graduated to a dog bed from the pack-and-play—her tail would thump as soon as my alarm clock went off. I'd get out of bed and ask her if she wanted to go downstairs to eat breakfast, but more often than not she'd remain on her back, tail not missing a beat. Breakfast could wait.

I couldn't help but compare everything Galen did during her first few months with us to Gryffin's behavior as a puppy and even as an adult. For instance, while walking Galen one day, I noticed that her body cast the same shadow when washed by the sun as Gryffin's had—a shadow that—to me, at least—looked like it belonged to a hyena.

I also noticed that Galen would sit on the deck and watch as rabbits or gophers meandered about our yard, while Gryffin had vanquished them. To Gryffin, they were invaders, and more than once a baby rabbit met an unfortunate end when he caught up with it. (When Galen got older she would give chase, but her intent always seemed to be to herd, not to catch, and certainly not to kill. She once shot down the backyard so quickly she bowled over a gopher that hadn't seen her coming. I think the collision shocked Galen more than it intimidated the gopher.)

But one thing Gryffin had rarely done was roll over to expose his belly. The action, according to canine behaviorists, is a sign of submission, and Gryffin didn't submit to anyone or anything. Galen, on the other hand, showcased every submissive action I read about, including exposing her belly, a dog's ultimate sign of deference.

I was thinking about Galen and Gryffin as I stood in Pet Valu one Saturday afternoon gazing at three eight-week-old puppies. They were sleeping—blocks of white and gray fur so entwined it was hard to tell where one started and another ended. A group of four, from the same litter, slept about a foot away. The puppies were so small—not much larger than the palm of my hand. Had Gryffin and Galen been that tiny? A middle-aged man who had been kneeling beside the pen stood and asked Buff their breed. "We don't know," she answered. "Maybe some kind of Australian shepherd mix." Each dog had been given a name, but that was the extent of their identity.

In a crate adjacent to the pen, two black puppies with white chests barked, demanding someone—anyone—pay them some attention. Their breed, too, was unknown.

A feeling of anxiousness washed over me as I surveyed the dogs. I wasn't seeing much foot traffic through the store, and, save for the one man who questioned Buff, there wasn't anyone looking at the puppies. I asked Linda, "Do you ever worry that you've pulled so many dogs from the South that you won't find homes for all of them?"

"They'll go," Linda said. "There's a shortage of puppies in New Jersey."

My face must have betrayed my disbelief. "We spay and neuter," she added. "The South doesn't."

Certainly that was a broad generalization, I said. But Linda insisted, asserting that the South has a dog problem—that because so many people don't fix their dogs, there are too many litters, leading to overcrowded shelters, which, in turn, results in healthy dogs being killed.

"Rescue is the back end of dealing with overpopulation," Linda said. "We need to work at the front end. That means getting animals fixed." If she had the money, Linda told me, she would buy a mobile spay/neuter van and drive all over the South, spaying and neutering every unaltered dog and cat she came across.

I left Pet Valu stunned by Linda's comments, and as I drove home, I kept replaying our conversation in my mind. I was having a hard time wrapping my head around two things: first, that New Jersey—or any state—could have a shortage of puppies; second, that not fixing a family pet could be happening in so widespread a way, when shelters are so overcrowded that healthy dogs are being euthanized every day.

Property with a Heartbeat

WHEN I WAS THIRTEEN my parents got divorced, and I got the dog I'd always wanted. It was August, and my sister and I were just off the bus after a summer at sleepaway camp. My parents drove us home, settled us onto the worn brown couch in the den, and delivered the news: Our dad had already moved his stuff—and himself—out of the house.

It was extremely important for my parents to instill in my younger sister and me that we had absolutely nothing to do with their breakup and that they loved us, even if they were no longer in love with each other. Thus, they were ready with peace offerings—I considered them bribes at the time—to help us through our shock. My offering: a dog. My sister's: a station wagon. (I never understood the appeal there.)

A couple of weeks after my parents' pronouncement, the four of us piled into our new Nissan wagon and drove to a breeder an hour from our West Orange, New Jersey, home to pick up an eight-week-old West Highland white terrier. We named her Sammie. Looking back, I'm not sure Sammie ranked all that high in intelligence—if she saw a squirrel from my bedroom window, which overlooked our front yard, she would dash downstairs to the den for a closer look, but since the sliders in the den faced the backyard, there would be no squirrel.

So she'd rebound back upstairs and back onto my bed for another look out the window. Upon seeing the squirrel, she'd dart right back downstairs. This episode would repeat itself several times a day, several days a week. But what Sammie may have lacked in smarts, she more than made up for in love and in that wonderful ability dogs have to make you feel as if you are the very center of their world.

After my conversation with Linda, I thought about Sammie. She'd been spayed—I knew that. But I didn't recall if, all those years ago, it was a decision my mother had struggled over. When I asked her about it she told me, "The breeder wanted Sammie to be shown, and show dogs usually aren't spayed or neutered. But since I didn't plan to show her, I knew I wanted her spayed." As it turned out, Sammie never would have made it as a show dog—the vet said she had an overbite.

Gryffin was already neutered when I adopted him, the surgery having been done immediately after he'd arrived at the shelter.

As for Galen, there was a clause in the adoption contract I signed requiring that Galen be spayed. Even without it, Kevin and I would have done so. To my knowledge, that's just what you did when you owned a dog—you fed it, you fixed it, you loved it. Period.

Turns out—and there's no surprise here—I am a product not only of the family I grew up in, but of the culture I grew up in, too.

THE 1970S WERE A DEVASTATING decade nationwide for dogs and cats that found themselves locked up in U.S. animal shelters. Euthanasia rates peaked at that time, according to the ASPCA, with up to twenty million dogs and cats killed in shelters each year. The price tag of that mass euthanasia, along with all the related hours of animal control work, was millions of dollars annually—all paid for by U.S. taxpayers.

In an attempt to slow the killing and save lives, animal welfare organizations started to encourage shelter adoptions and, in concert with veterinarians, began promoting the idea that responsible pet ownership included the spaying and neutering of companion animals. The American Veterinary Medical Association had established standards for spay/neuter back in 1923, but the procedure was far from common. By the 1970s, only 10 percent of pet dogs and 1 percent of pet cats were fixed.

New Jersey, overrun with its share of homeless dogs and cats, implemented a first-of-its-kind statewide spay/neuter program in 1983. Legislators hoped the Animal Population Control (APC) program would drive down the pet population and save taxpayers money by making spay/neuter surgery affordable for low income residents, who, it was assumed, weren't getting their pets sterilized because the cost was out of their financial reach. Funding for the APC program initially came from a $3 licensing surcharge levied on residents whose pets weren't sterilized. Today that money is supplemented by a share of the sale of pet-friendly license plates and voluntary donations via a check-off box on state income tax forms.

Dr. Faye Sorhage, who served as the state's Public Health Veterinarian from 1985 through 2013 and oversaw the program, said the implementation of the surcharge was relatively simple because the state already had an existing licensing system dating back to the late 1960s. That system—still in place today—requires residents to license their dogs in the municipality in which they live and to renew that license annually. When Kevin and I moved our family to New Jersey, I had Gryffin licensed with our township for $21. One dollar went to the state's Rabies Trust Fund, and the rest went to the township to pay for animal control services. Because I had papers from the DeKalb shelter showing Gryffin was neutered, I didn't pay the APC surcharge.

When the program launched, it got off to a slower-than-expected start. "At first it was hard to get those on public assistance to take advantage of the program because it was hard to get them in," Dr.

Sorhage said. "They are dealing with so many other issues. All the money allocated to the program wasn't being spent, so over the years, the legislature has expanded the program's eligibility." Now any resident who adopts a dog or cat from a state-licensed shelter or rescue group can have the surgery performed by a participating veterinarian for a $20 co-pay.

Linda had made a vague reference to a discount program when we adopted Galen, but we were unable to take advantage of it because our vet doesn't participate. We did receive a small discount since Galen was a rescue, but the price for the surgery and all that accompanied it—anesthesia, pain meds, an overnight stay, and an Elizabethan collar—was a hefty $250. But back in 2011, all I knew was that Galen needed to be spayed. I never inquired about cost. I just had it done, and, fortunately, we could afford it.

In terms of the APC program's effectiveness, statistics from the Department of Health show that shelter intake is down 45 percent since the initiative started in 1983, and the state's euthanasia rate is down more than 63 percent. Dr. Sorhage attributes much of the decrease in intake to the APC program, as not only has it made spay/neuter affordable, it has raised the procedure's profile, establishing it as just another routine aspect of pet care. As for the decrease in euthanasia, much of that, too, can be attributed to the program, but, Sorhage says, the decrease is also due to a steady increase in rescue work and a growing cultural attitude among New Jersey residents that shelters shouldn't euthanize healthy animals. This attitude, she said, has led shelters to step up their efforts to promote adoption.

Still, about 24,000 animals are euthanized in the state annually, a majority of which, Dr. Sorhage told me, are feral cats. In 2013, state shelters put down 4,500 dogs. That number—4,500—rang high to me, especially if animal welfare groups are right about 90 percent of the dogs killed in shelters being healthy and adoptable.

But as I began to investigate Linda's claim that "we spay; the

South doesn't," I learned that in Gryffin's native Georgia, local animal welfare groups estimate that shelters kill about 300,000 dogs and cats annually; in Galen's native North Carolina, the state's Agriculture Department puts the number at roughly 250,000. What's more, neither is an outlier among Southern states.

In 2009, PetSmart Charities—concerned with the problem of companion animal overpopulation nationwide—conducted a study designed, in part, to determine Americans' attitudes toward spaying and neutering and to gauge whether those attitudes differ by geographic region. According to the study, 40 percent of Southern dog and cat owners hadn't spayed or neutered their pets. That's about 10 percent more than in any other region. The study also found that 14 percent of Southern pet owners—twice as many as those in the Northeast—said they were unlikely to spay or neuter a future pet.

I wondered about the attitudes driving those statistics, especially because it seemed to me that the South's higher euthanasia rates are a direct result of those attitudes. Fortunately, having spent a decade living and working in Atlanta, I knew someone who not only was intimately familiar with the region but also had a very soft spot in her heart for dogs, notably for cocker spaniels of the rescue variety.

"MY DAD ALWAYS LIKED to pile the kids in the car on Sundays and go for a spin. In this fuzzy memory, he put a brand-new litter of puppies in a paper sack to bring along on the ride. I loved dogs and remember thinking how wonderful it was that the puppies could go with us. When we got to one of my favorite spots, where a tangle of muscadine grapevines grew near the creek, he stopped, set out the puppies in the tall grass by the side of the road, got back in the car, and drove off."

I was speaking by phone with my friend Lisa—she asked that I not use her last name—a Georgia native and videographer/editor with whom I collaborated during my years at CNN. Lisa and I clicked immediately despite—or perhaps because of—our diametrically different childhoods in the 1970s: mine in an upper-middle-class suburb of New York City, hers on a ten-acre property in the foothills of the Appalachian Mountains. My mother tended a small tomato garden in our backyard that, to her dismay, I never took an interest in; Lisa's family grew their own vegetables and raised pigs, chickens, cows, and horses. I once made a reference to the "farm" she grew up on, and Lisa corrected me. "We didn't own a farm," she said. "We just had some animals."

Today, Lisa lives in Atlanta with her husband and a nervous cocker spaniel named Harvey, a foster-turned-permanent member of the household. Because she's a lifelong Southerner and self-described dog person who volunteers with area shelters and rescues, I hoped Lisa might be able to give me a generalized sense of the Southern psyche when it comes to dogs and what might be driving those low spay/neuter rates.

"Growing up, we always had dogs at our house," Lisa told me. Most of the people she knew had dogs, too. But unlike Sammie, who lived inside our house, Lisa's dogs—and her neighbors' dogs—lived outside. They were "yard dogs." In fact, Lisa's father never permitted their dogs to set foot inside the home.

Lisa explained that where she grew up, as in many rural areas of the South, people didn't think of dogs as pets the way so many of us do—and the way she does today. "A pet is something you take care of, you spay and neuter. It stays indoors. It's a companion. Yard dogs, on the other hand, are for protection. They're just something you have in your yard. They were never spayed or neutered." To do so, it was believed, would undermine their very purpose. "Since our dogs were intended to guard our house, meanness was valued, and Daddy believed an intact dog was meaner."

Many people have long shared the belief that dogs—especially males—are more aggressive and more protective when they haven't been neutered, so, still today, all over the country, dog owners forgo fixing their dogs. This, of course, has implications for population control, which frustrates folks in animal welfare because the scientific consensus, they say, is that it's a dog's natural instinct to protect—that instinct is genetic, and while it's perhaps also driven by environment, it's been found not to be driven by sex hormones.

But the belief is so embedded in American culture that no one with whom I spoke, from veterinarians to experts in animal welfare, could pinpoint its origin. "The idea's just always been out there," one told me.

Julie Albright, an animal behaviorist at the University of Tennessee College of Veterinary Medicine, says perceptions often derive from a small kernel of truth that, because of human nature, gets generalized. This may be the case here because testosterone in males—canine or human—can increase aggression. And although testosterone wasn't identified by scientists until 1935, at some point in history someone apparently drew a connection between non-neutered male dogs and aggression that has become so widespread that, having been perpetuated for generations, it is still perpetuated today.

Lisa's dogs spent their days hanging out on the family's front porch or patrolling the property. Sometimes, though, they would abandon the home to wander the community. Most of Lisa's neighbors lived, like she did, on ten acres; most had dogs, and no one had fences. "Building a fence meant devoting way too much time and money to keep a dog around," Lisa said, "so they romped and roamed, and the females had puppies."

Few families could afford to care for all those puppies, so they dispersed them in various ways. In the best cases, the puppies found homes with friends and extended family. But when this was not possible, it was not unheard of for an entire litter to meet a quick end—puppies might be shot or put in a bag and tossed off a bridge into a local river or creek. Other times they were simply "set out."

47

"When one of our dogs had puppies," Lisa told me, "Daddy just set them out by the side of the road. If he could find homes for some of them, he would give them away, but then he'd leave the rest in a box."

"Set out" was a phrase I'd never heard before, but it is part of the Southern vernacular, even though the act itself is by no means limited to the South. "To 'set out' a litter is to drop it off in a neighborhood where people have money or to leave it on the side of a road," Lisa said. "The puppies either fend for themselves or are taken in by people who pass by." Lisa and her husband own a small, rustic cabin in Tennessee, and she said litters are regularly set out there because people presume the cabin owners are wealthy and can afford to take in a dog or two. Sometimes people even set out pregnant dogs. Lisa told me she's turned over many strays and litters to local rescues.

Some communities around the country have made setting out—or "dumping"—companion animals illegal. In Corpus Christi, Texas, dumping is considered animal abuse and carries a fine of up to $4,000 and one year in jail. Still, television station KIII reported in June of 2013 that "almost anywhere you go in town you will spot a stray dog or cat," and at least one private shelter has installed surveillance cameras to catch people dumping pets right outside the shelter's doors. In Tri-Cities, Washington, where the public shelter takes in some 5,000 dumped dogs each year, efforts to catch dumpers in the act were stymied in the fall of 2013, after cameras mounted on the shelter's roof were stolen.

I was familiar with the concept of dumping, even if the phrase "set out" was new to me. When I adopted Gryffin, the DeKalb County Humane Society had told me that his litter was found in a box on the side of an Atlanta-area highway. A Good Samaritan rescued the puppies and brought them to the shelter. I couldn't help but wonder if Galen's litter had similarly been set out—along a busy highway, in a park, in an upscale neighborhood in Gaston County …

Lisa said that when she was a child, most of the dogs her family owned were strays, or else they came from the litter of someone else's stray that had been set out near her home. She called it a "cyclical, ineffective form of population control." But really, it wasn't population control at all—it was simply a means of controlling the number of dogs living on one's own property, while doing nothing to address the overall canine population.

Still, this was the "population control" many rural families living near or under the poverty level could afford then—and, in many cases, that they can afford now. And it's a primary driver of shelter overpopulation. That poverty plagues much of rural America has been well documented, and the South is home to nearly half of the country's rural population. What's more, data from the government's 2010 Census finds that the South remains the poorest region in the country, with about one-fifth of the population living in poverty. Of course, these figures also count the South's urban poor, and animal welfare experts say they, like their rural brethren, often can't afford to spay or neuter their dogs—or their cats.

A 2009 study in the *Journal of the American Veterinary Medical Association* found that the single greatest predictor nationwide of whether a cat is fixed is annual family income. Homes with annual incomes under $35,000 per year were half as likely to spay or neuter their cats as those with incomes at or higher than $75,000. Animal welfare experts say there's no evidence to suggest that a similar study of dog owners would find anything different.

Compounding the economic challenges of spay/neuter in poor rural and urban environments is yet another obstacle: accessibility. Veterinarians just don't often set up shop in poor communities. In searching Veterinarians.com, an online directory that bills itself as the number-one directory for local veterinarians and animal hospitals in the country, I found that there are both rural counties and urban communities throughout the South that do not host a single veterinary clinic.

Lisa told me there may have been a veterinary clinic not far from her home when she was growing up, but she knows her dogs never went there. "They were lucky if they got rabies shots," she said. When they did, it was her father who gave the dogs their shots, or sometimes he would take them to a free rabies clinic at the local farmer's exchange. "For my family, for a lot of rural families, healthcare and wellness are luxury items, ones that they can't afford to extend to their animals."

A few weeks after our conversation, I received an e-mail from Lisa. Spurred by our conversation, she'd decided to ask some fellow Southerners about their perceptions of the human-canine relationship as it's been traditionally lived in the South. Lisa told me that a carpenter—a native Southerner working on her Tennessee cabin—summed up the long-established relationship this way: "Dogs are animals. They are not pets or family members. They are commodities used to hunt or guard the front porch. In exchange we give them food, but the rest is up to them."

Wendy Frandsen, a co-author of the book *Southern Culture*, says such attitudes evolved out of the South's long agrarian history, one that, despite its evolution over the centuries, still influences many aspects of Southern culture, right down to perceptions about dogs. Frandsen says that in agrarian communities, the farm was central to survival, and both people and animals had utilitarian roles in sustaining it. "No one was there for fun, not the kids, not the animals. Everyone was part of the tradition."

In many cases, dogs were less valuable than the chickens, sheep, cattle, or other livestock a farmer owned, especially if livestock was the economy that the farmer worked in. But no matter their value, all the animals on the farm had one thing in common: They were the farmer's property. "Southerners have a sense of what is theirs, what is theirs to take care of, what is their business," Frandsen says. "Even in terms of family, fathers owned their children legally. The children weren't exactly property, but they belonged to the man, not the woman."

Animals as property is not a concept unique to the South, nor is it a nineteenth-century Southern convention. In *For the Prevention of Cruelty,* a history of the animal rights movement in the United States, Diane Beers writes that although the Puritans passed the colonies' first animal welfare laws in 1641, they "and society as a whole at that time generally accepted the notion that domesticated animals were the property of humans." But the South seems to have held onto this notion longer than other regions of the country. As I started reaching out to people involved in dog rescue in the South, I heard over and over again that, still today, many Southerners perceive dogs as property. One person, a self-described animal lover who's called Tennessee home for nearly fifty years, framed the distinction for me this way: "In the North, pets are part of the family. In the South, too often pets remain property that just happens to have a heartbeat."

This longer embrace by Southerners of the idea that dogs are property may stem from the fact that the first inklings of an animal welfare movement in the United States—in the early to mid-1800s—coincided with the growth of the abolitionist movement, with both finding proponents in the states of the North. Following the South's defeat in the Civil War, animal welfare advocates were quick to adopt abolitionist ideology and strategies to promote their cause. According to Beers, they "perceived many common threads between the institutionalized oppression of a specific group of humans and the institutionalized oppression of nearly all nonhumans. Slavery had denied moral, social, and legal status to African Americans. Likewise, human society deemed animals unfit for such recognition ... Slaves and animals were simply objects to be purchased, used, and sold at will. The murder of either a slave or an animal usually resulted in no greater punishment than providing financial compensation for the loss of property."

Of course, urbanization and industrialization in the North also brought issues of animal cruelty and neglect into the public conscience in ways not replicated in the agrarian South. It wasn't uncommon, Beers notes, to walk down nearly any city street and to see drivers whipping teams of horses or to see dead horses left along the curb; to see stray cats and dogs scavenging for food or to see them clubbed to death or drowned in the name of public health.

It's perhaps not surprising, then, that the animal welfare movement advanced most rapidly in the North, with the South lagging decades behind. Beers writes that the South's earliest known humane societies—formed in the mid-1880s in Alabama, North Carolina, South Carolina, and Tennessee—had a hard time recruiting members. By the 1890s, they existed primarily on paper and would remain dormant until the 1940s. Today, humane societies proliferate across the South, but the notion that an animal is one's property proliferates, too.

In *The New Mind of the South*, Georgia native Tracy Thompson explores notions of property and property rights through a Southern lens. Regarding property rights, she states, "These are red-blooded American values, obviously, but Southerners defer to none in their passion on this subject." It's a legacy, she theorizes, that comes from both the region's slave-owning history and its Scotch-Irish heritage. "Those immigrants from the border area between England and Scotland were landless, quarrelsome folks who eked out an existence herding cattle or sheep. Societies where one's entire worldly estate might walk off during the night are societies that take the defense of property as a matter of life and death."

Thompson concludes that cultural attitudes born in the past "embed themselves in the collective unconscious and survive the economies that spawned them." It's not a reach, then, to conclude that at the core of many a Southerner's concept of the human-canine relationship is the belief that a dog—like everything else a person owns—is property to do with as the owner sees fit. And this may be what has made attempts to regulate that ownership highly controversial, and to pass legislation at any level of government—city, county, or state—regarding everything from outlawing the use of gas chambers at animal shelters to instituting licensing laws to mandating spay/neuter nearly impossible.

I was starting to see the human-canine relationship as something that can be expressed in two very distinct ways, depending on one's cultural milieu. There's the "family model," the model I grew up exposed to, in which dogs sleep on our beds and are considered our sons and daughters, brothers and sisters; in its most extreme, pampered pooches eat organic and wear cashmere sweaters and diamond-studded collars. This model certainly transcends region, but it's flourished most quickly in those areas of the country where the animal welfare movement also found its earliest adherents: the more developed areas of the Northeast, upper Midwest, and West. Then there's the "property model," the one Lisa experienced growing up, the one that still proliferates throughout large swaths of the South and the more rural areas of the United States.

And yet the relationship between Southerners and their dogs is rich with complexity. As a shelter director in North Carolina said to me, "From generation to generation, we Southerners have always had dogs. We don't necessarily know why. We don't necessarily care for the dog. But we just have to have one. There's a saying: 'Take my wife, take my kids, take my car, but don't take my dog.'"

PERHAPS NO ANIMAL has been romanticized in Southern art and literature more than the dog. Celebrated for protecting the homestead and leading the hunt, dogs worked their way into the poems and stories of some of the region's most renowned writers, such as William Faulkner, Flannery O'Connor, Mark Twain, and Eudora Welty, and into children's classics like *Old Yeller* and *Sounder*. In the book *Southern Dogs and Their People*, editor Roberta Gamble pays tribute to the bond between Southerners and their dogs by pairing black-and-white photographs of dogs—on porches and in pickups, on hunts and with their humans—with quotations culled from the literary works of more than fifty Southern authors. In his introduction to the book, best-selling author Clyde Edgerton explains that when you grow up in the South—he grew up in North Carolina—you grow up "in the culture of Dog."

"When I was sixteen," Edgerton writes, "my daddy's bird dog, Queen, had a litter of ten, and I was given a dog I named Ben … I spent as much time with Ben hunting quail as I did hunting with any friend. We got to know each other well. He developed almost naturally into a fine bird dog who would do it all—point, retrieve, back, hunt close. We had adventures together and when I left home at age twenty-two to join the Air Force, I left him behind almost like I might leave a brother, if I'd had one."

Edgerton's relationship with Ben harkens to Travis's relationship with Old Yeller in Fred Gipson's tale of a fourteen-year-old boy in 1860s Texas and the stray dog who becomes his loyal and beloved companion. I'd read *Old Yeller* as a child, but reading it again with a newfound curiosity about the relationship between dogs and their Southern owners, I saw more clearly how Gipson's story reflects the universality of the human-canine experience in the agrarian South.

Early in the story, Travis wants a horse. But his father, heading out on a months-long journey to sell the family's cattle, tells the boy that what he needs more than a horse is a dog. Travis, though not happy, concedes his father is right. "All the other settlers had dogs. They were big fierce cur dogs that the settlers used for catching hogs and driving cattle and fighting coons out of the cornfields. They kept them as watchdogs against the depredations of loafer wolves, bears, panthers, and raiding Indians. There was no question about it: for the sort of country we lived in, a good dog around the place was sometimes worth more than two or three men."

When Travis ultimately has to shoot Old Yeller—the dog's been bitten by a rabid wolf—the boy's heart breaks. But his father tells him the only way to deal with his grief is to move past it. "[Things] may seem mighty cruel and unfair, but that's how life is part of the time. But that isn't the only way life is. A part of the time, it's mighty good. And a man can't afford to waste all the good part, worrying about the bad parts."

This notion of learning to move beyond grief is a life lesson all children learn, but in an agrarian society children learn it early and often, particularly about animals.

"When I teach Southern culture," says Frandsen, a professor at Vance-Granville Community College, which is in a rural region of North Carolina near the Virginia border, "I have students do an interview with their grandparents. I always hear stories where a grandparent says, 'I had a pet chicken and we killed it and ate it, and I was so sad.' 'I had a pet pig and we killed it and ate it, and I was so sad.' You learned as a kid, don't get your heart set on an animal. It's a cultural thing."

Frandsen says today this attitude extends beyond farm animals to dogs. "I hear, 'We had a dog; it was killed. We'll get another one.' Or, 'Dogs don't live that long; we'll get another one.' You are taught that you'll get your heart broken if you try to act like it's not just an animal, so you are taught not to get attached. And this is the message that is passed down to children."

This view, that there is always another dog to be had, while reassuring, may also decrease the value of an individual dog, and animal welfare experts say it fosters a view that dogs are disposable. When a dog dies or is sick, when it is too old to guard or hunt, if it wanders away and doesn't return, there's always another one. And certainly, there is always another one in a culture that historically hasn't spayed or neutered its dogs.

In *Old Yeller*, Travis finds solace knowing that one of the pups that Old Yeller sires—"the speckled pup"—will one day take Old Yeller's place as hunting companion and guard dog. It's not a stretch to assume that, if the book were to detail Travis's life through adulthood, many of his future dogs would be Old Yeller's progeny.

But what of the puppies the adult Travis didn't keep? The most likely answer is that they would have been given away, much like the speckled pup was given to Travis—or perhaps set out as strays to be taken in by some family, much like the way Travis's family took in Old Yeller.

Still today, acquiring a dog from someone you know is common. A 2011 PetSmart Charities survey found that nationwide nearly 30 percent of dog owners obtained their dogs from a family member, friend, or neighbor; a post-Katrina study conducted by HSUS found that in Mississippi and Louisiana nearly 50 percent of dogs were acquired this way. Animal welfare advocates say knowing this information is important because studies also show that dogs obtained from people we know are less likely to be spayed or neutered than dogs adopted from a shelter.

For many people raised in the agrarian tradition of their parents and grandparents, whose dogs came into their lives as strays or from a neighbor's litter, or whose own dogs had litters, the idea of altering a dog is quite simply something to which they may never have been exposed.

Lisa told me about a conversation she had with a sixty-year-old neighbor who recently got a puppy. She asked the man if he planned to spay his dog, and he said, "No. I'm going to let nature take its course." When she asked why he would risk puppies, the man said he grew up in Louisiana, he had always had dogs, and they had never been spayed. It wasn't so much that he was opposed as it was just something that, for generations, his family had not ever done. Lisa persuaded him it was time to break with tradition; this dog was part of his family.

Kevin and I instinctually embraced the family model all those years ago when I adopted Gryffin. That's why, from the moment I brought him home, we referred to him as our son, and why I've taken to calling Galen a daddy's girl.

Of course, it took some time for that latter relationship to evolve.

I OFTEN JOKE THAT DOGGY DAY care saved my marriage, but what it really did was secure Galen's place in our family and set her on a path to becoming that daddy's girl.

After February's incident in the snow, I was desperately seeking ways to tame Galen of the wild energy she was unleashing on Lindsey and Dhani. One day, a friend mentioned that her dog attended day care. A day there, she said, wiped him out for the next several.

Enrolling a dog in day care—at least in the one near my home—takes more than a phone call. Galen had to pass two screening interviews—one in our home, one in the day-care center.

I tried to prep Galen for the interviews by explaining that she needed to be on her best behavior—that remaining in our home, in our family, rested on her performance. She'd cock her head and stare at me, clueless. "Let's go outside" and "Do you want a cookie?" she understood perfectly, but a discussion of good manners in the face of a make-or-break interview was completely beyond her cognitive grasp.

Fortunately, Galen came through for me, passing both interviews despite a performance at home that I feared might squash any chance of her becoming a day-care dog. (After repeated attempts to jump into the interviewer's lap, I relegated Galen to her crate in hopes of salvaging the situation.)

Playing with dogs for eight straight hours tired Galen like no activity I could do with her. She would come home, walk directly into her crate, lay her head on a stuffed Mickey Mouse—the only stuffed toy she hadn't de-stuffed—and sleep. Best of all, her mini-reign of terror over the girls ceased. And all that roughhousing with other dogs took an edge off her that carried over to her non–day care days.

What's more, Galen quickly fell in love with day care—each morning, she stalks Kevin as he dresses, hoping he'll take her there on his way to work. We've had to limit her to one or two times a week, though; good day care—for dogs, as for kids—isn't cheap.

Galen, of course, still had her quirks—refusing to pee anywhere but our backyard, which I assumed contributed to her recurrent urinary tract infections—and she remained leery of men, but, most important, she no longer posed a threat to our daughters. And they adored her. Dhani, who had spent her stuffed animal years collecting cats, was quickly becoming a dog person, showering Galen with a love that she had rarely shared with Gryffin. As for Lindsey, a dog-lover from the moment she fed Gryffin his first Cheerio, Galen made her whole again, and she told Kevin so in a child's inimitable way as she stood in our bedroom scratching Galen behind her soft, floppy ears. "I'm not glad Gryffin died, but I'm glad Gryffin died," she said. "Because now we have Galen."

As for me, I was feeling confident that I'd teased out of Linda every bit of information she knew about Galen's past. And Lisa had introduced me to a facet of the multifaceted human-canine relationship that had been, until now, foreign. But I wanted to know more; my journalist's instincts were telling me there was a lot more to this story.

Death-Row Dogs

"My neighbors know me as the crazy dog lady," Leah Lenox tells me as she picks at the cheese and crackers plated on the table in front of us. We are sitting on the patio of Lenox's Charlotte, North Carolina, home.

Lenox is one of Linda Wilferth's North Carolina connections to the Gaston County animal shelter. As a founding member of an all-volunteer foster organization, Lenox's group fosters dogs for Catnip Friends and for several other rescues in New Jersey, Pennsylvania, and Connecticut. She and her husband, Erich, own three dogs and are fostering a six-year-old Jack Russell mix from Gaston's shelter who will soon relocate to a Russell rescue in Tennessee. Lenox is in her thirties, is very pregnant with her second child, and works full-time in finance. She strikes me as one of those I-don't-know-how-she-does-it-all women.

Back in 2008, married but not yet with children, Lenox felt something was missing from her life. "I told Erich, I feel like we need to do something good for the world." Lenox had volunteered at an animal shelter while in college, and now she wanted to do so again, this time with her husband. At about the same time, the couple was considering adopting a dog, so they dropped by a local, privately run shelter in Charlotte. "The shelter was welcoming. The staff was all about adoption, asking, 'What are you looking for? What do you need?'" There was also something she found especially refreshing about the shelter: "They don't euthanize animals." The couple didn't adopt a dog that visit, but they did enroll in the shelter's dog-walking program, and they left with the first of many dogs they would foster.

"Then I met someone who said, if you want to make a difference, go look at Gaston County Animal Control. Go see where they gas the animals. I was like, I gotta go see this place."

Gaston County's shelter, in the town of Dallas, is about twenty-five miles west of Charlotte, an easy drive from Lenox's home. "I was dumbfounded," she says. "I had never seen anything like this. It was not as clean as the one in Charlotte. These beautiful animals were there, and they were dirty, had feces on them—poop was everywhere. No one approached us. There were no volunteers walking around to help you. It felt like a holding cell. I had to walk past a gas chamber to see the adoptable animals."

Lenox began pulling one or two dogs at a time from the shelter, fostering them, and trying to adopt them out to rescues or people she knew. "I went back once and asked about a puppy slated to be killed the next day. I was told, 'It's going to be euthanized tomorrow,' and I said, 'No, you don't.' I found that dog an awesome home with a friend." But, she says, "I didn't really know what I was doing. And I kept thinking there was something else I could do because just fostering dogs and begging rescues to take them wasn't enough." She also found she didn't like reading adoption applications and handling adoptions. "I just liked the dogs."

Lenox met Linda and members of other rescue groups through social media as she tried to find homes for the dogs she was pulling from Gaston's shelter. That's when Lenox decided she could have a bigger impact by fostering dogs and letting rescues in the North find them homes. "After four years of doing this, I know who adopts out what. Linda pulls puppies. Another rescue pulls older dogs. Then there are breed-specific rescues." To assist the rescues in finding the right dogs, Lenox goes online every night to see what dogs Gaston County Animal Control took in that day. If she sees one that she believes is the right fit for a particular rescue, she gets the okay from the rescue to foster the dog.

Lenox's operation quickly became too big for one household—she needed a network of people willing to take in dogs for up to two or three weeks at a time. And that's when she took a closer look at her community. Charlotte is home to the country's second-largest banking center, the headquarters of several Fortune 500 companies, and a growing number of energy-related businesses. It's brimming with young professionals who, Lenox thought, might not want the responsibility of owning a dog but would surely be willing to foster one—especially if she told them the alternative for the dog was death.

Thus, Dog Days of Charlotte was born. "We made it cool and fun to volunteer. We found some cool bars and restaurants that had never marketed themselves as dog-friendly, but they said, 'If you can get people here, they can bring their dogs.' So we're social in a way that combines liquor and dogs."

The fun part of fostering is the draw because there's a lot about fostering right from the shelter that requires much patience and time, and a willingness to take the most unsanitary of dogs into your home. "When we get the dogs, they are usually dirty, smelly—sometimes they have feces on them. They are extremely scared. Our fosters have to do the dirty work. They have to bathe the dogs and take them to a vet to be tested for heartworm, be vaccinated, and, depending on the dog's age, be spayed or neutered." The rescues pay the vet bills, not the fosters. "Once the dogs get to the Northern fosters or to their adopted families they are calmer, not so scared. They've had a few weeks to decompress."

The Jack Russell that Lenox is fostering seems perfectly at home in her backyard. He stops by my chair every now and then for a quick pat on the head; then he goes back to exploring the bushes lining the fence that rings her yard. Lenox says a shelter employee told her that the dog was surrendered by his owner, but Lenox doesn't know why. She says he's been a perfect gentleman while he's been living with them, leaving her to wonder what led the dog's owner to give him up.

It's usually impossible to know what kind of a situation a dog has come out of, but Lenox says sometimes the dog provides a clue. "I often will get dogs that have lived outside their whole life. You open the door to let them in the house, and they're almost confused."

Thinking back to my conversations with Linda about spaying and neutering, I ask Lenox if the Jack Russell is neutered. "No," she says. "Ninety-five percent of the time we pull dogs they aren't fixed, no matter their age." Often Lenox will have the dogs fixed at a low-cost clinic in the Charlotte area before sending them north, where the surgery is more expensive.

Prior to coming to Charlotte, during a telephone conversation, I had asked Lenox to comb through her records to see if she could find out who fostered Galen's litter. She had been optimistic that by the time we met she'd have the information, but as yet she hadn't said anything.

Now, I ask what she has learned.

Lenox pauses.

She had searched, she says, but it had been almost two years since Galen's litter had come through the organization. "I may have fostered them," she says. "So many litters come through my house, through the organization; it's just hard to know."

I leave Lenox's home knowing little more about Galen than I had when I came to Charlotte. However, I also leave entirely confident that whoever fostered the litter—whether it was Lenox or one of her fosters—the puppies had received the best of care.

I know where I have to go next.

I had once asked Linda if she ever wanted to visit Gaston County's shelter, to see where so many of her dogs and cats came from. She did not. "They are all on death row," she told me. "So you have to be able to pick which animals you are going to save, because you can't save all of them. I just couldn't do it."

GASTON COUNTY is in the Piedmont region of North Carolina, along the South Carolina border. Long an agricultural community, the county gained national prominence in the late nineteenth century, when it forged a central role in the ascendant textile industry, earning the moniker "the combed yarn capital of the world."

Today, Gaston is the state's seventh most populated county, and it finds itself under heavy pressure to reinvent itself. Global outsourcing, followed by the recession of 2007, hit the county hard. Mills closed; manufacturing workers lost jobs. And the impact on the economy stretched far beyond the textile industry, as the double blow forced many companies out of business.

Driving from my hotel to the shelter, I pass signs of the struggling economy—boarded-up buildings, stores with FOR SALE signs in windows, and small patches of construction. But what strikes me most is that my GPS—loaded with the shelter's address—isn't taking me toward the outskirts of town, where I expected I'd find the shelter. Many public shelters are located in out-of-the-way areas of the cities and towns they serve, near railroad tracks or next to landfills—on streets named Landfill Road or even Dump Road—making them largely inaccessible and inconvenient for people who might otherwise consider adopting a shelter dog. Gaston's shelter not only is not out of the way, but it sits on prime real estate, just past the entrance to Dallas Park, a 100-acre recreation area.

A senior center marks the entrance to the park, behind which rolling green hills stretch as far as I can see. Signs signal the way to ball fields, equestrian facilities, picnic areas, and the shelter. On the day of my visit, the sky is blue, the sun is shining, and as I drive toward the shelter, I am having a hard time believing the house of horrors Lenox described could exist in such a family-friendly environment.

Then I pull into the shelter's parking lot.

A chain-link fence, about ten feet tall and locked, separates the parking lot—and the park—from the shelter and an adjacent building that houses Gaston College's Veterinary Technology Center.

I stand in front of the fence for what seems like several minutes, hoping someone inside the shelter will see me, despite that being wholly unlikely, as the fence and the building are several yards from one another. Then I begin digging in my purse for my cell phone. Fortunately, a student attending the college arrives, and while she tells me she isn't permitted to let me enter, she does say she will find someone who can. Moments later, she returns to unlock the gate. I walk past that gas chamber Lenox had spoken about during our conversation and then into the shelter.

REGGIE HORTON RISES from behind his desk to shake my hand. Horton, who stands more than six feet tall, with broad shoulders, white-gray hair and a matching mustache, and a smooth Southern accent, is an imposing figure. He's been the shelter's administrator for nearly two decades; he's worked at the shelter for three, starting out as an animal control officer. I had e-mailed Horton requesting an interview, and he'd agreed to it quickly, but I immediately get the impression he's wary—very wary, actually. We begin our conversation with him asking me questions: What brings me to the shelter? What information am I hoping to learn? What exactly do I plan to do with that information? I get the strong sense he's sizing me up, trying to figure out what, if any, agenda I may have.

I'm not all that surprised. Shelter workers, especially those in public shelters, are often skewered by the public and the press—sometimes fairly, sometimes not—over how animals are treated and the very fact that healthy cats and dogs are euthanized, often in excessively large numbers.

I quickly learn that Horton has received his share of criticism and condemnation over the years. He relates a story that he says reflects the way many people feel about public shelters. "A lady called complaining about some horrific thing she heard about happening in Dallas, and it was heartfelt, but she was absolutely vilifying us, telling me how terrible we are to allow this to go on. And as I'm listening, I'm thinking, 'I have no clue what she's talking about.' Then she reads from the article, and I come to find out she's talking about Dallas, Texas. So I said, 'Ma'am, that's not us.' Do you think she said, 'Oh, whoops, sorry'? No. She said, 'It doesn't matter. You're probably doing something just as bad.' Click." He mimes the woman slamming down the phone.

There is no national shelter system in the United States or even a nonprofit umbrella organization that oversees the country's animal shelters. Rather, U.S. shelters are a hodgepodge of public, private, and public-private entities that operate under the auspices of the municipalities, counties, and states in which they are located. And even within states, there is little, if any, coordination among shelters.

The first modern animal shelter in the United States—modern in that it provided medical care, sought homes for its cats and dogs, and engaged in humane methods of euthanasia—opened in 1869 in Philadelphia. Called the City Refuge for Lost and Suffering Animals, it was conceived of by Caroline Earle White, the founder of the Women's Pennsylvania Society for the Prevention of Cruelty to Animals (WPSPCA). White, along with the better-known ASPCA founder, Henry Bergh, is considered one of the leaders of the country's then-fledgling animal-protection movement.

At the time, Philadelphia and other American cities and towns relied on impoundments—better known as pounds—to house stray animals. These were the successors to the country's first pounds, which came into fashion during colonial times, primarily to house livestock that wandered from a family's farm—but colonial pounds took in stray dogs, too. Owners wanting to reclaim a lost animal paid the pound master a redemption fee. This fee, along with what the pound master could earn from slaughtering unclaimed livestock and selling the meat, was how the pound master made his living. Dogs rarely generated revenue, so they were usually killed quickly and in no way humanely.

Dogs didn't fare better when cities and towns took over control of the pounds, which happened around the Industrial Revolution. The inhumane treatment—clubbing and drowning stray dogs to death—outraged people like Bergh and White. But whereas Bergh refused to allow the ASPCA to take over New York City's pound—he didn't believe the city would provide enough money for the ASPCA to run the pound as he saw fit—White embraced the challenge.

Under White's direction, the WPSPCA not only raised enough money to build the country's first shelter, the organization took over Philadelphia's pound, and White persuaded the city to contribute $2,500 to run it. Thus, the City Refuge for Lost and Suffering Animals distinguished itself from the pounds of the day as the first-ever shelter to receive a municipal appropriation and for creating a safer haven for animals. I say "safer" because many dogs were still killed—often using chloroform—to create cage space for the next ones who would enter the shelter. Thus, this "gentle killing," as it was called, was perceived as acceptable—a necessary evil—as the only tool communities had to control overpopulation and provide for public safety.

Over time, the lexicon has changed—the city pound has become the public shelter. But in the last several decades there's also been a paradigm shift in the way most Americans view the role of an animal shelter. No more do they want it to act in its historic role—as a hold-and-kill facility—but rather as a facility that cares for animals until they can be found permanent homes.

Herein lays the challenge for many public shelters, say shelter administrators like Horton. They say older facilities—those thirty, forty, fifty years old—were not built to hold animals for extended periods of time, nor do most counties and municipalities provide the funds or the employees necessary to run shelters as adoption agencies. Further, what has not changed, they say, is the primary mission that most counties and municipalities do budget for: rounding up stray animals for the welfare of public health and safety.

As a division of county government, Gaston's shelter is funded by taxpayers and staffed by twenty-three county employees—animal control officers, shelter and administrative staff, and Horton, the administrator. And like most, if not all, public shelters, it is open admission—it must accept every animal that comes through its doors, whether the animal is surrendered by its owner or picked up by an animal control officer, whether the shelter has space or does not. Private shelters, on the other hand, can decline to accept dogs for any reason or no reason. Those turned away—usually the least adoptable due to age, breed, or disposition—often find their way into public shelters. Then—and this is what really frustrates those employed by public shelters—after turning dogs away, private shelters tout themselves as "no-kill," a designation that sets them apart from the public shelters, which, by default, get referred to as "kill" shelters, a black eye in the eyes of much of the public. The administrator of a public shelter in New Jersey put it to me this way: "The private shelters do all the feel-good work, and that's what the public sees. Then I have to answer to the media because people will say that we don't do enough to save lives."

The no-kill moniker isn't just divisive; it's also controversial because its definition is not universally agreed upon within the animal welfare movement. To some, a no-kill shelter is one in which no dogs are euthanized to create space but where a dog may be put down if it is deemed too aggressive to be adopted or too ill to be made well—designations that advocates say account for about 10 percent of shelter animals. Then there's the position promoted by Nathan Winograd's No Kill Advocacy Center, which holds that the term "unadoptable" is defined too broadly by most U.S. shelters. A no-kill shelter, according to the center, is one in which dogs are rarely euthanized, the assumption being that there is a home for every dog no matter how dangerous or how sick, and that if a home can't be found, it is because shelter employees are not working hard enough to find it. Euthanasia, the center states in its online literature (www. nokilladvocacycenter.org), is indicated only for dogs whose condition is so grave that they cannot live without "severe, unremitting pain" or who are so aggressive that they "have been adjudicated to be vicious by a court of competent jurisdiction and ordered killed by that court."

Gaston's shelter has been labeled both a "kill" shelter and the more derogatory moniker, a "high-kill" shelter, because of its euthanasia rate. Since its construction in 1969, the shelter has been inundated with more animals—primarily cats and dogs, but every now and then it will take in rabbits, raccoons, or various rodents—than it can legally hold. The only means of relieving overcrowding are adoption, rescue, and euthanasia, and in Gaston County's shelter, as in many overcrowded public shelters around the country, euthanasia has long been the most reliable means of creating kennel space. In the late 1990s and early 2000s, the euthanasia rate at Gaston's shelter regularly hit 90 percent. Over the last several years, however, the trend has been toward more adoptions and rescues, and in 2011, for the first time in the shelter's history, the euthanasia rate dipped just below 50 percent.

Kennel supervisor Sue King is tasked with euthanizing the shelter's animals, and she does this—along with several staff members—every day of the year, except weekends and holidays, mostly via lethal injection and mostly to create space. Hers is not the type of job, she says, that you share with people you meet at cocktail parties or that you want to discuss in the majority of social settings.

When King, a veterinary technician, started working at the shelter sixteen years ago, she and the staff were euthanizing 13,000 animals a year, according to a 2008 article in the *Gaston Gazette*.

Although I can't fathom the emotional toll that euthanizing healthy dogs and cats must take on a person, King tells me she did it then, as she does it now, because it has to be done. She says there just aren't enough people adopting dogs and cats from the shelter to free up needed space. And each day the shelter is open, more people come in surrendering their pets. I hear in her voice that familiar frustration that I've heard so often when talking with Linda Wilferth. But, King says, softening a bit, just because the job has to be done doesn't mean it ever gets easier. "To do it, I choose to not fully open my heart. But there have been a few dogs I couldn't kill, and someone else has had to do it."

Perhaps not surprisingly, a 2005 study in the *Journal of Applied Social Psychology* on the psychological ramifications of euthanasia-related work found that shelter employees engaged in euthanasia suffer higher levels of job-related stress, work-to-family conflict, sleeping problems, and substance abuse than do their fellow employees. Researchers say these findings are reflective of the strain resulting from what's been called the caring-killing paradox. They write that shelter workers face "a daily contradiction between their ideal occupational selves (i.e., protectors of animals) and the reality of having to kill healthy but unwanted animals," and that this strain is often amplified "given the social stigma attached to the killing of companion animals."

King and I are talking in her cramped office. It's small and dark; there are stacks of boxes, filing cabinets, and a desk strewn with piles of paper, some tucked into folders. King, like Horton, seems wary of me; rarely has good come out of a reporter's visit to the shelter. To redirect our conversation, perhaps, King tells me a story.

In 2012, animal control brought into the shelter a mom and her thirteen puppies. They were found, along with a bag of dog food, in an abandoned house. Shelter employees named the mom Ellie. "She was a Lab mix—a plain Jane on the outside but spectacular on the inside. She was extremely intelligent. You could just look in her eyes and see her thoughts. 'Do I trust them? Do I not trust them? My past wasn't so great.'"

King took Ellie on walks outside and inside the shelter. "The shelter can be pretty confusing to newcomers, but Ellie always knew how to get back to her babies. She put her heart and soul into them." Twelve survived.

A rescue organization ultimately pulled Ellie and her puppies from the shelter. Seeing them leave was tough, King tells me. "Ellie got past those barriers built around my heart. I cried when she got loaded out. She was special."

I soon realize that what makes Ellie's story so unusual is not just that she and her puppies beat the odds by making it out of the shelter alive; it's that they lived in the shelter for about a month while animal control tracked down the dogs' owners. King called the fact that it took so long a blessing. All that time allowed Ellie to nurse her puppies to good health, and it allowed a rescue group to organize foster and adoptive families for thirteen dogs.

Most dogs don't stay in Gaston County's shelter for nearly that long. Legally, animals surrendered by their owners need only be held for one business day before they can be euthanized. Strays must be held for three, since a stray may be someone's lost pet. Those extra two days, King says, give owners the opportunity to find and reclaim their dog or cat. The holding times are set by the county.

One day. Three days. Either way, that seems like so little time. But King says the shelter doesn't have a choice—by law it can only hold a limited number of dogs, and cages fill up fast. "During a typical summer week, we take in about two hundred dogs and cats. During the winter, it's about half that." But even if the shelter wasn't overcrowded, King says it's not healthy for dogs to remain caged for long periods of time. "They can't stay here long term; their temperament changes. They need human interaction, and we don't have the volunteers. We're just not built to be a long-term facility."

The bottom line, as King sees it, is that too many people don't think through all the implications of owning a dog: There are financial obligations—a dog should be fed and vetted—and societal obligations—a dog should be spayed or neutered. The spaying and neutering isn't happening to the extent it needs to be, she says.

A comprehensive animal welfare study commissioned by Gaston County in 2002 sought to determine the cause of what one of the study's authors called the county's "pet population problem." The study's findings mirror those of national studies: Neither legitimate breeders nor puppy mills were driving shelter overpopulation. What was: accidental litters from the indiscriminate mating of "backyard dogs." Later, I would learn a new term for these accidental litters: "oops litters," as in, "Oops! I didn't intend for my dog to get pregnant."

"I'D SAY NINETY-EIGHT PERCENT of our litters are 'oops litters,'" Mona Triplett tells me. "It's amazing how many repeat customers they have at the shelter."

Triplett, who lives in Stokes County, North Carolina, along the Virginia border, is as passionate a protector of dogs as I've met. In 2004, county commissioners appointed her to the position of humane investigator, a volunteer role that allows her to assist animal control officers on cruelty and neglect cases, a position that takes up a lot of her time. "I'm working on a case now where some yahoo stabbed his nine-year-old German shepherd eight times because he was pissed at his girlfriend. We see hoarders who call themselves rescuers. And then we had a case where this yahoo decided it was cool to tattoo his dog all over her belly." She raises her voice, as if to underscore the absurdity of such an act.

A petite blonde with a penchant for cigarettes and dogs, Triplett is sitting on a sofa in her living room, legs tucked beneath her. Maya, a small black Lhasa apso mix, is curled beside her, hidden under a green throw pillow. Maya's mother, Mimi, makes a quick appearance in the living room before returning to Triplett's bedroom. Kai, a fifteen-month-old Weimaraner, lies on the carpet, coming to me every now and then for a little attention. He's a drooler. "He was just cast out," Triplett says of the large gray dog she thinks is a purebred. "We tried to find an owner but never could."

Thelma, who Triplett thinks is a whippet mix—"she can run like the wind"—tries to hop onto the loveseat with me. Triplett found Thelma, pregnant, along the side of a county road and took her in to have her litter. "Thelma raised the puppies until they were ten weeks old because I think puppies need to be around mama for as long as possible." When Triplett couldn't find homes for the puppies locally, she had them transported to a shelter outside New York City. "All the puppies were adopted that first weekend." Thelma will be heading north soon, too. "After the puppies left, she lay on her bed and looked out the window for three days, which just broke our heart. But it had to be done. She'll do fine. We thought about keeping her, but we already have the three."

In Triplett's backyard, in a large run, are two very active Belgian Malinois—siblings, a male and female—whom she came across at the Stokes County shelter. "There was something about them laying there in that kennel that broke my heart. I shouldn't have them. They're just broken. But I tend to take in those kind more often than not. They'll need a lot of work before they can be adopted out."

Triplett is also the founder and director of the nonprofit Stokes County Humane Society. The organization has a dual mission—to educate dog owners about low-cost spay/neuter opportunities and to save dogs' lives by pulling them from the county's animal shelter and putting them into foster homes until permanent ones can be found. These days, Triplett says, she does more pulling than educating. It's a predicament many in rescue find themselves in: They would prefer to spend their time working to stop the flow of those unintended litters, but with shelters euthanizing for space, they devote their time to finding homes for the animals whose lives already hang in the balance.

The Stokes County shelter is at the entrance to the county landfill in the small community of Germanton. Triplett calls it "an aesthetically depressing place." The thirty-year-old rectangular building is concrete and much smaller than the shelter in Gaston County, but then Stokes County's population is also more than four times smaller than Gaston County's. Inside the front door is a reception desk much like you would see in a doctor's office. The waiting area is tiny, with room for just four chairs. Beyond the desk and through a closed door is the canine kennel, with twelve dog runs, six on each side of the room, a walkway through the center. There are two and three dogs in a single run; Triplett says she's seen up to seven. Most of the dogs are large—shepherd and pit bull mixes. Some sit, some stand, mostly near the front of the run. Some bark, some watch me, silent, as I walk by. It's my imagination, I know, but they seem to be pleading, "Get me out of here!" An overwhelming sense of guilt washes over me. There is nothing I can do to help them. They need homes, and homes are not something I have to offer.

I overhear Triplett tell one of the animal control officers that she hasn't seen some of the dogs before. She asks if their pictures have been taken and posted on the shelter's Facebook page. Not yet, she's told. The shelter closes in fifteen minutes—not enough time to take the pictures today. The woman behind the reception desk tells Triplett they'll try for tomorrow, then adds, "But you know how crazy things get around here."

Most of the dogs I've just seen will likely be put down.

In 2011, the Stokes County shelter euthanized 61 percent of its dogs. In 2012, it didn't submit its numbers to the state. In April of 2013, county officials ordered that all of the shelter's dogs and all incoming dogs without vaccination records be euthanized following an outbreak of parvovirus. The chairwoman of the shelter's advisory board told the local newspaper that the shelter's out-of-date construction—it lacks an area to quarantine sick dogs—means it is practically impossible to rid the shelter of the virus. "Because of the way this shelter is set up we cannot clean properly. You can't get it out of the environment no matter how hard they try, it's just not happening." (A nonprofit group has been raising funds for a new shelter with the hope of breaking ground in 2015.)

Triplett has found it nearly impossible to find homes locally for all the dogs she rescues from the shelter, so she's established a partnership with North Shore Animal League America in Port Washington, New York. She sends about thirty dogs to North Shore each month. One of her dogs was adopted by actor Kevin Spacey, she says, a note of pride in her voice. "We sent Larry, Curly, and Moe. He took Curly."

I've become fascinated by what turns a dog lover—there are so many of us—into someone willing to make rescue a part of each and every day of her life. So I ask Triplett if she has a sense of where her passion comes from. She hesitates ever so slightly. "My dad killing about every animal I had growing up, right in front of me. Dogs, cats, rabbits. He was an abusive alcoholic who did mean, cruel stuff to control his family. If one of our animals did something wrong while he was in his spell—like if my grandmother said the dog pooped on the porch or the cat scratched something, he'd stomp it right there in front of us. He took a tire iron to a rabbit one time. He's dead now. Died when my son was born; I was twenty-one. Car crash, drunk. I've worked as a substance abuse counselor, and I have more understanding and more forgiveness for it now, as an adult. It's just sad what humans will do to one another because they can. And to animals. I'm just very passionate about that."

Triplett pauses before continuing.

"What really got me thinking about starting the Humane Society, though, was my neighbor had a little golden mix that got pregnant every time she went into heat. Once, my husband found a puppy in a ditch between our houses. It was very cold outside, and the puppy was maybe two or three weeks old; it was dirty. My husband returned it, and the guy says, 'My dog had thirteen puppies. She keeps getting pregnant, and I can't afford to get her spayed.' Now I don't believe that. There's a low-cost spay/neuter center forty minutes away. He also told my husband he was thinking about taking the puppies into the woods and letting nature take its course. So, I started watching for the puppies around his yard. Then one day, I didn't see them, so I grabbed my daughter and we started walking into the woods—it's all state park behind us. There they were, on a blanket, all the puppies. We brought them home, put them on the back porch, and I called a vet. She put me in touch with a rescue."

When Triplett looked around her county, she saw there were a lot of dogs who weren't fixed and a lot of dog owners like her neighbor—people, she says, who "are not able or not willing to be responsible." I ask to what she attributes the unwillingness.

"There's a lot of old money in this county, and old land. People don't sell it. They pass it from one generation to another, so a lot of people are raised on farms. They see life and death with animals every day. Animals are used for our food, for our needs. I think that desensitizes people to the plight of dogs, and they just don't value them. It's too simple to have animal control take care of an unwanted litter or a dog you don't want anymore."

Triplett would like to see county leaders put in place a spay/neuter ordinance, but, she says, there is little chance of that happening. "They don't want to disturb taxpayers. And anyway, dogs are considered personal property, and around here, the feeling is, 'Don't mess with my property.'"

Compounding the problem, county lawmakers don't require that dogs adopted from the shelter be spayed or neutered. So dogs that enter the shelter not having been fixed return to the community the very same way. The dogs that Triplett rescues will have the surgery, but they will likely live out their lives in New York, not in Stokes County.

"WE'VE DECIDED WE won't be part of the problem," Reggie Horton says when I ask about the shelter's policy regarding the spaying and neutering of the dogs it adopts out. All dogs adopted from Gaston County's shelter are fixed before being released, just as Gryffin was all those years ago, before I adopted him. More and more public shelters are requiring that animals have the surgery before being released because they've learned that they can't rely on the public to follow through with getting their pets fixed, even when given vouchers for free or low-cost surgeries, even when appointments are made for them. In Gaston County, new owners retrieve their dogs post-surgery from a local veterinarian's office. Horton says it's a win-win for the community and the vets, who are introduced to potential new clients.

Dogs pulled by rescue groups, however, are not sterilized. Horton says it's not fair to ask Gaston County's vets to do low-cost surgeries on dogs who will live outside the state. That's why Galen wasn't spayed. In the last seven years, the number of rescues has skyrocketed from zero in 2005 to more than 2,900 in 2012. One member of the shelter's administrative staff told me she gets an average of 100 inquiries a day from rescue groups, 70 percent of which are about the shelter's dogs. In 2012, local adoptions numbered 863, down more than 300 from 2011. "The reality is that we've saturated the local market, and we're seeing a stagnant number of adoptions," Horton says.

Horton attributes the boon in rescue activity at the shelter to two things. First, animal welfare has become a higher priority among society at large, and with that has come vocal opposition to the practice of euthanizing healthy dogs. Second, in 2006, the shelter lifted a "no rabies vaccination—no adoption" policy. Prior to that, all dogs who entered the shelter without proof of having been vaccinated for rabies—every stray and some surrenders—were euthanized. The policy was put in place in 1999, after the county saw a spike in rabies cases, from five in 1998 to thirty-two the following year. Even after the number of rabies cases fell, the policy remained in place until 2006, despite challenges by animal welfare groups to overturn it.

These days, Horton feels optimistic about the direction in which the shelter is moving—euthanasia on the decline, rescues on the rise. But he's cognizant of the obstacles that could halt this trend. "My impression, from conversations I've had with shelter directors in the Northeast, is that they are not necessarily in favor of this influx of our dogs because with more dogs to select from, it's more difficult for them to place the pets that they have in their shelters."

Perhaps the more immediate challenge facing the shelter, though, is the facility itself, which, at forty-five years old, is not only run down, it is just too small. Structural improvements made over the years have helped, but only so much, Horton says. "Quite frankly, I think we're hampered by the outmoded, outdated facility. We, in effect, have ten pounds of potatoes in a five-pound bag. A fresh coat of paint is fine, but it's still old, and I think the aesthetics of it—not only the creature comforts for the pets and staff but for someone coming in and seeing this more or less depressing sight—that's not a lot of incentive to want to come back and bring your friends with you."

Touring the shelter, I find that "depressing" is not quite a strong enough word, especially once I enter the main canine kennel. I'm hit first by the smell, a putrid melding of wet dog, feces, and urine, which I suppose makes sense as the dogs relieve themselves in their runs, which then get hosed down, inevitably getting the dogs, as well as the run, wet. I find myself holding my breath. In several of the runs the dogs sit or stand just inches from their own excrement. I don't see anyone making a move to clean it up, and leaving it no doubt makes the already foul smell fouler. Sue King tells me the runs are cleaned morning and night—that she doesn't have the staff to do more than that. It's no wonder Leah Lenox's rescues leave here so filthy. I can only imagine how nasty Galen and her siblings must have been when they were taken from the shelter—seven puppies, six weeks old, not housebroken, in one run, climbing all over each other, sleeping in a mound of fur and, very likely, feces.

In July of 2013, the shelter failed a biannual state inspection. Regarding the dog runs, the inspector wrote, "Many of the canine kennels had feces and urine during inspection … Facility has strong odor throughout and needs general cleaning/sanitizing throughout." And the inspector noted that the shelter was "understaffed by 50%."

Horton says plans to build a new shelter are in the works, but the county has run into several roadblocks. The first was the economic downturn. The second came from members of the community who rejected a proposed location change for the shelter. The shelter needs a larger property than it has now, and it can't, by law, expand into surrounding Dallas Park, Horton says.

"Community members were coming out and saying, 'We don't want to hear all the barking. We don't want all the smells.' It would have been a modern facility. They wouldn't see, hear, or smell anything. We would have been good neighbors. But the county backed off due to the opposition. 'Not in my backyard' is alive and well, not only for jails but for animal shelters."

Now county commissioners are suggesting a new shelter be built near the county landfill.

"I'm adamantly opposed to that," Horton says. "Some folks already see pets as a disposable commodity. You put an animal shelter next to the landfill, and at some level that reinforces it. Garbage, unwanted pets." He pauses. "But if the only way to realize a modern new facility is there … " Horton shrugs his shoulders, and his voice trails off.

Wherever or whenever a new shelter is built, Reggie Horton won't be there to oversee construction. That work will be left to his successor. Horton retired in the spring of 2014.

I WALK OUT OF THE SHELTER just as it's opening to the public. A woman from a South Carolina rescue group is sitting in a chair just inside the entrance, in front of the welcome desk. She tells me she stops by the shelter routinely to see if there are any dogs or cats she might be able to adopt out. She's retired.

It dawns on me that one reason that local adoptions might be stagnant is that the shelter's hours aren't amenable to people with full-time jobs. It's closed on weekends, and during the week it opens in the morning at eleven and closes early in the evening, at five on some days, six on others. Sue King says there's been a push by the public to extend the hours past six, but she's skeptical about whether that would increase adoptions. "When you expand your hours, it's not just the opportunity for adoption that increases, it's also the opportunity for people to dump more animals."

When King and I were talking in her office, I'd told her about Galen—about how I adopted her in New Jersey, and that the rescue group said she and her siblings were pulled from Gaston County's shelter. I gave King all the information I had—the date in 2010 on which Linda Wilferth said the puppies were rescued and the size of the litter—and asked if she could tell me how the pups came to be in the shelter. King had turned toward her computer and started typing.

"You said she was one of seven?" King asked.

I nodded.

King paused, then said simply, "Owner surrender."

"Do you know why?" I asked.

"We don't collect that information," King replied.

My head was still spinning as I stared out the airplane window during my flight home. If Galen's owner surrendered the litter, that meant the shelter was obligated to hold the puppies for only one day. After that, they could legally have been euthanized. It was my family's incredibly good fortune that Linda Wilferth or Leah Lenox or one of their colleagues saw the puppies and acted so quickly. I closed my eyes and sighed deeply. I saw Galen's pretty gray face, but only momentarily. The faces of the dogs I'd seen in Gaston County's animal shelter quickly crowded her out. There were so many of them, and they had so little time. Yes, rescues are up—a promising trend—but Sue King was still euthanizing perfectly healthy, adoptable dogs nearly every day. And this wasn't happening just in Gaston County. Or Stokes County. The story, I'd come to understand all too well, was the same in nearly every community in the United States where animal shelters simply don't have the kennel space for all the dogs and cats that are coming through their doors.

And then it hit me. I knew nothing about my local shelter—not its name, its location, how it treats its animals, how many it euthanizes each year. I had never even thought about looking there for a dog after Gryffin died. As the plane made its descent into the Newark airport, I knew I needed to find out all I could about the animal shelter servicing my own community.

Never-Ending Flood of Need

HILLSBOROUGH, NEW JERSEY—a town of about 40,000 people—doesn't have its own animal shelter, nor does the county I live in. So for the past four decades, Hillsborough has been outsourcing animal control and animal sheltering services to St. Hubert's Animal Welfare Center, a private nonprofit organization based in nearby Morris County. St. Hubert's runs three shelters: a primary facility in Madison and two smaller satellite facilities, one in North Branch—where stray and lost dogs picked up in Hillsborough are taken—and another, acquired in 2013, in Ledgewood. Hillsborough's health officer, Glen Belnay, says not to outsource would be to waste taxpayer dollars. "We paid just over one hundred and ten thousand dollars to St. Hubert's in 2012 for a full range of animal services. To do animal control and sheltering ourselves would cost three or four times as much."

I was somewhat familiar with St. Hubert's, as I'd first learned about the shelter in 2010, when a student in one of my public speaking classes gave a persuasive speech urging his fellow students to donate to it. To punctuate his plea, the student brought in the golden retriever he'd recently adopted. The young dog, its wavy coat more red than gold, sat obediently beside the student throughout the speech. Persuaded—as much by the dog as by the student—I made the first of what would become several donations to the shelter. But it wasn't until I learned that St. Hubert's serviced my town that I took a closer look at the entirety of the organization.

St. Hubert's has a storied history dating to 1939, when it was founded by Geraldine Rockefeller Dodge, the daughter of William Rockefeller, who, with his brother John D., founded Standard Oil Company. When, at twenty-five, Geraldine married Marcellus Dodge, the president of the Remington Arms Corporation, the *International Herald Tribune* hailed them "the richest young couple in America." Dodge brought $60 million to the union; the new Mrs. Dodge brought $100 million.

One of Geraldine Dodge's passions was dogs, and she had more than enough money to indulge it. Dodge devoted four acres of her vast New Jersey estate, Giralda Farms, to kennels, where she bred dogs, many of whom would go on to compete and win Best in Shows. Her search for the finest canines took her across the Atlantic Ocean. From Germany and Austria, she brought back German shepherds, becoming one of the breed's leading proponents in the United States and writing what was, at the time, the definitive book on the breed. From England, she brought back English cocker spaniels and persuaded the American Kennel Club to recognize them as their own breed—separate from the American cocker. When she took an interest in Doberman pinschers, she sent her most trusted dog handler to Germany to bring her home a winner. He did, and in 1939, the dog, Ferry v Rauhfelsen of Giralda, became the first Doberman to win Best in Show.

Dodge's dogs—in addition to being of the finest stock—received superior care. In her biography of Dodge, art historian Barbara Mitnick writes that the kennels "were described as 'nothing short of palatial'... [They] were hosed down twice a day, and the dogs were kept scrupulously clean and given plenty of exercise." Dodge's eye for elite dogs made her a sought-after judge at the country's major dog shows. According to the foundation that bears her name, Dodge judged shows in every state, as well as the premier shows in Germany, Canada, Ireland, and England. In 1933, she became the first woman to judge Best in Show for the Westminster Kennel Club. Mitnick writes that Dodge "came to be known as the 'first lady of dogdom' and 'the dog fancier of the century.'"

But over the years, Dodge also must have been thinking about dogs who were less fortunate than hers, because in 1939, she established a foundation for lost and injured dogs. She named it St. Hubert's, after the patron saint of dogs and hunters, and she had a cow barn on the property converted into a shelter. "Practicing what she preached," Mitnick writes, "[Dodge] spent a good deal of time at the new facility and continued occasionally adopting some of the strays and orphans herself."

Today, St. Hubert's Animal Welfare Center is engaged in a wide variety of animal welfare activities that stretch beyond sheltering, but it remains true to its original mission, and it remains right where Dodge envisioned it—on sixteen acres of Giralda Farms, in a nineteenth-century cow barn that's been renovated many times over the years.

The day I visit, St. Hubert's is a buzz of activity. Dogs enrolled in doggy day camp play in a fenced-in space at the entrance to the property. The day-camp program is much like the day-care program Galen attends, but a primary purpose behind this one is to raise some of the revenue needed to run St. Hubert's shelter program. Revenue from an on-site dog-training school, grants, donations, and fees from the nine municipalities that outsource animal control and sheltering services make up the rest. Interestingly, the Geraldine R. Dodge Foundation—the philanthropic organization Dodge established in her will—does not provide any money to St. Hubert's. In 2006, the foundation stopped issuing grants in the category of animal welfare, much to the chagrin of those who run the shelter.

Walking along the sidewalk that leads to the main entrance, I pass a group of children—they look about eight years old—along with several teenagers, playing games on a patch of grass. During the summer months, St. Hubert's offers weeklong day camps for children in grades two through six that teach them to value animals and introduce them to the work of the shelter. The highlight, of course, is the time the children get to interact with the shelter's dogs and cats, birds and bunnies.

Inside the shelter, in a cramped foyer that hosts cages of cats and birds available for adoption, there's a welcome desk and, crowded behind it, several more desks, each piled high with papers and files. I count eight women, some seated behind the desks, others standing and talking, all wearing T-shirts of various shades of blue emblazoned with ST. HUBERT'S. Nora Parker, who will be my tour guide and who's been with St. Hubert's for more than three decades, tells me staff wears dark blue and volunteers wear light blue so people can quickly tell them apart. I only recall seeing one volunteer—she was helping out behind the welcome desk—at the Gaston County shelter. What I remember is Sue King telling me she wished more members of the community would "step up." The only "volunteers" working regularly with her staff were inmates serving time at the "prison down the road" and one individual, who, she said, was part of a welfare-to-work program. At the same time, I'd heard grumblings from people like Leah Lenox that shelter employees weren't quick to embrace volunteers or rescue groups. (In 2014, the Gaston shelter hired a volunteer coordinator—a paid position—to begin building a structured volunteer program.)

Parker, eager to show off St. Hubert's, greets me without a hint of that wariness I encountered from King or Reggie Horton, and she leads me down a narrow hall. Our first stop is a walk-in closet filled with collars, leashes, and a large white board listing the names of about forty dogs and when they were last taken out for a walk. "This is where our canine coaches and dog walkers come to dress the dogs before taking them out," Parker tells me.

Canine coaches are volunteers with training in dog handling; they walk the bigger dogs and the rowdier ones. After a dog has been walked, the volunteer writes up a short report on how the dog behaved. "In addition to it being wonderful that the dogs get out and get socialized, it gives us more information about the dogs as we look for homes for them," Parker says. This is essential because every adoptable dog who enters the shelter will be placed in a home, no matter how long it takes—and sometimes it takes a while. To manage its canine population without having to euthanize to create space, St. Hubert's relies on a network of foster families who allow dogs to rotate through their homes when the shelter reaches capacity.

Next, Parker opens the door to the canine kennel, steps inside, and instinctively reaches into a plastic "treat cup" that is secured near the top of the first dog run we come to. "Sit," she says to a large brown dog, a Lab mix. As soon as he does, Parker shouts, "Yes!" and pushes her hand through the metal bars to give the dog a cookie that is not much larger than a peanut.

Treat cups hang on every run, and as we walk by each dog, Parker commands and rewards in a stern, gravelly voice. One dog—a sign on his run warns he's aggressive—looks at Parker expectantly, tail wagging. He spies the cookie, but he's standing, so Parker refuses him. "Are you going to sit?" Parker asks. The dog wags his tail. "Sit," Parker says again, firmly. "Sit." When he does, Parker shouts, "Yes!" and carefully tosses the cookie into the dog's mouth.

To me Parker says, "This reinforces what they're learning."

St. Hubert's dogs come from all over the state—and from outside of it. The shelter has an open admission policy for municipalities, like Hillsborough, that outsource animal control services to it. When space is available, it also accepts surrenders from New Jersey residents who live outside those municipalities and from residents living in nearby New York and Pennsylvania. But surrenders make up only about 10 percent of the shelter's population, according to Colleen

Harrington, the shelter's director. Harrington also says the shelter doesn't take in many strays, as there aren't many in Madison and its surrounding communities. There are also very few accidental litters. "Spaying and neutering has become the norm of ownership in this area," Harrington says. "It's just common, it's just, 'Of course my animal is neutered.'" So despite the fact that St. Hubert's services a population more than twice the size of Gaston County's, intake to the shelter remains consistently lower.

St. Hubert's will also take in dogs from New Jersey shelters that sporadically find themselves overcrowded—usually those in cities like Camden, Newark, and Jersey City, and those in rural counties, like Cumberland, in the southern part of the state. And it participates in PetSmart Charities' Rescue Waggin' program, which transports dogs from overpopulated regions of the country to those areas where there's demand. In the case of St. Hubert's, it receives dogs from the South, most often from West Virginia.

From 2001 to 2013, St. Hubert's worked with the Humane Society of Parkersburg, a private nonprofit organization that operates animal control and sheltering services for Wood County, West Virginia, to find homes for homeless animals and to drive down the county's pet population. The relationship—the organizations referred to themselves as "sister shelters"—worked this way: Parkersburg would send dogs to St. Hubert's, which would adopt them out to Jersey residents, and St. Hubert's would send money—$25 per dog—to help pay for the spaying and neutering of those canines adopted into Wood County and surrounding communities. (It's a similar relationship to the one Mona Triplett has with North Shore Animal League America, except North Shore doesn't send Triplett any money.)

St. Hubert's relationship with Parkersburg evolved out of Parkersburg's desire to save more lives than it could by relying solely on local adoptions. The idea of moving dogs out of the state was, at first, a hard sell to the organization's board of directors, who were leery about sending their dogs to a shelter they'd never seen. But St. Hubert's reputation, along with the alternative—continuing to euthanize large numbers of dogs—was enough to change minds. The relationship ended when Parkersburg was accepted into the Rescue Waggin' program. Having lost its "sister," St. Hubert's is in the process of searching for another shelter with which to build a similar relationship.

Kim Saunders, St. Hubert's vice president of operations and communications, says this sort of partnership is a model that isn't being replicated widely enough. "The source community needs funding. Without it, the community can't address its overpopulation problem. Part of the problem with a lot of groups bringing pets up from the South is that they aren't solving the problem. They believe they are doing a good thing. They believe they are helping. But they are helping the individual animal that they are taking out, and they are never going to stem that tide."

The influx of Southern dogs into the Northeast, whether by "mom-and-mom" rescues like Catnip Friends or long-established animal welfare organizations like St. Hubert's, has its share of critics throughout the region. The criticism has grown louder—and coarser—on social media sites over the last decade, as the number of dogs brought north has grown larger. For example, a Virginia television station's report on ten dogs transported from Roanoke to Atlantic City, New Jersey, yielded comments on Facebook such as, "Really? We don't have enough here?" and "I'm fed up with out-of-state facilities justifying exporting their animals by perpetuating the myth that we have a shortage of dogs and puppies," and "Screw these people importing animals and getting paid for it." I didn't read a single comment in support of the transport.

Anne Lindsay, founder of the Massachusetts Animal Coalition (MAC), says it is a myth that the Northeastern states have a shortage of dogs and puppies, but it's a myth, she says, that gets perpetuated even by Northeasterners. "The line people use is that we've spayed and neutered our way out of the problem, but we haven't. We are putting on blinders regarding the dogs who live in our states and need our help."

MAC is a not-for-profit organization that works to foster collaboration among both public and private animal welfare groups. And it serves as an incubator for ideas to reduce the state's numbers of homeless, neglected, and abused animals. Lindsay says that in 2006, after repeatedly hearing complaints from Massachusetts residents that the state had no puppies, no small dogs, no adoptable dogs, and that shelters housed only pit bulls, she decided to poll animal control officers about what dogs were actually in their shelters. "Their response was, 'Thank God you asked us. We don't know what to do with all our dogs. We have no money, no support, no respect. After seven days we're killing them.'" So MAC designed AniMatch, a program that connects in-state shelters that often have limited resources with rescue groups that are better equipped to find dogs homes. "We've facilitated the movement of almost seventeen hundred dogs," Lindsay told me, "and only thirty percent are pit bulls. So do not ever tell me that we don't have dogs who need help."

Sherry Heisler, a New Jersey animal control officer and cruelty investigator who founded Sad Eyes Animal Welfare Society, echoes Lindsay's sentiments. "We have our own problems in New Jersey," Heisler told me in an e-mail. "Thousands of dogs are euthanized right here each year because of not enough homes or cage space at our local shelters." Heisler tries to move dogs out of South Jersey–area shelters by finding them permanent homes or fosters willing to keep them until an adoptive family can be found. But, she says, finding fosters is getting increasingly difficult as rescue groups bring up hundreds of dogs from the South who also need to be fostered and who also need permanent homes. One group, not far from where Heisler lives, brings up about 150 puppies and young dogs to New

Jersey each month from a shelter in southeast Georgia. The group even owns a five-acre property there, where its dogs are quarantined, temperament tested, vaccinated, and spayed or neutered before being transported north.

Heisler, like other critics, believes that simply transferring dogs out of overpopulated communities doesn't address the underlying problem and that it has the unintended consequence of making problems for the destination communities. Heisler would prefer to see an increase in efforts targeting the spaying and neutering of unfixed animals in communities with overpopulation issues and a decrease in transports.

"What a sad day it is for me when I receive the message from the shelter I volunteer at that one of our dogs will be put to sleep because we have absolutely nowhere to keep the dog," Heisler's e-mail continued. "We local shelters and animal rescues need to get our overpopulation crisis under control before I would even consider bringing more animals into New Jersey."

Colleen Harrington doesn't agree that bringing out-of-state dogs to St. Hubert's displaces New Jersey dogs. "If they did, then I would push back. Hard," she tells me. Harrington and I are talking with Kim Saunders in Saunders's office as a full-figured gray pit bull, pink tongue drooping, pants loudly. Saunders, who joined St. Hubert's after more than a decade at Petfinder, tells me that not only do Southern dogs not displace Jersey dogs, the Southern dogs often get people in the door, making adoptions of New Jersey dogs more likely.

"Studies have shown, and we see this to be true, that when you have a nice assortment of dogs in the shelter, you bring in more people," Saunders says. "So if someone looks at our pet list and all they see are large, block-headed-type dogs that they're not interested in adopting, they may not even come in. But if they look at our list and see all these different animals, they may end up leaving with a large, block-headed dog after all. And they'll tell their friends, 'Go there.

They'll have a dog for you.' And now, we're at a point where people in the community call us and ask, 'When is the next truck coming?'"

The "block-headed-type dogs" Saunders is referring to are the pit bulls and pit bull mixes that are crowding so many of New Jersey's—and the country's—shelters. They are the only dogs that St. Hubert's doesn't transport in from the South. "We're not breed-ist," Saunders says. "It's just that we get our pit bulls from our New Jersey partners." And, she could have added, New Jersey has an abundant supply.

For example, about 70 percent of the dogs coming through the doors of the Atlantic County shelter in South Jersey are pit bulls, a trend that has been on the upswing over the past decade, according to Kathy Kelsey, the shelter's manager. "When I started here, in 1995, we had German shepherds, we had rottweilers, we had chows, Labs, mixes. Now we have pitties, and we also have little designer breeds." The designer dogs are not much of a problem, Kelsey says. They get adopted quickly. The pit bulls, however, are a much harder sell. "Pitties will stay in our adoption room for five, six months, because people have a notion in their mind that these are not good dogs, that they are not good pets."

Many of the pit bulls that make their way into New Jersey's shelters come from the state's inner cities, where some see the dogs as status symbols and where they are used in the illegal but all too prevalent underworld of dog fighting. Kelsey told me that the majority of the pit bulls that make it into her shelter are found by animal control officers in abandoned properties in Atlantic City, where they are housed by young men who breed them and fight them. Kelsey says her dog, Maya, a mid-size white-and-brown pit bull, was likely a bait dog, because she came into the shelter with her body "totally ripped to shreds."

The gray pit with the loud, rhythmic panting in the cage behind Kim Saunders's desk is much larger than Maya. I want to ask Saunders if she knows the dog's history, but Saunders has another meeting. My time is up, and she ushers me out of her office.

St. Hubert's is deep into a multimillion-dollar renovation that will quintuple its size and turn the century-old cow barn into a state-of-the-art center for animal welfare. It will boast impressive features like "get well" wards to isolate sick animals, cat and dog kennels with fresh-air ventilation systems, indoor and outdoor play areas, and separate areas for cat and dog adoptions. A training center and a spay/neuter suite are already operational.

But what strikes me as I stand in what will be the new lobby, and as Nora Parker talks about the natural light that will stream in and the boutique whose sales will help fund the operating budget, is how much St. Hubert's has accomplished out of Geraldine Rockefeller Dodge's century-old cow barn. With its training classes, children's summer camp, and doggy day camp, it's as much community center as dog shelter. And as dog shelters go, it's remarkably clean and inviting, despite its age. I never smelled the stench of wet or dirty dog. I never saw feces in a dog run. I never felt the need to hold my breath. Yes, I hated seeing dogs locked in runs, but I didn't feel as disheartened as I did at Gaston's shelter. These dogs, I knew, were just months or weeks or even days away from finding a home.

Of course, St. Hubert's isn't a public entity, reliant solely on taxpayer funding. Municipalities like mine pay for its animal control and sheltering services, but its funding also comes from private donors, foundations, and grants. As such, it is a ruthless fundraiser. It hosts an annual 5K run/walk and events like wine tastings and auctions. It makes donations—of everything from money to pet food, toys to cleaning supplies—possible with just a few clicks on its website. You can even get a St. Hubert's Visa Card courtesy of Capital One, and the shelter will receive cash back on some of the items you buy. I became a recipient of its aggressive fundraising strategy after making my first donation. Now solicitations arrive in the mail every few months with heartrending photos and emotional stories about dogs and cats whose lives have been saved, along with a plea to donate yet again. Kevin jokes that the more I donate, the more requests I get. One of the more recent solicitations even asked me to "consider including St. Hubert's in [my] will or other estate plans." I have to admit that's not anything I'd ever thought about.

But St. Hubert's efforts seem to be paying off. Over the last several years—during the course of its capital campaign to renovate the shelter—it's raised about $2 million annually. That St. Hubert's is located in Morris County, a community with a median household income of just over $77,000, nearly twice as much as the median income in Gaston County, can't be overlooked—or understated. Still, St. Hubert's has something that is priceless: a groundswell of public support that reveals itself not just in the donors who give their money but in the volunteers who give their time.

Before I'm accused of being a Northeastern elitist for touting an exceptionally well-run shelter sitting figuratively in my backyard, it's important for me to note that shelters operating under such public-private partnerships aren't limited to New Jersey or to the Northeast. You can find them throughout the country, including in the heart of the South, where the challenges far surpass those faced by St. Hubert's.

MORE THAN 700 MILES southwest of Madison, New Jersey, in Maryville, Tennessee, Darlene Bakos sits on her kitchen floor inside a metal dog pen, nine boxer-mix puppies competing for her attention. Newspaper, scattered with chew toys and a couple of dog beds, lines the floor. One puppy is crated beside the pen. Bakos thinks he may be sick, so she's separated him from his siblings. The puppies' mother, Sugar, stands in front of the pen's open door.

"Come in, Sugar," Bakos says. "Come see your babies."

Sugar gently steps into the pen, and two puppies dart over to her; one nips at Sugar's front right paw.

"The people moved out of their house after it burned down,

but they left Sugar and her litter," Bakos tells me. "The house was destroyed around them. There was all sorts of debris, broken glass. The dogs couldn't get out. Neighbors were throwing food in for them. When the dogs were found, there were twelve puppies. Ten survived. The owner is in jail now. He wanted to sell the puppies." She shakes her head incredulously.

Bakos and her husband moved to Maryville, which is about fifteen miles south of Knoxville, from western New York in 2006, the day she retired from a thirty-year career teaching home economics. The couple liked the milder climate and the fact that Tennessee residents don't pay a state income tax. Bakos planned to settle into retirement making and selling custom quilts. She launched a business—Gingersnap Quilts—and received several commissions, including one from the Tennessee Valley Authority. "Then the dog thing happened, and I went from walking dogs to doing anything and everything that needs to be done."

Bakos had read a news story about a local dog-hoarding case that was overwhelming the Blount County Animal Center, a local shelter. The center needed help dealing with the sudden influx of dogs, so Bakos, a tall woman with short, red, spiky hair and seemingly boundless energy, volunteered. Now, "doing anything and everything" includes working as an amateur veterinary technician—"I'm a sewer, so I'm good with my fingers, and I think that's helped me to feel for veins"—manning the front desk, fundraising, and fostering. One of the couple's two dogs—a terrier mix—is what's known in the rescue community as a "foster failure." Fostering failed because the family kept the dog. While this may seem like a success—the dog now has a home—the problem is that once a foster family adopts a dog, it often, though not always, stops fostering.

"I fostered for three years before I adopted a dog. But Ernest, he came into the shelter shaking. It was five-thirty, after intake hours were over, but I couldn't turn him away, so I took him home with me. The next morning I didn't bring him back."

Bakos says the Blount County Animal Center takes in about ten dogs each day—strays and surrenders—though she does recall a day it took in twenty-eight. To avoid overcrowding, the center relies on fosters like her. There's been a recent peak in surrenders, and for that, Bakos blames the economy—but only in part. "The problem down here is that people don't see pets as a family member. A dog is disposable."

I ask Bakos about her "down here" reference. I'm still grappling with the notion that regional differences might play a role in shaping how people experience the human-canine relationship. Are attitudes in Tennessee really that different from those held by folks in Corfu, the tiny town between Buffalo and Rochester where she'd lived most of her life?

"There are going to be some people who say there is no difference between the South and the North, but I lived in the North. I talk to my friends in the North. There is a difference. It's a whole different culture here. I had a man come into the shelter with eight two-week-old puppies. He said his cousin told him, 'I'm gonna splat them against the tree, so if you want 'em, take 'em.' The man brought them to the shelter."

I have to ask: "What does it mean to 'splat a dog against a tree'?"

Bakos says she'd never heard the expression before either, but she's heard it since. "You hold the puppy by the tail and whack it against a tree to kill it."

Bakos continues, "I asked the guy, 'Where's the mother?' He said his cousin is keeping her because she's a bear-hunting dog, and he said his cousin also kept one puppy. I asked the guy to ask his cousin to bring in the mother—and the puppy—so the mother could nurse all her babies."

Bakos says she had an ulterior motive for wanting the mother in the shelter: She wanted to persuade the owner to have the dog spayed. Clearly, the owner didn't want this litter. Bakos didn't want to even consider what might happen should there be another one, or two. "Sure enough, the cousin brings in the mother—she's in a wooden box—and turns her over to us. I get a good look at her, and I see why he's decided not to keep her. She was limping. She was filthy. I had to bathe her five times. One of her mammary glands had gangrene. She had never interacted with people, so I kept her in an office with me. Volunteers had to bottle-feed all nine puppies. The mother is now in a foster home with a retired vet, and he's taking her to a behaviorist."

The puppies have since been adopted out.

"We try to save as many dogs as we can, and we do a good job. But I'll tell you, I've never cried as much in my life as I do, doing what I do now."

THE BLOUNT COUNTY ANIMAL CENTER grew out of a perfect storm of government mismanagement and grassroots activism. Prior to 2007, Blount County outsourced animal control services to the county's largest city, Maryville, which ran a shelter of its own. In the early 2000s, overwhelmed by the number of animals coming through its doors, Maryville started tracking its intake and discovered that about two-thirds of its dogs and cats were coming not from the city but from the county. So in early 2006, Maryville hiked its contract fee by nearly 50 percent. Blount County's commissioners declined to fund the increase.

"I think the city of Maryville felt justified in asking for more money based on the usage, and the county government just saw an increase, and they just pushed back. They balked," says Chris Protzman, who led the fundraising effort for what would become the Blount County Animal Center.

In addition to letting the contract with Maryville lapse, county commissioners didn't seek out alternative animal control services.

So on January 1, 2007, Blount County residents woke to a new reality: They had no access to animal control services of any kind, a particularly acute problem for a county with a sizable stray dog population—a result, Protzman tells me, of people dumping dogs along outlying roads and county highways. In no time, the stray dogs were creating havoc. "We had a llama viciously attacked by wild dogs; it died on the front porch of its owner's property. We literally had herds being attacked. We had bite reports—little kids taking a walk in their subdivision and being approached by aggressive animals."

Blount County's then-mayor, who had inherited the crisis from his predecessors, decided he needed to act quickly to find immediate and long-term solutions to a problem that was growing increasingly untenable. He reinstated an animal control officer to collect strays, but where to put the dogs once they were in custody posed a bigger challenge, as striking any kind of deal with Maryville was out of the question.

A temporary solution emerged via a partnership with neighboring Loudon County, which had opened a new shelter in 2006 and whose elected officials agreed to accept Blount's strays and owner-surrenders. Protzman says the deal wasn't just good for Blount County's citizens but for its animals, too. "Loudon's facility was new. Maryville's was police-run. It was more of a pound, and it was very crude." Loudon's county commission made it clear that the partnership was for a limited time only, that Blount County needed to look elsewhere for a permanent solution to its self-made problem. So Blount's mayor issued an appeal to the public and to the private sector to bring the commission new ideas for how to deal with the county's animal welfare situation.

As it happened, issues of animal welfare had been on the minds of a group of citizens, including Protzman, who had come together in the late 1990s to discuss ways of making Blount County an all-around better place to live and work—the kind of community into which businesses relocate. Jon Grubb, a member of the group, which called itself Citizens United for a Better Blount County, says that including animal welfare in the group's discussions was a no-brainer. "Businesses look at school systems. They look at social life. They look at social resources. We have the Smoky Mountains. We have Gatlinburg. We have Pigeon Forge. We have the University of Tennessee. We have Oak Ridge National Laboratory. Blount County now has a really good school system. We have a nice library system that's Wi-Fi integrated and online. And we had a little block house—the Maryville shelter—where they put down animals. The shelter had a ninety-percent-plus kill rate. Now what's wrong with this picture? To the animal welfare community, that was outrageous. And that was completely unnecessary."

Days after the mayor's plea for ideas, Protzman and three members of that original group sat down to dinner at Aubrey's, a local restaurant, and concluded it was time to step up. "When citizens are a part of a government, a part of a community, it's our government and our community. We felt a need, a call to mission to do something." The foursome laid out their ideas on the back of a cocktail napkin, and the Smoky Mountain Animal Care Foundation (SMACF) was born.

Several weeks of research and feasibility studies later, Protzman says, "We contacted the county mayor and said, 'We've never started a foundation, but we got one incorporated here. It's a one-hundred-percent volunteer effort, but we want to help you out, and we think we've got an idea.'"

That idea was a public-private partnership. SMACF would raise the capital to build a state-of-the-art facility that would be run by the county. Importantly, the shelter would not be like the pounds of the past—or even like the present one in Maryville—it would be a refuge for dogs and cats on a journey to their "forever" home. And it would fill that hole in county services that Citizens United for a Better Blount County believed was so large that it hindered the county's ability to lure in new business.

In April, the county commission endorsed the plan and set the project in motion by providing the land—a vacant field behind the local Boys & Girls Club—and by finding $350,000 in seed money in the county's coffers.

SMACF took over from there, raising $1.3 million through donations of cash, material, and services over the course of a two-year campaign. "When I started, I went to the business community first," Protzman tells me. As senior vice president of the Journal Broadcast Group's Knoxville operations, Protzman himself was a member of this community, and he knew, or knew of, many of the people he was targeting. "My closing comment was the same at every presentation. 'As a community we have a moral obligation to take care of these companion animals. They've never been wild. We've created this bond with them that goes back centuries. We have an obligation to reconnect the bond. They did nothing wrong. We severed the bond; we created the problem. And as the caretakers of these animals given to us, entrusted to us, we have a moral and ethical obligation to fix this.' And I would make that very direct, and I would make a lot of eye contact when I delivered that last line to a lot of gentlemen and ladies who control businesses and who were leaders in the community. Then I would say, 'These are companion animals. You can't drop a dog on the side of the road and expect it to go feral and figure out how to hunt again. It won't. It will die.'"

Protzman also sought contributions from the county's citizens, many of whom were still irate over having gone several months without any animal control services. "I make a very specific point when I talk about our campaign. It ran in 2008 and 2009, in the heart of the recession, when people were pulling back and the county was struggling. Yet in our little county, we raised $1.3 million to build an animal shelter. You have to give credit to the people of East Tennessee because all the dollars were from East Tennesseans. These are people born and bred here, who've been here for generations. Southern families, many of them founding families, who said, 'Our animal welfare situation is no longer acceptable to us.'"

The Blount County Animal Center opened to the public in two phases. The first, completed in late 2009, consisted of a simple bare-bones facility with little more than functional kennels, but it was operational, and that's what mattered to the county commission. By November of 2011, when phase two was completed, the once-skeletal building had been transformed into a 9,000-square-foot state-of-the-art animal shelter with rooms for bathing and grooming; indoor/outdoor kennels to make cleaning easier for staff and to ensure dogs have daily access to fresh air; adoption rooms where people and their future pets can get acquainted; and a high-tech surgical suite for on-site spay/neuter surgery. It also has the most advanced computer system of any animal shelter in the country, courtesy of Jon Grubb. "To do all we wanted to do, we needed a computer system that was smart," Grubb says, but none existed that could be tailored to meet all of the center's needs, so he built one.

Grubb, an Illinois native who's lived in East Tennessee since 1967, is the type of animal lover who can't remember a time in his life when he lived without one. "You see those pictures on the Internet of babies kissing shar-peis—that was me. I've always had animals. I've been in animal rescue my whole life. And I've always been associated with people who have the same connection to animals that I have." But it was an intimate understanding of computers and computer systems garnered over a career spent as a cryptologist at the Pentagon's Oak Ridge National Laboratory and as an academic at the University of Tennessee that made Grubb the go-to guy to create a one-of-a-kind computer system. When he'd retired from the Pentagon in 2009, Grubb told his wife that he never again wanted to build another computer system. But SMACF had a vision for the center that was grander than its budget. So, he says, "I thought, what's one more?"

Jon Grubb walks me through the center early one morning before it opens to the public. I have the same feelings touring it as I'd had inside St. Hubert's. The volunteers—and I see many—seem happy, and the dogs—while they certainly would prefer not to be locked in cages—don't have that look of fear, of sadness, that I truly believe I saw in the eyes of the dogs in Gaston County's shelter and in Stokes County's shelter. Each dog has a bed, a bowl of fresh water, and a strikingly clean kennel—the shelter's kennel director, I later learned, won't have it any other way.

"There's an attitude here that says if an animal can be adopted, it will be adopted—if it can be saved, it will be saved," Grubb tells me as we make our way into the center's education room, a space that's used to teach schoolchildren and community members how to better care for companion animals. "We've had animals that have been shot, that have been burned. We get a lot hit by cars. We had one animal whose face was literally torn off. He was hit in such a way that he was sideswiped. But other than that, he was a perfectly good animal. So we raised the money and put him back together and adopted him out. That's what we do."

The "we" to whom Grubb refers over and over again are the volunteers—nearly 300 of them—who are the engine of the enterprise, as the county employs just three full-time staffers, one of whom, an animal control officer, spends most of his day off-site, and two part-timers. "We have retired folk, the unemployed, the underemployed, and soccer moms who want their children to understand the importance of pets. The sheriff's department has also decided we are a good place to put trustees—nonviolent juveniles."

I meet one of the trustees that afternoon. He's tall, slim, in his twenties, and paying the price for "something stupid I did a couple of years ago." He spends his day in the puppy room, keeping the metal crates—three high against three of the room's four walls—spotless, and making sure the puppies have fresh water, food, and a friendly face to look at throughout much of the day.

Seeing a puppy in almost every crate, I understand why Bakos has Sugar's litter at her house—there's not enough room at the shelter. The previous day, Bakos had introduced me to a couple, also retirees, also from upstate New York, caring for a litter of puppies in their garage. Not unlike Bakos, the couple began fostering after volunteering at the shelter. Since taking in their first litter, the couple has taken in more than 100 dogs. "It doesn't take long to hit one hundred when you foster puppies," the wife told me matter-of-factly.

All those puppies—as well as every dog and cat that enters the Blount County Animal Center, either as a stray or an owner-surrender—get a medical screening and vaccinations, all of which is overseen by Jon Grubb's wife, Amy, in her unofficial position as volunteer medical director. A retired hospital lab technician, Amy supervises intake and teaches volunteers—like Bakos—to do the work that in a vet's office would be done by veterinary technicians. A lack of state regulations regarding vet tech certification makes such activity possible, Grubb says. "We do as much as we can at the center because it's free, and the vets trust Amy. If something is beyond our capabilities, then the animal goes to the vet."

To pay for those vet visits, SMACF funds a $60,000 per year vetting pool, which is much like an insurance pool. "The money is used for vetting any animal that is savable—to make it whole and make it adoptable. Sometimes it costs one-fifty; sometimes it's fifteen hundred. It was thirty-four hundred dollars for the dog who had his face torn off. You can't predict it."

But it's Grubb's computer system, which serves as the center's all-knowing brain, that makes a shelter run by so many volunteers—impassioned though they may be—operate as smoothly as it does. "The computer system is designed to aid the humans and to prevent the humans from screwing themselves up or screwing anything else up," Grubb tells me. "It was designed and built to extend and enhance the capabilities of the volunteers because we try to do more programs than we have the physical resources to pull off."

The system tracks every animal from the moment it enters the shelter until the moment it leaves. But it's more than simply a mechanism for data storage. On days the spay/neuter suite is operating, the computer can be used to calculate the amount of anesthesia each animal will need for its surgery. And volunteers can access the system from anywhere, at any time. "The computer is a lot like Google," Grubb tells me as he demonstrates the system. "What you see on the screen can be accessed on any browser, smartphone, or tablet. So if you need to find out where an animal is supposed to be at any time, you can. Without it, we couldn't do all that we're doing. So it's a team effort, with the computer system being one of the members of the team."

The team is having remarkable success. The Blount County Animal Center is open admission, but since becoming operational in 2009, it has never euthanized an animal to create space, and its live-release rate, which hovers around 94 percent, is one of the highest in the state—and the country. But you don't find a whole lot of people slapping themselves on the back around here.

"It's difficult, even when it's working well," Grubb says. "We're always on the edge of failure. We worry about saturation. There are only so many homes for all the animals we have here. They're making them twelve at a time and we're adopting them out one at a time. So, we've got a math problem. That makes for long days and long nights."

It also makes for the perfect environment for compassion fatigue—an emotional burnout experienced by caregivers exposed, day in and day out, to patients' traumas. The term was coined in the early 1990s in reference to clinicians and nurses, but the veterinary field began discussing compassion fatigue among its own ranks in the early 2000s.

Chris Protzman says anyone who runs an animal shelter has to have a thorough understanding of compassion fatigue. "Working in a shelter is the hardest job anyone will ever do. It's emotionally draining and exhilarating. If you have the right people, you will have burnout. That's an ironic statement, but it's true."

"When we see a volunteer who's starting to get frustrated, we try to get somebody else trained to jump in and share the responsibility or take over the responsibility," Grubb tells me. "Sometimes volunteers just have to stop. They can no longer do this. And they were great volunteers, but they take a mental health break, and they don't come back. We recently had one of our vets kill himself, and it was a kind of jaw-dropping, numbing, stunning thing. People couldn't even talk about it."

Volunteer Cindy Faller puts it this way: "This business can break you because there is a never-ending flood of need." So much so that Faller organizes weekly transports to rescue groups in the Northeast and upper Midwest. The transport program is entirely run and funded by SMACF. The foundation owns two vans, each of which are outfitted to hold about thirty animals. Volunteers do the driving now, but SMACF would like to hire professional drivers to bring down insurance rates. Protzman says the transports are vital; the county simply can't absorb back all the dogs and cats that come into the shelter.

SMACF didn't intend for its financial relationship with the shelter to extend beyond the initial capital campaign, but it has—it's had to, Protzman says. "As soon as the capital was raised, we were still in the middle of a recession. The county was under incredible financial pressures. They weren't hiring teachers. Schools were not being funded for textbooks. There was a herculean amount of financial pressures on the county which, frankly, have not subsided. We quickly realized that the funding to support the operation, five hundred to five hundred fifty thousand dollars, was not going to materialize. The county's animal control budget was originally set aside years prior. It was going to be modestly increased, but would not be more than about three hundred fifty thousand. There wasn't the political will to raise the rest."

So SMACF and the county cut another deal. The foundation agreed to augment the county's money with private money to retain the level of service that SMACF believes is essential. That includes funding the spay/neuter suite. "We had put a hundred thousand dollars into that suite, and we didn't want it to be idled," Protzman says. In return, the county created an Animal Advisory Board to oversee the center and seated on it three members of SMACF, a veterinarian, the local director of the SPCA, and county commissioners. "We hope that eventually the county will fully fund the center, but no one is holding his breath."

One revenue source that Protzman would like to see tapped but that has faced opposition from county residents, is the licensing of companion animals. A $10 license fee, he says, would make up most, if not all, of the difference between what the county pays and what SMACF pays to fund the center. But right now the environment is not favorable. "Talk about another license or tax, and the constituents in the county push back hard on it. Perhaps if an economic recovery kicks in, this is something we would tee up. You know, we've gone a long time throwing Hail Marys and catching them, but we're going to run out of volunteers and luck."

I ask Protzman what it will take to slow the flood of dogs and cats into the shelter. "I see it in economic terms," he answers. "The solidly middle, upper-middle class has a compassion for companion animals. There's an attachment that this is a member of the family. This is not cattle. This is not property. This is regardless of whether you're in the North, South, East, or West. I think where you start seeing the greater neglect is where there isn't a highly literate population that's never been exposed to what is socially the norm of caring for companion animals. They see them as extensions of the livestock—to help herd the cattle, to help mind a small child—but absolutely disposable.

There's always exceptions, but the majority is economic based. And then some of it is cultural, in the sense that there's a 'don't tread on me,' strong anti-federal government sense. I think the South has gone through and is still going through abuse dating back to the Civil War and Reconstruction. And so Southerners"—of whom Protzman is not one, having grown up in the Midwest—"have a distrust, I think, and rightly so, that is just inbred with outside forces coming in and telling them how to run their government and their community, and how to conduct their family and their culture."

Since the center opened, it's seen its intake numbers decline by about 40 percent; it's now taking in about 2,600 animals annually. Protzman attributes that to a host of factors: the shelter's presence in the community and the local media attention it's garnered; an overall increase in awareness nationwide of animal abuse and neglect, driven by celebrities like Sarah McLachlan and Willie Nelson; and a booming retail sector of pet products that drives the notion of the pet as a family member. But for so many of the volunteers, like Darlene Bakos, who've made volunteering a full-time job, progress isn't happening fast enough, and that can be both frustrating and infuriating. "I came in great guns of fire, and I had to learn my place real quick. I'm in the South. Change, I'm told, comes slowly."

Grubb says change can come through education, and an education program is in the works—or at least the germ of an idea is, with a focus on children. "Right now we bring third graders in, and we show them the animals, and we talk to them about how making their pet so that she doesn't have babies or so he can't make babies is much healthier for the pet and much healthier for the world. And the kids take that to heart. But we need to do more, and we haven't mounted that major battle yet."

Generational change, which is what comes through educating children, takes time, I say.

"Time is both our friend and our enemy. In the long term, people will get used to the idea of the shelter, and good habits will become ingrained into the community's culture. Short term is against us. We still don't have spay/neuter laws, so we still get litter seasons in the spring and the fall, and then we are just totally overwhelmed."

The private-public partnership that undergirds the Blount County Animal Center is similar to the partnership between St. Hubert's and the towns, like mine, that outsource animal control and sheltering to it. In both cases, the funds raised by the private partner are an essential buttress to what the public entities can provide, and the volunteers are a vital supplement to the paid staff. But what if the money dries up, if volunteers get discouraged at the never-ending flood of dogs and cats coming through the door? As much as finding homes for the country's shelter animals is a priority, so, too, has to be finding ways of stopping those animals from entering the shelters in the first place, whether that means doing more to prevent unintended litters or finding ways to help pet owners keep pets they can't afford. As Protzman says, "The shelter is the back end of the equation. People need to realize these animals are not the shelter's problem; they're the community's problem."

At the front desk, a young woman fills out paperwork as her four-year-old daughter hangs on her leg. Her husband gently swings a car seat to keep the couple's infant son asleep. The family is adopting a three-month-old beagle-Chihuahua mix that entered the shelter as a stray. His name is Marley. The little girl tells her mother she wants to take the puppy home now, but her mother tells her she will have to wait—the Blount County Animal Center won't release a dog until it's been spayed or neutered.

It's a little after eleven, and the center has scored its first adoption of the day. The volunteers hope there will be more because, according to Darlene Bakos's count, the shelter can expect at least ten dogs to make their way in before the day is done.

If You Build It, Will They Come?

"FOSTERS QUIT ALL THE TIME," Linda Wilferth said to me one Saturday afternoon as we talked about the challenges of running a rescue. "No one wants to get their house dirty. No one wants to stay up all night." I got the sense, as I often did while talking with Linda, that she would like to see more people share her level of commitment—to dogs certainly, to cats definitely.

"The people burn us out," she added, "not the animals."

Spend any time on social media sites frequented by shelters and rescue groups, and you see an infinite demand for fosters. It's not just that fosters save lives by buying more time for a dog whose shelter stay has expired or by creating space for more dogs, it's that they provide dogs with socialization and an environment that is less stressful than being trapped in a kennel in a loud and busy shelter.

Atlantic County's Kathy Kelsey told me that it's not uncommon for dogs to experience kennel stress after prolonged stays in a shelter—even if a dog gets daily walks and experiences human interaction. Dogs are social animals, she said, and they are not meant to be placed alone, in cages. "When you see a dog that has been sweet and happy suddenly one day smearing its feces all over the kennel run and chewing on the gate, you know that animal has lost its mind.

And if it has crossed that line where it is no longer aware of what it's doing, it's not humane to keep it caged." More often than not, such dogs are euthanized.

As my understanding of the scope and complexity of the problem grew, I was beginning to feel guilty that the extent of my engagement was simply to mail off a few small donations to St. Hubert's. So I began toying with the idea of fostering. One night, as Kevin and I lay in bed talking, I ran the idea by him.

Loki came home with us a couple of weeks later.

We had gone to Pet Valu as a family, and as I talked to Linda and Buff, Kevin and the girls volunteered to walk a five-month-old mix from the Gaston County shelter who had been passed over for adoption for three weeks straight. Then they started conniving to bring the dog home with us. Since I'd already mentioned my desire to foster, Kevin figured there was no reason to wait. Besides, he and the girls were smitten. So he bought a crate and food, and I explained to the girls that Loki was coming home with us as a foster pup, not a permanent addition to our family. What if Galen and Loki didn't get along? I asked them. The girls nodded, but I wasn't sure they were listening.

In some ways, we lucked out with Loki as our first foster. He was house-trained, and he was as well behaved as he was funny-looking. His shelter papers identified him as a husky–pit bull mix, but he didn't look as if there were any husky or any pit in him. He had a black-and-gold coat, much like a Doberman pinscher's, with a thin line of white fur running from his neck to his chest, and a Lone Ranger–style mask that wrapped around a pointy gold snout. His ears launched straight up from his head, but three-quarters of the way up, they flopped forward. He took an immediate liking to Galen, and she seemed to move from indifference to pleasure at having a playmate.

Unbeknownst to me, Loki came with some health issues. One I immediately suspected. The others I learned about when I took him to our veterinarian. I initially made the appointment because Loki was hacking, and I was concerned he had kennel cough, a highly contagious respiratory disease that Galen had been infected with twice. Gryffin had also had that telltale hack when he entered my life.

The vet concurred with my diagnosis and prescribed Clavamox twice daily for both Loki and Galen. Then, a day after our visit, the vet called to say that Loki's stool sample tested positive for three intestinal parasites: coccidia, giardia, and whipworm—whipworm being the most concerning with regard to Galen's well-being. Apparently whipworm eggs contaminate the soil via a dog's feces and can live anywhere from three to five years. Dogs can become infected simply by licking their paws after walking on a contaminated site. I returned to the vet's office to pick up more meds and was told to make sure I thoroughly clean up after Loki every time nature calls.

I e-mailed Linda immediately. She needed to let Loki's former foster know about his situation, as it was very likely that he hadn't been the only dog living at the house. Linda's response surprised me. "Wow. None of us heard that at all," she e-mailed back, "and he has been with four other dogs in foster ... one senior beagle and one puppy, and none of them have it." How, I wondered, could she know that the other dogs aren't infected if she hadn't even known that Loki was? I just hoped the foster had done a thorough job cleaning up Loki's poop for the sake of those other dogs.

A frequent argument against bringing Southern dogs north is that they carry with them infectious diseases, including heartworm, which can be expensive to treat and which is more prevalent in the South. But rescue groups say diseases caused by the most common parasites, like the ones Loki had, are shelter contagions not limited to any region. Because parasites are easy to treat, rescues argue, they are no reason to stop or even limit the transports.

Alan Beck, director of Purdue University's Center for the Human-Animal Bond, says the potential for disease to spread always exists when there are major migrations of animals, and presently, the most common animal migration in the United States is this movement of Southern dogs up the Eastern Seaboard, which increased exponentially in the wake of Hurricane Katrina.

A 2011 study in the *Journal of the American Veterinary Medical Association* sought to determine whether canine and feline diseases endemic to the Gulf Coast increased in areas of the country that took Katrina animals into their shelters. While researchers determined that significant numbers of Katrina animals did test positive for these diseases, what was less clear was what impact, if any, they had on animals with whom they came in contact. The study states that conclusions are difficult to draw, in part, because the animals were distributed so widely throughout the country. Still, it concluded that while the Katrina animals may not have contributed to the spread of infectious disease in a statistically significant way, transporting animals to parts of the country where certain diseases are not typically found "could contribute to new geographic ranges for these organisms."

Accordingly, a spokesperson for the Connecticut Department of Agriculture told the *Hartford Courant* in 2011 that veterinarians throughout New England were seeing an uptick in heartworm and parasites not typically found in the region, an increase, he said, that dates to Katrina.

In July of that same year, in an attempt to curb the number of sick dogs coming into Connecticut, the state passed legislation, over the strong opposition of the rescue community, requiring that animals imported into the state be examined by a veterinarian within forty-eight hours of arrival and be re-examined every ninety days until adopted. Violators would face fines up to $500. A group called the Federation of Responsible Rescues argues that the regulations—which also require rescues to register with the state, pay an annual $100 fee, and advise the Department of Agriculture and municipalities of adoption events at least ten days prior to the event—will drive responsible rescues out of business. Supporters of the bill, which was passed overwhelmingly in the state's House and unanimously in the Senate, say the law is intended to have little impact on legitimate rescue groups and to make it more likely that adopters bring healthy dogs into their homes.

I gave Loki his meds and left not a trace of his feces in the yard by scooping up the grass and dirt surrounding it to ensure the soil did not become contaminated. Rather quickly, Loki became parasite-free, and Galen, I'm happy to report, escaped infection.

Each day Loki was with us, Lindsey and Dhani grew more attached to him, as did Galen. Four days into Loki's stay, Kevin ushered the dog into his crate—set up in our family room—for the night. Then he and Galen retired upstairs, to our bedroom. Instead of the few seconds of whimpering we had grown accustomed to, Loki cried … and cried. I shot Kevin a look: I didn't want Loki waking the girls. Before we could come up with a plan, Galen ran downstairs. I winced. I expected to hear more crying, louder crying. But instead, Loki went silent. At about 11:30, when I presume Galen was confident Loki was sleeping, she came upstairs. Thursday night she slept downstairs with him.

By now Kevin and the girls—and I presume Galen—were prepared to keep Loki, but something deep in my gut said I wasn't yet ready for another dog. I also knew I couldn't return Loki to Linda—he'd been through too much already. So I turned to my mom. She hadn't owned a dog since Sammie, and I thought Loki would do wonders for her and for my stepdad, who's survived one too many heart attacks. (In a scientific statement published in 2013, the American Heart Association reported that owning a dog may reduce the risk of heart disease. Perhaps, I thought, it might also prevent an existing condition from getting worse.) I knew if I could persuade them to meet Loki, to live with him for a few days, he would win them over. He did.

Dhani was devastated. She drew a card for Loki that read, "If they end up keeping you, I'll miss you sooooooo MUCH!!!!! Always remember us. Love, the Skole family." I had to keep reminding her that Loki was only moving to Grandma's house and that we would see him often.

I came away from our foster experience with the deepest regard for people who take in one dog after another, one litter after another. The more I thought about the fosters, the rescuers, the shelter volunteers, the transporters, and the dogs—so many dogs—the more I couldn't get the image of a hamster running on a wheel out of my mind. As long as accidental litters were being born, as long as shelters were overcrowded, as long as healthy dogs were being euthanized, there was no way that wheel would ever stop spinning.

"WE'VE GOT TO TURN OFF THE SPIGOT," Becky Moser says emphatically. "We can't rescue ourselves out of this problem. We can't adopt our way out of the killing."

I'm having dinner at Tequila's on Main Street in Gastonia with Moser and Kathy Cole, both of whom have been involved in animal welfare in Gaston County for about four decades. In the late 1970s, Moser was a founding member of the Gaston Humane Society. "There was no humane society here, and even though I didn't know the extent of our problems, I just knew we needed one."

Early on, the group's primary mission was to investigate animal abuse allegations, and Moser says they did so "here and there." But it was a fire at a commercial breeder—the women called it a puppy mill—in 2000 that set in motion the events that led a faction of people, including Moser and Cole, to break away from the Humane Society. The women say that in the wake of the fire, a group of Gaston County residents tried, unsuccessfully, to persuade the county to place regulations on breeders. What appalled many of the people who had been with the Humane Society for decades was that the organization didn't get as involved in the fight as they believed it should have. An internal battle broke out, with present members feeling besieged by past ones.

Unable to heal the battle's resultant wounds, the old-timers established a new animal welfare organization—the Animal League of Gaston County—in 2002. Early on, the Animal League set relatively small and largely attainable goals. It persuaded the county to establish a five-acre off-leash dog park in Gastonia and began pressuring Reggie Horton to open the county shelter to rescue groups, which it had yet to do. Moser told me that at the time she was working closely with a Great Dane rescue, and she found it easy to adopt Danes out of area shelters but difficult to adopt out of Gaston County's. This was, in large part, because the rabies ban instituted in 1999 had yet to be lifted.

All too aware of the overcrowding at the county's shelter, the Animal League decided on a two-pronged approach to relieving it: encourage more adoptions and decrease the number of dogs and cats coming in. But to achieve that second part, the Animal League needed to figure out a way to persuade more people to embrace spaying and neutering. So for the first time in the group's short history, members dared to dream big: They would find a way to bring a veterinary clinic to Gaston County that did nothing but spay/neuter surgery at a cost to clients that was far less than what area veterinarians charged. It had been done before. The city of Los Angeles opened the first public low-cost clinic in 1969—it was so busy pet owners waited four months for an appointment—but it wasn't until the early 1990s that clinics started sprouting up throughout the United States. The thinking behind the clinics is that the high cost of veterinary care prohibits many pet owners from fixing their pets. Make fixing affordable, and that price barrier will disappear—and so, the hope is, will the population problem.

For the Animal League, the seeds of the idea were planted when it began sending unaltered dogs and cats from Gaston County to be spayed and neutered by veterinarians at a low-cost clinic in Asheville, about 100 miles away. The clinic, run by the nonprofit Humane Alliance, was the area's closest low-cost clinic. Opened in 1994, it started out as a small spay/neuter clinic serving Asheville and surrounding communities. But it has since blossomed into a 13,000-square-foot medical and training facility whose mission includes working with humane organizations nationwide to open their own low-cost clinics and teaching veterinarians from across the country to do what it calls "high-quality, high-volume spay/neuter surgery." An Alliance-trained vet can do up to thirty-five spay/neuter surgeries a day.

In 2000, the Humane Alliance launched a free transport program, which the Animal League enthusiastically took advantage of. The transport program operates by sending one of two vehicles—an extended cargo van that can hold up to thirty companion animals or a climate-controlled box truck that can hold up to eighty—to communities that don't have their own low-cost clinic or even one that's conveniently located. Animal welfare groups in these communities encourage pet owners who haven't had their pets fixed to have them spayed or neutered by an Alliance vet for what is often a fraction of the cost charged by the community's full-service veterinarians. The dogs and cats are picked up by the Alliance in the morning, operated on in the afternoon, and returned the following day. Pet owners pay only for the surgery—$65—and a rabies shot—$10. According to the Alliance's assistant director, the vehicles are on the road five days a week, and transports make up nearly three-quarters of all surgeries done on-site.

The Animal League was grateful for the Alliance program, but keeping it operational was challenging. "We did for it a few years," Cole told me, "but it was hard getting enough volunteers to help the morning of the transport and the next day when the truck came back. Then we had to wash all the kennels and dry them, and sometimes there was thirty to forty of them. Some people would do it for a couple of months and then quit." The Animal League also faced an obstacle it hadn't anticipated. "For some folks, having their pet gone overnight was too much for them, and they would cancel."

To the Animal League, having a spay/neuter clinic of its own—where dogs and cats were dropped off in the morning and picked up that same afternoon—was the only solution. So, Cole says, "We asked the Alliance for help."

The Humane Alliance had the know-how—it has helped more than 125 animal welfare groups bring low-cost, high-volume spay/neuter clinics to cities and counties across the country. But the Animal League didn't have the money—it needed at least $100,000—and it didn't have anyone on its board who had experience raising a sum so large. So, members held tight to their dream and ran small-scale fundraisers, banking the money in hopes of realizing a clinic sometime in the future. To their good fortune, the future came sooner than expected.

ON SUNDAY, JUNE 29, 2003, Gastonia attorney Terry Kenny began her morning as she does each day, with coffee, yogurt, and two newspapers. As she settled into her favorite chair, a front-page story in the *Charlotte Observer* caught her eye. Its headline: "Death at the Pound—Animals in the Charlotte Region Are Killed at More Than Twice the National Average, and Little is Being Done to Stem the Problem."

"It continued inside the paper," Kenny recalls. "The article was long for a newspaper. Those are the ones that I usually skim. 'Death at the Pound' was different. I read every word, and I cried."

A decade later, Kenny's eyes still fill with tears. What shocked her, in addition to the high euthanasia rates reported—90 percent in Gaston County in 2002, 91 percent in Caldwell County, 89 percent in Iredell County—was how the dogs and cats were killed. According to the *Observer*, thirteen of fifteen counties in the Charlotte region were euthanizing dogs and cats with carbon monoxide, and Gaston County was one of them. What's more, the article stated that "the Carolinas require no training for the shelter workers who administer the gas, and some animals have to be gassed twice because it doesn't always kill them the first time."

Kenny was horrified. "I immediately knew that I had to do something. I knew that gassing helpless animals alongside their buddies was wrong."

That Kenny would, as she says, "find her niche in life helping animals," surprises no one more than Terry Kenny herself. "When people would ask me if I had children, my response was always, 'No kids, no cats, no dogs, no fish.' I was happily married, serving on this committee or that committee with no furry friends to tie me down. Happily naive. And although I have always been involved in volunteer work, I had never even considered animal welfare as an issue."

From the offices of her eponymous law firm on Main Street in Gastonia, Kenny began researching animal shelter gas chambers—who used them, who didn't, why—with the same fervor and attention to detail with which she tackles her legal cases. "I read everything I could. I was on a personal mission. Oddly, I never thought about enlisting the help of other like-minded people. I didn't even know any like-minded people." Ultimately, Kenny, a petite woman with short blonde hair, a sharp Southern accent, and a get-down-to-business attitude, presented her findings to Gaston County's commissioners at one of their monthly meetings. Her message: Get rid of the gas chamber at the county shelter; it's inhumane.

The commission's reaction was far from what Kenny had anticipated. "The response was like, 'Aah, sweet little lady wants to help the animals." After she spoke, Kenny recalls, Reggie Horton addressed the commissioners and told them that use of the gas chamber was not inhumane—that in some cases, as with highly aggressive dogs, it was more humane than lethal injection—and that it was financially cost effective, that the per-animal cost of gassing dogs and cats was less than euthanizing via lethal injection. And he told Kenny that she didn't understand the situation. "And he was right," she says. "I didn't. Not yet, anyway."

It just so happened that an employee in the county's finance department was watching the commissioners' meeting on television that night. According to Kenny, when she began her presentation, he called to his wife, "Come down here! You have got to see this. There's a lady talking about doing away with the gas chamber." The man's wife, like Kathy Cole and Becky Moser, was a founding member of the Animal League of Gaston County. And she, like many people in the animal welfare community, was struck by Kenny's forthrightness and depth of knowledge. Journalists at the meeting were struck, too, by the petite woman in the well-tailored suit and high-heeled pumps determined to take on commissioners over the issue of the gas chamber. The following day, the *Gaston Gazette* ran a front-page story in its Hometown section about Kenny; it was picked up by newspapers around the state.

"I started getting phone calls from folks who saw me on TV or heard about my speech," Kenny says. "Many told me I had to join the Animal League. I said, 'What is the Animal League?'"

Hungry now to learn all she could about Gaston County's animal welfare situation, Kenny attended one of the Animal League's board meetings, where much of the talk focused on the members' desire to build a low-cost spay/neuter clinic. The *Observer* article had noted that not a single county in the Charlotte region put any public money toward increasing spay/neuter rates, and no one involved with the Animal League thought that would change anytime soon, at least not in Gaston County. Thus, if there were any hope of bringing low-cost spay/neuter to the county, the nonprofit community—the Animal League—would have to step up.

Kenny listened to members talk and decided there was no reason she couldn't do two things at once—work to rid the shelter of its gas chamber and raise the money needed to build the clinic. She volunteered to head up the effort and learned quickly that she could be quite the rainmaker. "I would write grants to anyone who would read them," she told me as we talked in her spacious law office. The money started coming in, "and I found out I'm a pretty good grant writer."

By early 2009, the Animal League had the money, and it had a veterinary-clinic's worth of equipment, thanks to a vet who sold most of what he had to Kenny when he shut down his practice. "I offered to take everything he didn't want, and we cleaned up. We took anesthetizing machines, kennels, a desk, prep tables, operating tables, file cabinets, a refrigerator, all for $12,500." But the equipment was put in storage because the Animal League had yet to find a suitable building.

There was something else Kenny knew needed to be done before the Animal League opened the clinic, and that was to inform area veterinarians of the organization's intention to offer low-cost spay/ neuter services—and to persuade them to get on board.

Despite animal welfare being a goal of both veterinarians and the nonprofits that run most low-cost spay/neuter clinics, some veterinarians oppose the clinics—whether they are stand-alone, tucked inside animal shelters, or mobile. The issue, perhaps not surprisingly, comes down to money and the fear by private practitioners that they will lose clients to the clinics. In some states, aggressive lobbying by the veterinary community against spay/neuter clinics has landed the issue in state legislatures. For example, a bill in South Carolina, supported by the South Carolina Association of Veterinarians, would require that clinics provide services only to low-income pet owners and would require mobile clinics to secure an affiliation agreement with any veterinary practice within twenty miles of where the mobile unit operates. In Alabama, debate during the 2013 legislative session over a bill that would permit nonprofit organizations to run low-cost spay/neuter clinics—the state currently has four under threat of closure—grew so contentious that the president of the Alabama Veterinary Medical Association called the situation a "PR nightmare" for the state's veterinary community. That bill stalled in committee, but it was introduced again in 2014, and again it was opposed by the state's three largest veterinary organizations, including the Alabama Veterinary Practice Owners Association, which sent a letter to its members urging them to contact their representatives. Failing to act, the letter stated, "may result in the Greater Birmingham Humane Society's Mobile Bus being parked in the parking lot across from your office."

Such organized opposition has led many in animal welfare to accuse veterinarians who are opposed to low-cost spay/neuter clinics of being greedy. They charge that the vets are putting money before the innocent lives that will be lost if unfixed companion animals procreate and their offspring end up in already overcrowded shelters. Besides, clinic proponents say, veterinarians' concerns about competition are unfounded because the clinics and the vets are not targeting the same clientele: People who go to low-cost clinics would never show up at a private practice because they can't afford the fees, and those who can afford the fees are unlikely to go anywhere else. Said one program director at a low-cost clinic in Florida, "What you have to remember is that people with money like the service they get at their vet. They don't care if they're paying five hundred dollars for a fifty-dollar surgery because their vet is convenient to them; they have a relationship with them. And they don't want to go to a clinic in a depressed part of town. They don't want to sit in the lobby with people who are poor. I hate to say that, but some people are snobbish.

They want to go to the clinic where everybody knows their name and where the clinic will call you at home and ask, 'How's Fluffy doing today? And do you want to come back for this or that?' So if you are fine to pay full price, you are going to go to your private practice. Plus, there is still this mindset that a low-cost clinic means low-grade quality. That's not true. Our vets are specialists in high-volume spay/neuter. But that's the mindset."

There have been few studies to determine if low-cost spay/neuter clinics do indeed lure pet owners away from private veterinary clinics, but a 2007 study in *Ecological Economics* suggests they do not. Using data from Alabama and Utah and from counties in Arizona, California, and Florida, researchers found an overall increase in spay/neuter in these communities rather than a substitution of services from private to low-cost clinics. They write that the finding "may seem counterintuitive that offering a discount spay/neuter program would increase regular spay/neuter procedures performed in a community"; however, "the results show a positive relationship, not just the lack of a negative one." The researchers attribute the overall increase in spay/neuter to marketing done by low-cost clinics touting its benefits and to the promotion of sterilization as socially responsible pet care. The publicity, the authors point out, reaches everyone in a community, not just those with lower incomes.

Rachel Barton, the veterinarian at the Tallahassee-Leon Community Animal Service Center, a municipal shelter in North Florida, believes communities that want to decrease shelter killings need low-cost spay/neuter clinics—she'd very much like to see one in Tallahassee. But, she says, writing off vets as greedy isn't entirely fair, and vets' concerns about competition aren't entirely unfounded. In fact, Barton says, some in animal welfare are themselves responsible for veterinary opposition because of what she calls mission creep. "The clinics start out doing spay/neuter, but then they begin to administer vaccines. Then they do dental cleanings because they see there's a need, and they want to help these pet owners, but they start to drift from their mission, and pretty soon, they turn into a low-cost, full-service hospital. And then veterinarians see their clients going to the clinic for a dental cleaning because it costs less. So now, in the minds of the veterinarians, a low-cost spay/neuter clinic equals a low-cost hospital that's going to compete with them in the future."

Barton has heard veterinarians in the Tallahassee area cite this drift as the primary reason they oppose a low-cost spay/neuter clinic coming to the city. But she disagrees with them—the city, she says, needs a clinic because her shelter gets overcrowded, and healthy dogs and cats do get euthanized for space—but she understands where they're coming from. "A veterinarian's livelihood comes from the services they provide and the money that they charge, and veterinarians are not making lots and lots of money. We go to school for just as long as a human doctor. We have tuition fees just as high as a human doctor. We graduate with ridiculous amounts of debt, and if we're lucky, we make half of what a human doctor makes. And then there's the reality that when the economy is not doing well, vet care is seen as a nonessential expense." Add the threat of a business doing what you do for less money, and that's cause for concern.

Barton says this mission creep concerns her, too, and not just because it leads to animosity between vets and clinics but because it undermines the clinics' very mission. "If our goal is spay/neuter, then every time we are doing something that is not a spay, not a neuter, then we're not working towards our goal."

"Before we opened, we sent a letter to all the vets in town and invited them to a meeting to answer questions," Kenny says. "Many were very concerned. The dilemma for them was if they pushed against us too hard, I would open a full-service, low-cost clinic, and that was something they truly would have hated." But it was something Kenny made clear then and still makes clear today is always an option. "I continue to mention the possibility of a full-service clinic in the event that vets begin to trash us. I am near retirement age, and I would quit and make my goal opening a very successful full-service clinic if that happened. Little carrot and stick—but all truthful."

CONTRACTOR RICK BAILEY stood inside the former home of a Papa John's pizza franchise and tried to see past the holes in the floor, the cracks in the ceiling, the dirt, the grime, the pizza grease, to see what Terry Kenny saw: a bustling low-cost spay/neuter clinic. It was the spring of 2009. "If I'd told her that it couldn't get done in that building, then the next day I would have been looking at another one," Bailey says. "Ms. Kenny don't take no for an answer. If something don't work, it ain't, 'No, you can't do it.' You find a solution."

While on a daylong whitewater rafting trip, a friend in commercial real estate had suggested that Kenny consider the Papa John's property. The rafting hadn't interested Kenny—she hadn't wanted to go—but the property did, so she toured it the following day. The location was ideal; the building is on Franklin Boulevard, the main artery through Gastonia. And the price was right; Kenny's friend offered to donate the first year's rent and charge $500/month thereafter.

Bailey began construction on June 10, 2009, with a team of volunteers, including Becky Moser and Kathy Cole, and with instructions to complete the job in two weeks. "Ms. Kenny is the kind of person that once you get the ball rolling, she don't want the ball going around no curves," Bailey told me. "You get the job done and move onto something else." To ensure the ball remained on course at all times, Kenny turned a pop-up picnic table in the parking lot into a makeshift law office so she could keep on top of contractors and inspectors.

The clinic opened the first week of July with Kathy Cole, who had become a certified vet tech five years earlier, overseeing day-to-day operations. "I can be a nervous Nellie," she said, "and I was totally a nervous wreck that first day. The clinic had come to fruition, and we had six lives we were responsible for. Now we do thirty a day, and I know that these babies are going to leave better than when they came in."

By its fourth anniversary, the clinic had fixed almost 15,000 dogs and cats. Kenny would like to see the clinic reach 5,000 annually.

The clinic charges from $65 to $125, depending on the weight of the dog, but because Kenny pulls in every grant she can, clients often pay less. For instance, the clinic regularly offers discounts to pet owners on public assistance. It's offered free fixes to pit bull owners. And in January of 2014, it received a PetSmart Charities grant allowing the clinic to offer two hundred $20 neuter surgeries to owners of male dogs and cats as part of a "Happy Neuter Year" program.

To get the word out about special programs and the clinic's very existence, Kenny says, "We do everything I can think of." That includes advertising in the local newspaper, online, and at community events; posting flyers in county offices; direct-mailing information about special programs; speaking to community and church groups; and bringing in youth groups, like the Girl Scouts, to tour the clinic.

Listening to Kenny tick off all the promotion being done, I couldn't help but wonder if Galen's previous owner knew about the clinic. After all, Galen was born about sixteen months after it opened. There was certainly more than enough time to have had her mother spayed and to have prevented a litter that I could only assume wasn't wanted by the very fact that it was surrendered to the county's animal shelter.

But it turns out that reaching the people who would most benefit from the services offered by low-cost clinics—low-income pet owners—are often those who are the hardest to reach. A vet who works out of a mobile clinic in North Carolina's Guilford County told me advertising itself is challenging: First, it costs money, and most nonprofits aren't flush. Second, many potential clients don't buy newspapers and are not necessarily on the Internet, so traditional modes of advertising are not always effective. "The bottom line," the vet said, "is that it's very difficult to reach those people who most need our service."

It is standing room only at a seminar on how to drive low-income pet owners into low-cost clinics. The seminar is one of several being offered at the Best Friends Animal Society's 2013 annual conference, held this year in Jacksonville, Florida. Best Friends is perhaps best known for running an animal sanctuary in southern Utah, where it cares for and rehabilitates more than 1,500 animals, primarily dogs and cats but also pigs, parrots, horses, and rabbits, until each can be found a permanent home. But it's also involved in initiatives nationwide, all of which are working toward making the United States a "no-kill" nation. For Best Friends, a "no-kill" nation or "no-kill" community is one in which all adoptable animals who enter a shelter have a "live outcome." Statistically, Best Friends says this translates to a 90 percent live release rate, which accords with the statistic that 90 percent of dogs and cats that enter shelters are healthy and adoptable.

The focus of the conference—which brings together the disparate members of the animal welfare community, from shelter workers to rescue groups to veterinarians—is on ending shelter euthanasia of all those healthy and adoptable animals. And it's come up with a catch-all phrase for the effort: "Save Them All."

Rick DuCharme, founder of First Coast No More Homeless Pets, a low-cost spay/neuter clinic in Jacksonville, leads this seminar. First Coast opened its doors in 2002, and in its first seven years, it performed an average of 5,500 surgeries annually. In 2009, in a larger facility and utilizing the Humane Alliance's model for high-quality, high-volume surgery, it increased the number of annual procedures to more than 24,000. All those surgeries, DuCharme says, have had a direct—and positive—impact over at the city's shelter. By First Coast's tenth anniversary, he reports, the shelter saw its intake drop by half, to just below 17,000. Its euthanasia rate fell by 78 percent.

But here's where things get interesting—and complicated. DuCharme says not all spay/neuter surgeries are created equal when it comes to driving down canine population rates. He distinguishes between those surgeries that are simply low-cost and those that are targeted. For example, a low-cost surgery done on a dog whose owners would have gone to a private vet if the low-cost clinic didn't exist doesn't drive down population because it was simply a question of where, not whether, that dog was getting fixed. Targeted surgeries are done on dogs whose owners, but for the low-cost clinic, would not get their pets fixed.

DuCharme also says that First Coast's experience, along with that of several other communities nationwide, has found that to yield a reduction in shelter admissions, a clinic must do a minimum of five targeted surgeries per 1,000 residents each year. The more impoverished the community, the more targeted surgeries per 1,000 residents he recommends.

How does a low-cost clinic determine whom to target? It asks its public shelter which zip codes its dogs—strays and surrenders—are coming from and which breeds are being euthanized at the highest rate. This is why it's essential that shelters keep statistics. Not surprisingly, what shelters find most often is that the poorer the community, the more dogs enter the shelter. This is where targeting comes into play. A clinic needs to make sure that the targeted community knows about the clinic. But knowing isn't enough. A clinic must also make sure that pet owners can afford the surgery, and sometimes, DuCharme says, that means making it free or subsidizing the cost below list price, which in the case of First Coast is a flat $50. Additionally, a clinic may have to provide transportation to pet owners who live a distance from the clinic or who do not have transportation of their own.

The money First Coast uses to keep clients' costs down and to run a transport program comes from partners, like the Animal Farm Foundation, which provides funds for the spaying and neutering of pit bulls; grants; and the city of Jacksonville, via a $20 license levied on companion animals. (The penalty for non-compliance is $250, making not licensing a pet a really bad idea.) In January of 2014, First Coast received grants to fix dogs and cats at no charge to pet owners living in two Jacksonville zip codes where census data shows median household incomes hovering around $25,000 and more than a third of residents living below the poverty line. To get the word out, First Coast direct-mailed every household in each zip code a postcard announcing the free service. Beyond the postcards, First Coast does little paid advertising. Rather, advertising comes from word of mouth, and word is getting around. First Coast's four-person phone bank takes in about 1,000 calls daily.

To extend its reach even further, First Coast's vets became some of the first in the country to offer non-surgical neutering, playfully known as "zeutering," before the procedure became commercially available in the United States, in February of 2014. The primary targets are those pet owners—most often men—who object to castrating their dog. I spoke with one veterinarian after another who told me they have clients whose husbands won't allow the couple's male dog to be fixed. The reason: It's emasculating. My favorite story comes from a North Carolina vet who told me that when he told a male client that he should get his dog neutered, the man instinctively crossed his legs. "I'm not talking about you," the vet told the man. "I'm talking about your dog!"

"Zeutering" involves injecting Zeuterin, a solution of zinc gluconate and arginine, directly into a dog's testicles. Zinc is a spermicide, so the solution travels through the testes, destroying the sperm and rendering the dog sterile. The appeal, beyond the non-invasive nature of the procedure, is that unlike with neutering, a dog retains its testicles; thus, Fido only looks like he could impregnate the ladies. What DuCharme likes about the procedure is that it's cheaper and faster than neutering. He estimates that First Coast could increase its volume by about 15 percent with no additional staff or equipment.

First Coast also provides services to help low-income owners keep their pets, as a common reason for shelter surrenders is that owners who adore their pets just can't afford food or vet services. In 2010, it launched a volunteer-run food bank that distributes donated dog and cat food to families on public assistance. The only catch: Pets must be fixed. If they are not, volunteers will help owners register their pets for a free spay or neuter. First Coast also runs a low-cost veterinary clinic that charges 40 percent less than area vets for routine services like vaccinations, microchipping, X-rays, and dental care—it's one of those clinics that many veterinarians oppose. But Cameron Moore, First Coast's program director, says that there was no mission creep here—DuCharme never hid his intent to operate a full-service clinic. And Moore doesn't believe First Coast infringes in any way on private vets. Beyond being located in what she calls "the ghetto, not the Beverly Hills of Jacksonville," where many middle- and upper-middle-class pet owners don't want to venture, she says the city has an incredible need for low-cost services. "The Jacksonville Humane Society also has a clinic in the city. We could open up ten more, and each one would still have plenty to do."

Despite First Coast's efforts to increase spay/neuter, keep pets in homes, and facilitate adoption events large and small—one "mega" event resulted in nearly 950 adoptions—the city shelter still gets overwhelmed with dogs and cats, an indication of how deeply rooted the city's problem is. In May of 2013, the *Florida Times-Union* reported the shelter had 170 dogs, nearly three times its capacity. Five months later, the FOX affiliate reported the shelter was in the midst of "an adoption and foster care emergency." The shelter pleaded with the public to adopt or foster, saying it would have to euthanize healthy animals if the community did not step up.

For DuCharme, though, the long-term trends in Jacksonville are moving in the right direction. But he's quick to acknowledge that the progress hasn't been First Coast's alone; it's been a community effort. In 2005—after years of animosity and an "us against them" attitude among First Coast, the Jacksonville Humane Society, rescue groups, and city government—animal welfare advocates and city leaders came together and decided that if they were going to save lives, they needed to work together. To someone who exists outside the animal welfare community, this revelation seems wholly unremarkable. But the animal welfare community, with its history of internal animosities and infighting, has, at times, undermined itself, a point made by the fact that DuCharme led a second seminar—this one on the importance of collaboration. He told audience members to let go of their egos, to stop vilifying one another, and to walk in each others' shoes. Common-sense teachings, perhaps, but apparently lessons that conference planners felt were worthy enough to devote an entire session to. DuCharme also connected the collaboration taking place in Jacksonville to a prediction: The city, he said, would be "no-kill" within five years.

BASED ON CONVERSATIONS with folks in and around Gaston County, that spirit of collaboration has been slow to take hold between rescue groups and the Gaston County shelter. The consensus of the animal welfare community is that the shelter historically hasn't done enough to promote adoption or rescue; rather, it has stymied efforts. They point to the difficulty they had persuading Reggie Horton to overturn the 1999 rule that no animal could be adopted out unless it had evidence of being vaccinated for rabies. That left, they say, few animals available for adoption and a euthanasia rate that, at times, topped 90 percent. When Terry Kenny got wind of the issue, she said, "I started my research again, and found that other counties didn't require the rabies vaccine for adoption. And I learned that ours was imposed temporarily but had been in place more than seven years."

Another reason for the animosity remained the issue of gassing animals to death at the shelter. Kenny's appeal to county commissioners to stop using the gas chamber had reaped little more than a few newspaper stories on her efforts. There was no state pressure to end the practice, either. A 2009 bill that would have banned gassing in North Carolina never made it out of a House committee. The bill, known as Davie's Law, after a puppy who had survived being gassed, was opposed by the state's Department of Agriculture and Consumer Services, which oversees shelters. The department argued successfully that it be permitted to implement and enforce regulations that would allow the continued use of county and city gas chambers, so that what happened to Davie would not happen again.

North Carolina isn't the only state that has permitted the use of carbon monoxide gas chambers for shelter euthanasia. Nationwide, only twenty-one states have passed legislation banning their use, while several others lack legislation but do not gas. Still, the national trend is toward lethal injection, a method preferred by most animal welfare advocates and both the American Veterinary Medical Association and the National Animal Care & Control Association. Feeling the pressure from Kenny, the animal welfare community, and concerned citizens, Gaston County's commissioners adopted a resolution in the fall of 2010 making lethal injection the primary means of euthanasia at the county shelter. But for many, the resolution didn't go far enough because it allowed for continued use of the gas chamber in instances in which animals were "deemed wild, dangerous, or otherwise unmanageable through designated safe handling practices." It wouldn't be until the fall of 2014—nearly a decade after Kenny

addressed the commission—that the shelter would officially cease
using the gas chamber to euthanize animals. That November,
commissioners had the large stainless steel structure loaded onto
a flatbed truck, hauled off to a local recycler, and reduced to scrap
metal. Then, in December, North Carolina's newly named animal
welfare director announced the state would institute a ban on gassing
at all public shelters beginning in early 2015.

I have to admit that I can't help but think that this debate inside
and outside Gaston County over how to euthanize shelter animals
takes time and attention from what seems to be the real issue: How
do we reduce the number of animals that end up in shelters in the first
place? Yet I do understand activists' concerns that euthanasia—when
it is done—be done humanely. That is why there seems to be promise
in the growing number of low-cost spay/neuter clinics opening up
around the country—that is, so long as pet owners know about them
and take advantage of them.

Dr. Robert Neunzig, a retired veterinarian who performs spay/
neuter surgeries at the Animal League's clinic, is doubtful that clinics
in themselves are the answer because they can't drive down costs
enough to motivate some pet owners. "You can't make the surgery
less expensive than free," Neunzig says, "and still, some people just
won't take advantage." When he was a young vet working in South
Florida in the late 1970s, Neunzig told me, members of the South
Florida Veterinary Medical Association agreed to spay or neuter
one pet per month for free for anyone on public assistance; he was
responsible for administering the program. The vets pledged to do
up to 5,000 free surgeries, but there were so few applicants that at
the end of the year they had only performed a few hundred. "Sadly,
it seems people must be stimulated to do the right thing with the
risk of penalties if they don't. That is why children can't go to school
until they get their vaccines, tickets are given out for not wearing a
seat belt, penalties are raised for not paying property taxes. At the end

of the day, it seems like we are not a very responsible or disciplined society, and that certainly spreads into the pet population issue."

Terry Kenny believes that the combination of the ALGC's low-cost spay/neuter clinic and differential licensing—in Gaston County, licenses for spayed and neutered dogs and cats run $10 per year or $25 for three years, whereas licenses for unfixed pets are $35 a year—is what is beginning to drive down shelter admissions. That's why Kenny wants to see the clinic's annual number of surgeries continue to increase.

To Kenny's surprise, the clinic has been getting referrals from an unexpected source—private veterinarians. Although some detractors remain, Kenny said that by and large, the clinic is winning over its critics. In an e-mail to me she wrote, "One vet wrote a wonderful letter saying how sorry he was to oppose our opening the clinic and that it was purely greed on his part. (Yes, he used the word greed.) He went on to say that we were doing a good service for the community and for the animals, and he was embarrassed by how he acted. He sent a $250 donation and said he hoped that would help our programs."

As I finished reading Kenny's e-mail, Galen caught my eye. She'd been lying in a sunbeam on the dining room rug across the foyer from me, and she stood to stretch. I was at my desk in the living room, whose hardwood floors she still disdains. I once went so far as to place Gryffin's dog bed beside my desk—several dog treats scattered on top—in hopes of luring her in. I think I was trying to create my own Norman Rockwell–like vision of the writer and her dog, but Galen would not have it. She stood in the foyer and looked at the bed, looked at me, and retreated to the dining room.

Kenny's e-mail got me wondering if Galen's mother, somewhere there in Gaston County, had had another litter—or two. Or whether her owner might have learned of the Animal League's clinic, might have taken Galen's mother there, and perhaps Galen's mother had since been spayed.

Pet Deserts

"THE ANIMAL WELFARE COMMUNITY needs to get over ourselves," says Amanda Arrington. "It's not, *build it and they will come.* A new spay/neuter clinic could open a mile down the road, and folks will have no idea it's there. We have to reach people in a different way to get to our target audience. We need to be on the ground, flyers in neighborhoods, doing hand-to-hand marketing. It's on us to change the way we do things. We can be a little holier than thou."

Listening to Arrington, it's a little hard to believe she's employed by the Humane Society of the United States (HSUS), one of the country's largest and most mainstream animal welfare organizations. But it's this affiliation that makes it possible for Arrington to test some of her renegade ideas, which stretch beyond merely saving the lives of companion animals to improving their lives—and the lives of their humans. It is this acknowledgment of the problems underlying the country's dog problem that makes her so different from so many of the people I've met on my journey. For Amanda Arrington, it's not just about the animals—it's about the people.

I caught up with Arrington at a Starbucks just outside Durham, North Carolina, where the slender, brunette thirtysomething lives with her five dogs—that is, when she's not on the road, which she is about nine months of the year. Arrington is the director and force behind Pets for Life, an innovative program within HSUS that takes a "boots on the ground" approach to improving the lives of people and pets in some of the country's most impoverished urban neighborhoods. To Arrington's way of thinking, where people are suffering, their companion animals are suffering, though she says, "Sometimes I think the people are living worse than their pets."

Arrington grew up in Douglass, Texas, a tiny rural town in the eastern part of the state, population: 500. Her father ran a cattle ranch, and the family's ten-acre property was filled with all sorts of animals—horses, pigs, chickens, dogs, cats—all of whom lived outside. "Never did our dogs or cats come indoors. Ever," Arrington tells me, echoing my friend Lisa. "And it was the same way for everyone."

Arrington knew kids who had an affinity for their animals, and some for whom a dog was a best friend. But it wasn't that way for her, not on the ranch. "They were just there. Some dogs I liked more than others, and I would pet them or play with them. But they were really just part of the landscape."

In the summers, Arrington's parents had her put flea powder on the dogs; there were no vets around, so none of the dogs were vaccinated; none were spayed or neutered. "I didn't even know what spay or neuter even meant until I was eighteen or nineteen years old." When a female gave birth, the litter simply disappeared. "I think there were probably shootings, drownings. I don't think I would ever get my father to admit it, but the puppies would just be gone. And it was never discussed. I don't remember explanations from my family or me inquiring. It just was."

Arrington says she didn't think much about the plight of any of the animals on the ranch. "I was much more into human issues when I was young."

Douglass was, Arrington tells me, "very segregated," and she witnessed racism daily. "I don't think there was a day that went by that I didn't hear the n-word. That was just how my family was and how everybody around me was. I remember in third grade there was a black girl in my class—we had only eleven or twelve people in it—and I wasn't allowed to go to her birthday party. And that really upset me, so from then on, that was always an issue with me."

In 1998, when Arrington was in high school, another incident, occurring just ninety miles southeast of Douglass, left an indelible mark. "The James Byrd situation happened." Byrd, an African-American man, was murdered by three white men who beat him and then chained him by the ankles to the back of a pickup truck, dragging him for three miles before dumping his broken body in front of an African-American cemetery. The murder drew national attention—and outrage—as did the autopsy results, which suggested that Byrd was alive for much of the dragging. For Arrington, Byrd's murder was more than horrific; it was emblematic, albeit in its most extreme, of the racism she grew up around and that she never understood.

It wasn't until Arrington graduated from college—she attended a public university just twenty minutes from home—and moved to Houston that she began to experience life, and dogs, in a way she had never experienced either before. "I got my first dog from a flea market. He was a Japanese Chin, and I know now that he was a puppy mill dog. I absolutely fell in love with him, and I think that's where things started changing for me."

After a year in Houston, Arrington returned to Douglass to help her parents deal with some family issues. She not only brought the Japanese Chin home with her, she brought him into the house. "My parents thought it was crazy, bringing him inside the house. But having the dog, having lived in Houston, I saw everything differently. That is the key to me: exposure, seeing the bigger world, and I never had that before. I was extremely sheltered, and I had an extremely limited view of the world."

Back in Douglass, Arrington started noticing all the stray dogs. She started picking up dogs she'd encounter "along the side of the road." Then came a relationship with a veterinarian in the nearby city of Nacogdoches, who gave her a price break on spay/neuter surgeries. After that, she began building an ad hoc rescue network, seeking permanent and foster homes for the newly fixed strays. If Arrington couldn't place a dog, she kept it. "I ended up keeping seven myself, which is what happens." She even started pressing her parents to spay and neuter the dogs and cats who lived on the family's ranch.

Arrington's brief taste of the world outside Douglass whetted her appetite for a new life in a new city. After Hurricane Katrina struck the Gulf Coast in 2005, Arrington and her then-husband decided it was time to leave Douglass. The two agreed they wouldn't move too far north—Arrington's husband was a mail carrier and he didn't want to deliver mail in the snow. But Arrington says she wanted "to get the hell out of Texas," so they settled on Durham, North Carolina, a city she says she readily considered because she is a Duke Blue Devils fan.

"I fell in love with Durham. There was so much opportunity, and I was just a sponge. I started jumping into everything going on in my neighborhood." *Everything* included the InterNeighborhood Council of Durham, a coalition of neighborhood and homeowners' associations working to increase the vitality of the city's diverse residential areas, some of which are near the bottom of the socioeconomic ladder. Soon Arrington was serving on the council's board and instituting a spay/neuter program unlike any other. The idea: Don't wait for people to come to you; go directly to them. "I wanted to get out and start walking through neighborhoods, talking to people. That was my inclination. I didn't know enough to know that that wasn't what animal people did. So it was good I was a little bit naive or ignorant."

Arrington's inclination to go straight to pet owners derived, in part, from seeing dogs chained up in backyards, especially in the poorer parts of the city, like East Durham, where more than half the population lives below the poverty level. "It's just what everybody did. It was the norm. And if they even thought about the problems tethering caused, most other options were out of reach."

The consensus of the animal welfare community, veterinary organizations, and even the federal government is that chaining is harmful to dogs and, by extension, people—especially children. In a statement in the July 2, 1996, *Federal Register,* the U.S. Department of Agriculture stated that the "continuous confinement of dogs by a tether is inhumane. A tether significantly restricts a dog's movement. A tether can also become tangled around or hooked on the dog's shelter structure or other objects, further restricting the dog's movement and potentially causing injury." In addition to physical harm, tethering can cause changes in a dog's personality. According to the American Veterinary Medical Association, when kept continuously chained even a friendly dog can become neurotic, depressed, and aggressive. This is because dogs are pack animals—tethering is akin to solitary confinement. Dogs are also territorial, so they grow ever more protective of the small area in which they eat, sleep, and relieve themselves, increasing that potential for aggression even more. A study by the Centers for Disease Control found that chained dogs are nearly three times more likely to bite people than are unchained dogs, and children who don't know to avoid them are most often their victims.

Despite these well-documented dangers, many communities around the South, and the country, don't have anti-tethering laws. The InterNeighborhood Council wanted to change that in Durham County, so in 2006 it started pressing county commissioners to pass a no-tethering ordinance. Arrington, however, recognized the need for a two-pronged approach to the problem because for many pet owners the issue was financial—it wasn't that they wanted to chain their dogs so much as they couldn't afford to do otherwise. An ordinance would do nothing to change that.

So Arrington came up with a plan that tied directly into her desire to see more pets spayed and neutered. She would go door to door offering a deal to pet owners whose dogs she saw tethered in their yards: She would build a fence for their dogs if they would permit her to take their dogs to a vet to be spayed or neutered. Oh, yes—and she would pay for it all. The money would come from donations to her newly established nonprofit, the Coalition to Unchain Dogs.

The very first house Arrington arrived at on the Saturday she kicked off the program heralded one of the challenges she would face getting Unchain Dogs, and later Pets for Life, up and running. The woman, who was home, refused to come to the door; she simply peeked at Arrington from behind the curtains of a window. Arrington stared back, and their eyes locked. Not to be deterred, Arrington returned the following Saturday and the Saturday after that. On each visit the woman became less cautious, more talkative, and more open to Arrington's offer, until one day, the woman agreed to have her three dogs fixed.

Some pet owners hesitated only slightly; some jumped at the offer. Arrington put out press releases, and local news outlets started telling the Unchain Dogs story. The publicity brought in donations and volunteers. As for the non-tethering ordinance, that passed two years later, in August 2008.

Eight years after Arrington built the first fence, the Coalition to Unchain Dogs has grown to four chapters in North Carolina, and she's received inquiries into how to get similar programs off the ground from as far away as Oregon. Unchain Dogs's goals are twofold: Set dogs free by exchanging their chains for wire-mesh fences that provide them with room to run—and reduce the number of accidental litters caused when free-roaming males impregnate chained females, which happens all too often because so few of the dogs in impoverished areas are fixed. "It's interesting how predictable it is, but study after study shows that in areas of systemic poverty it is the cultural norm not to alter your pet. We need to change that cultural norm."

The way to do that, according to Arrington, is simply to talk to people, earn their trust, and make it possible for them to access the services that are financially and physically out of their reach. "We have to show compassion to the people, not just their pets. Many people assume that no care means no love. That's not necessarily true."

When people are treated respectfully, when they are not judged, when they are provided with options, they are often open to help and they are grateful. Best of all, their relationships with their pets improve. "Most of my philosophy for Pets for Life came from Unchain Dogs. I just went door to door and talked to people. It was such an education for me."

TIM FREEMAN'S BEIGE Chevy Venture is stocked with large and small crates, bones, dog food, leashes, and Pets for Life T-shirts. It also has that baked-in scent of dog that comes from transporting dogs from their homes to veterinary clinics and then home again several days a week. As Freeman drives, Rachel Thompson runs down the list of dogs to be picked up for spay/neuter surgeries and vaccinations.

Tim Freeman and Rachel Thompson are Pets for Life's representatives in Atlanta, one of four cities—the others are Chicago, Los Angeles, and Philadelphia—in which HSUS is piloting the program. Pets for Life targets urban communities it regards as "pet deserts." These are communities where a majority of residents live below the poverty level and where pet owners lack access to basic pet-care resources, such as veterinarians and pet stores. Such establishments rarely put down roots in poorer communities, and since many residents who are financially stressed lack transportation, they can't reach those in communities outside their own.

"It's shocking," Thompson says. "There are no resources available. There's only one grocery store. If I go three miles toward my house, I have everything I need."

I join the duo on an overcast day in March as they hit the road at seven-thirty in the morning to pick up eight dogs for spay/neuter surgery and one dog, already neutered, who needs his rabies shot. They will drop the dogs at a private veterinary clinic in Midtown Atlanta—the Ark Animal Hospital—which provides Pets for Life with a discount on its services because of the volume of animals Freeman and Thompson bring in, and then the two will deliver the dogs back to their homes late in the afternoon. On a good day, Thompson tells me, twenty dogs will be fixed—ten that they drop at the clinic, ten dropped off by their owners.

Six of today's dogs belong to a seventy-nine-year-old woman they refer to as Miss Helen. As the van pulls up to the curb in front of her house, Miss Helen, one of her four sons, and several grandchildren stand on the porch waiting for us. Her dogs—Rocky, Kipper, Jo Jo, Scrappy, Chi Chi, and Chloe—Chihuahuas, terriers, and mixes of the two who span three generations, are in crates, ready to be loaded into the van. Miss Helen gives Thompson a hug hello, and because I'm with her, I get one, too. She is thrilled her dogs are getting fixed. It's difficult keeping the males and females apart every time a female goes into heat, she tells me. She does her best, but there have been times she hasn't been successful. Rocky, her virile Chihuahua, has fathered several litters. She would have gotten them fixed, she says, if it weren't so expensive. As it is, the dogs cost her $40 per month for food, and that's with the coupons Kroger gives her. She's retired after twenty-nine years working in the housekeeping department of Georgia Baptist Hospital, now Atlanta Medical Center, and lives on social security. But, she says, she's not complaining. When she was a young girl in Alabama, her family had twenty-three dogs. "We were so poor we could hardly eat ourselves, but we'd feed our dogs. We loved them." And she loves the six she has now. "They are my children. I spend more time with them than with anyone else."

As Freeman carries the crates to the van, Miss Helen says goodbye to each dog, adding, "You be good." As the van pulls away, she remains on the porch, smiling. She waves. Her dogs will be returned this afternoon. They will be fixed. And it won't cost Miss Helen a cent.

Pets for Life got off the ground in the fall of 2011, after Amanda Arrington spent a couple of years lobbying the leaders of HSUS. She'd been with the organization for three years, hired originally in 2008 to be state director for North Carolina. It was a job she applied for on a whim. "When I found out they were hiring, I thought there was no chance in hell I would get it. I had never had a job in animal welfare. The lady who hired me said, 'On paper there was nothing, but when I met you, I knew you could do it.'"

After less than a year as state director, she became the spay/neuter initiatives director, working in Mississippi and Louisiana to further research started post-Katrina into why the Gulf Coast was so overwhelmed with companion animals and what actions HSUS and the broader animal welfare community could take to increase spay/neuter rates there and, by extension, across the country. That work, her experience in Durham with the Coalition to Unchain Dogs, and her childhood in Douglass persuaded Arrington that the animal welfare community needed to be more proactive if it was going to get to the heart of the pet overpopulation problem. That meant going into the most underserved communities where spay/neuter rates barely top 5 percent, building relationships with pet owners, and educating them and empowering them to care for their pets.

In Atlanta, Pets for Life chose the 30318 zip code, just northwest of the city's downtown. In the program's headquarters on Hollywood Road, across from an auto-parts dealer and behind a cell phone store that doubles as a check-cashing depot, a huge street-level map is tacked to the wall. This is one of the city's poorer communities, with a third of the residents living below the poverty level, an unemployment rate 50 percent higher than the city's and nearly double the state's, and a college completion rate just under 20 percent. It is also the most rural zip code in the four pilot cities, Rachel Thompson tells me, in that most people live in single-family houses with backyards, and few people have fences. Add to this mix Atlanta's mild climate, and that means dogs spend much of their time outdoors, creating ideal mating conditions. Not surprisingly, accidental litters are a problem here.

Lucky, a brindle pit who needs his rabies shot, is very likely the product of such a litter. Thompson encourages Lucky's owner, Lily, to tell me the dog's story. "I was walking around the neighborhood one day," Lily says, "when I came upon a litter of puppies in a paint bucket. I asked why the puppies were in the bucket, and the man standing there says, 'Because we're gonna drown them.' I said, 'Not all of them.' And I took him." She nods her head in Lucky's direction. "I named him Lucky." Lily already owned Princess, a small black Chihuahua with great big brown eyes, or, she says, she might have taken another one. Princess is heading to the veterinary clinic, too, to be spayed and vaccinated against rabies, parvovirus, and distemper.

Stories like Lucky's and those HSUS canvassers heard in Mississippi and Louisiana confirmed for Arrington something she'd believed for a while—that shelter euthanasia numbers don't reflect the full scope of America's dog problem. There are thousands, perhaps hundreds of thousands, of dogs in poor rural and urban communities in the South, and across the country, who are killed—sometimes by their owners—whose deaths are not counted because they never make it into a shelter. "If we only focus on shelter numbers, we're going to think we solved the problem when we really haven't. Our team tries really hard to address the problem more broadly."

In Atlanta, Freeman and Thompson are embedding themselves in the community. They frequent the grocery store and convenience shops, speak about the importance of spay/neuter at local churches, and run outreach events like group dog walks, picnics, basketball games, and vaccination clinics that have turned out upwards of 400 people. All the while they are educating pet owners about a higher standard of pet care and making it possible for them to access it. In addition—and this is what really sets Pets for Life apart from other programs—they are walking down every street and knocking on every door to identify pet owners whose dogs and cats are not spayed or neutered. And then they work diligently to persuade those owners to sign up their pet for a free spay/neuter surgery, offering to drive the animal to and from the veterinary clinic if transportation is an issue. Between the two of them, they are in the community six, sometimes seven, days a week. The best time to canvass the neighborhood, they say, is Saturday afternoon, when most people are home, but they go most weekday afternoons, too.

"You only get one chance to make a first impression," Freeman says, "so you don't want to wake anybody up."

Rachel Thompson and Tim Freeman are each in their mid-forties, outgoing, friendly. She is white; he is black. Neither is a native Southerner. She came to Atlanta via New Jersey, he via Wisconsin more than thirty-five years ago. They share a love of animals and an empathy for people, two basic requirements of the job. When they are in the community, they are walking billboards for Pets for Life, wearing T-shirts advertising the program, handing out cards and flyers. They want everyone to know who they are and what Pets for Life is all about.

When they go knocking, not everyone answers the door. Not everyone signs up a pet for a free spay/neuter surgery the first time they speak. In fact, most don't, but that's okay. They are not going anywhere; they've been schooled in patience and persistence by Amanda Arrington. Freeman and Thompson tell pet owners to think about their offer, that they'll come back. "We have to establish their trust," Thompson tells me. "Trust is very important. These people hand off their dogs to us, and we walk out the door with them."

"Some clients are resistant up to a year," Freeman adds. "Our approach is to stick with them, keep informing them about the benefits of the surgery. Other organizations have come in and said, 'We'll give you this or we'll give you that if you spay or neuter your dog,' and then they never come back. For us, follow-up is religious. No one falls through the cracks. The only way we lose you is if you move out of state or die. And so many people are surprised we follow up. People always say, 'I didn't expect to hear from you again.' They're not used to that."

"And we open up a discussion," Thompson says. "We don't judge. I may not agree with someone's decision, if he doesn't want to spay or neuter his dog, but I keep it to myself. Then I'll try to help by making sure the dog is healthy and well trained. And each time I see the person, I'll bring it up again."

Thompson tells me the story about a client I'll call John, who initially refused her entreaties. "For more than a year we asked him if he wanted his dog spayed. The first time, he was having none of it. He just shut us down. But we didn't give up. Sometimes we'd drive by, and if he was outside, I'd roll down the window and yell, 'Hi. Change your mind?' One day we were driving by, and I'm not sure why we stopped. By then the dog had had a litter, and we told John that she looked tired. I said, 'Look at her. She loves her puppies. She loves you. But she's thin. She's tired.' He finally agreed to have her spayed. A few months later, he called Tim to say he got another puppy, and he wanted her spayed. Now the first one has gained weight, and their life together has improved. It's a phenomenal story."

Thompson's exhilaration sounds as fresh as if the events occurred yesterday. "John has a better quality of life now, and so do his dogs. It elevates the relationship to that from just pet to companion."

Freeman estimates that roughly 60 percent of the pet owners they meet want to spay or neuter their pets, but they don't have the funds or they haven't had the opportunity. "Once we offer it to them, and they think about it, it gets done." The majority of those who don't want to do it "are black males, and their dogs are male. They say, 'I can't do that to him.' Or, 'Let him have one litter.' Or, 'I don't want to cut his nuts off.'" In fact, research on attitudes toward spay/neuter by HSUS has found that opposition, primarily to neutering, tends to be highest among black and Latino men whose cultures value machismo.

"I often explain that it's like a vasectomy," Thompson says, "and that the surgery is easier on the males than the females."

It was that reluctance that was keeping a client I'll call Lewis from having his pit bull, Stripe, neutered. "Stripe was knocking up all the ladies in the neighborhood," Freeman told me. "He probably fathered seven or eight litters." The problem was, in part, that Lewis's backyard wasn't fenced, so Stripe would break loose from the tree he was tethered to when he got wind of a female in heat. Neutering would lessen Stripe's instinct to chase the girls, but eight months of conversations couldn't persuade Lewis. What did was an accident: One night when Stripe broke loose, a car hit him. Freeman told Lewis that he was lucky this time, but that not neutering Stripe could kill him. Lewis's love for the dog finally changed his mind.

"I want to see a dog make it past four or five years old," Freeman told me. "Too often a male senses a female in heat, and he breaks his chain and runs away. He gets lost or hit by a car or ends up in the shelter. You just don't see a lot of dogs living 'til old age around here."

On this day, Freeman and Thompson choose a street in the Grove Park neighborhood to commence the daily ritual of door knocking. This is one of the prettier areas of 30318. The homes, built in the early 1900s, are typical of the American bungalow style of architecture that was popular at the turn of the twentieth century. I don't see many of the boarded-up or burned-out houses that proliferate in other areas of the community.

At our first house, a woman answers the door. She has a pit bull in her backyard, she says. No, he's not fixed. Yes, she will take their information. No, she will not sign up the dog for surgery, at least not today. "I used to think I was bad at this," Freeman says as we head back toward the sidewalk. "I would canvass a whole street, and no one would sign up. But a week or so would pass, and the calls would start coming in."

It's not surprising to me that people respond with hesitation, even outright suspicion. What Pets for Life is offering—like what Coalition to Unchain Dogs offers—seems too good to be true. Think about it: If strangers showed up at your door asking if you had pets and wanting to know if they were fixed, would you answer their questions? Would you even open the door? And if you had pets that weren't fixed, would you believe these strangers when they told you that they would not only pay for the surgery but that they would provide transportation? This is why follow-up is essential—and word of mouth. If Freeman and Thompson can get one pet owner on one street to get her pet fixed, others are likely to follow.

We come upon several guys hanging out and chatting in front of a house; one is working on the engine of a Dodge SRT. Thompson strikes up a conversation. One of the men just got a toy shih tzu, and he would definitely like to get her spayed. He takes a voucher for a free surgery and gives Thompson his wife's number to set up a time. He also gives her his friend's name and number—the friend owns the shih tzu's brother. Thompson tells him she will follow up—and she will.

One woman comes out of her house as Thompson and I approach; Freeman has crossed the street to cover more ground. The woman tells us she's heard of the program and wants her cats fixed. One is a three-year-old male; the other, a black-and-gold tabby, is a one-year-old female. The woman doesn't want any litters, or, she says, her home will be overrun with cats, like a house across the street where a neighbor keeps seventeen. The woman would like Thompson to do the transporting to the veterinary clinic because she lacks transportation—she says she sold her car to buy a new stove.

By doing the bulk of the transporting to and from the clinic, Pets for Life makes sure that dogs and cats signed up for surgery get their surgery. If an owner agrees to take a pet himself, Thompson will call every few days leading up to the appointment to ensure follow-through. This approach has yielded the four-city program a 90 percent completion rate.

Thompson keeps impressive notes, recording the number of houses she and Freeman hit, the houses to return to because an owner isn't ready to alter her dog or cat, the houses where no one is home but where they see a dog in the yard or hear one barking inside the house, the houses where they learn a dog is pregnant and know following up will be essential not just to get the mom spayed but to track the puppies and get them fixed, too.

We come upon one of those latter houses about halfway down the street. A young woman in her twenties answers the door along with a "Chiweenie"—a Chihuahua-dachshund mix—she'd adopted from a Los Angeles shelter. The Chiweenie is fixed, but the twentysomething says her sister's three shepherds are not, and one is pregnant. "She got that way accidentally," she says. Thompson hands over her card. As we're walking away, she says, "I often feel like we're too late, that if we could only have knocked on that door earlier. Tim tells me I can't think that way. But when you see how many there are, I feel like we need to walk as fast and as furiously as we can."

In 2013, Pets for Life's Atlanta program fixed 1,761 dogs and cats. After the surgery, many pet owners become spokespeople for the program, persuading family, friends, and neighbors to take advantage of it. That's how Miss Helen learned of the program—a church friend who'd had her dog fixed sang the program's praises. Other satisfied clients become volunteers. "Afterward they want to help," Thompson says. "They ask, 'What can I do?' One little old lady tried hard to give me five dollars one day."

Back in Freeman's van, on our way to retrieve the dogs from the

Ark Animal Hospital, we spot a young man, seventeenish, eating a bag of potato chips and walking down the street with a two-month-old pit prancing behind him. Freeman pulls over and introduces himself to the teen, who says his name is T.J. Freeman gives T.J. a leash for the puppy and asks T.J. if he's interested in free dog training. Freeman runs training sessions out of Pets for Life's headquarters as yet one more way to help owners build stronger, healthier relationships with their dogs. T.J. texts his phone number to Freeman, then asks if Freeman can teach his dog to bite on command.

Thompson jumps into the conversation. "No," she says. "We won't teach her that." Then she smoothly changes the topic, asking T.J. if he's thought about whether he's going to get his puppy spayed. T.J. says he wants the dog to have puppies because he likes pit bulls. By now Thompson is out of the car, petting the puppy. "I can get you a free pit at the shelter any time you want one," she tells him, and explains that the shelter is overcrowded with pit bulls. Then she says, "Look, everyone loves puppies, and when she's pregnant, everyone is gonna tell you, 'I'll take a puppy. I'll take a puppy.' Until you show up at their door with a puppy. Then they don't want one. And what are you going to do? We already have too many dogs and not enough homes. Why don't you think about it?"

Thompson gets back into the van, and Freeman tells T.J. that he'll be back in the neighborhood tomorrow afternoon with Blue Boy, his seven-year-old pit. They and a group of locals are going for a group dog walk. He asks T.J. to join them; T.J. says he will.

I mention to Freeman that I am surprised by the number of pit bulls I am seeing—pits and Chihuahua-sized dogs. I wasn't seeing any of the breeds that proliferate where I live—full breeds like golden retrievers and Labrador retrievers; boutique mixes like Labradoodles and golden doodles; and mixed breeds like Galen and Gryffin, who often have a bit of retriever or shepherd in them. Freeman said people in the community like small dogs for purely practical reasons—they can own several, and, because they are small, they can live inside the house. As for the pit bulls, Freeman, who owns two, in addition to a rottweiler and a German shepherd, sounds almost philosophical.

"The more I've thought about it, and I've thought about it a lot, I just think that the pit bull embodies everything that black people have been through. The sheer strength of the dog and his willingness to keep fighting no matter what. His drive. Also, his compassion. And I think that's why black people just took that particular dog almost as their mascot. You know, this is the dog that we're going to embellish and breed."

Freeman has driven no more than several hundred feet when Thompson spies a yard with a rottweiler and two pit bulls. She asks Freeman to stop the van. "Last stop," she says. "I promise."

When Thompson returns, she's smiling. She's signed up the rottweiler for surgery. The pits are already fixed.

PETS FOR LIFE ASKS nothing financially of its clients. Rather, everything it provides, from leashes to pet food to dog training to spay/neuter surgery, is paid for by the program. The money comes from HSUS's operating budget, grants, donations, and anywhere else Amanda Arrington can find it. And that's where much of the pushback comes from—both from inside and outside the animal welfare community. As critics see it, people who can't afford to feed and vet a dog shouldn't own one, and certainly not two or three or more.

"That's when I say get over yourself," says Arrington, "because what your opinion is doesn't matter. This is reality. We are never going to pass a law that has income requirements on people owning pets. Even if it could pass, I wouldn't want it to happen because I think people living in poverty are deprived of so many things that make you a human being. And I think that sometimes the less you have, the more important a pet can be to you, even if it doesn't appear that way to an outsider who doesn't understand your life. And I think it makes people feel better to say that because the alternative is to say, 'There are all these people living in poverty. So many of them have pets, and we need to help them.' And a lot of people don't like that because of the discomfort, because it's really sad. Because when you really open your mind and heart to this, you see how hard it is to be poor and what it does to someone's self-esteem. To say someone doesn't deserve a dog is an unbelievable judgment to make."

Teresa Fisher shares many of Arrington's ideas, so much so that if I close my eyes I could easily be listening to her. Fisher directs the Companion Animal Initiative of Tennessee (CAIT), an animal welfare program run out of the University of Tennessee College of Veterinary Medicine that works to reduce the state's surplus of dogs and cats and promote responsible pet ownership. When I ask Arrington if she knows Fisher, she tells me the two once crossed paths at an animal welfare conference. "She heard me talking and came up to me afterwards. We bonded."

Like Arrington, Fisher is slender, brunette, in her mid-thirties, and she, too, grew up around animals—Fisher's grandfather raised hogs and grew tobacco on a farm in southern Virginia, near the North Carolina border. Echoing Arrington's experience, Fisher says, "Animals were for eating. They did not come into the house because they'd bring in filth and fleas." Both women are now vegetarians.

Even as a young girl in Martinsville, Virginia, a city small in size and population, Fisher says she felt like she didn't fit in with everyone else. "Life was very religious-based, and I was sheltered. The culture was, 'You'll marry and take care of the house.' Education was not pushed. My mom only got through sixth grade. But I was raised in a single-parent home, so I was taught I didn't need a man."

The only way out of Martinsville, Fisher told me, was to attend college or join the military, and for her, the choice was clear. "I had a strong urge to go to college. I always felt I wanted to see more, know more. I barely made it into college, but I made it."

Fisher attended East Tennessee State University, where she studied computer animation. There were twelve students in her program, and they spent a lot of time together waiting for their projects to render. "These were the days before rendering was quick and easy," she says. During a conversation one day, the only other female in the program mentioned she was a vegetarian. "I had never even heard that word before. She had to explain it to me. She told me why she became a vegetarian, and after that, I chose to become one, too. And I began to think about animal husbandry and animal stewardship."

It was also during her college years that Fisher adopted her first cat. Today she and her ex-husband "split their herd" of three cats and five "Chihuahua-type dogs" Fisher calls "doglets." They are all rescues; four are victims of abuse. One of the dogs was so starved when he was rescued that his bones protruded from his tiny body; two dogs found with him were dead. "I took him home with me so he could die in a loving place; seven years later he's still with me."

After graduation Fisher and her ex, who was then her fiancé, moved to Charleston, South Carolina, and she got a job doing "boring IT stuff." She spent her free time online perusing the alphabet soup of animal welfare sites—PETA, HSUS, ASPCA—"trying to come up with ways to make the world a better place." It quickly became clear that IT was not her calling, but that animals are. "I told my fiancé I wanted to pursue an animal science degree. I got accepted to UT, got a job in the vet school as a student computer worker doing graphics work and presentations, and they have yet to get rid of me."

Today Fisher runs CAIT while working toward her Ph.D. in anthropology. "I'm 'that girl,' a vegetarian in this animal science, ag world. I take classes with people who raise animals for food. But I'm proud I don't eat or wear animals."

CAIT evolved out of a grassroots initiative launched in 2000 to better the all-around quality of life in a nine-county region that has

Knoxville, home to the University of Tennessee, at its core. Strikingly, out of a long list of concerns culled from nearly 9,000 ideas, animal welfare ranked fifth. A task force was created to explore the complex problem of pet overpopulation, which seemed to be at the heart of the animal-related concerns, and to seek both public and private sector solutions. In 2004, when the initiative dissolved, CAIT picked up where the task force left off, affiliating itself with the university's vet school and expanding its focus statewide.

In Tennessee, the problem of pet overpopulation is particularly hard to quantify. The state doesn't require that municipalities or counties run animal shelters, so it's left to local governments to determine their needs. Some have shelters—like Blount County, with its public-private partnership—and some don't. In some counties, private citizens have opened nonprofit shelters to house stray and surrendered dogs. Some shelters, perhaps all, track the disposition of every animal, but there is no public or private entity collecting that information. CAIT is trying to determine how many shelters exist across the state, but it is work that is ongoing. In a slide presentation for a 2013 animal control conference, Fisher listed the number of shelters in Tennessee as "unknown." What is known is that in 2013, the public shelter that services Knox County and the city of Knoxville euthanized just over 6,500 dogs and cats—about 50 percent who entered that year.

It's numbers like these that frustrate Fisher and animate her, too. "Animal shelters exist because we fail as a society," she says. "Especially in the South, I think, we've taught our children that animals are disposable, and they're not. But you teach your child that when your German shepherd has fourteen babies, and you dump them in a shelter or put them in a free-to-good-home ad and don't know what happens to them. And in Tennessee we're big on property rights and the government not telling you what to do with your property. So I say, 'Keep your property on your property.' But too many people don't, and we have this overpopulation problem. And then people turn against shelters when they euthanize animals, saying shelters don't care, they're evil. Well, the shelter would not need to exist if you would just spay and neuter your animals."

I ask Fisher for her take on why spaying and neutering isn't happening in large enough numbers to more quickly slow the population rate.

"Lack of education," she tells me. "It's not that people are stupid, it's just that they don't understand basic reproduction, so they don't know what to do, and many can't afford it anyway. There's also a lack of urgency because people don't see the importance, so they book surgeries and then don't show up. Or we hear a lot that they want their children to experience 'the miracle of life.'"

This is where CAIT's engagement with the community comes into play; CAIT is working to educate pet owners about why spaying and neutering their companion animals is important not only for their own relationship with their pets but for society as a whole. Fisher even has a message for those who fix their pets. "Some people say, 'I spay and neuter all of my animals.' Okay, well, why don't you sponsor an animal at the shelter, sponsor the little old lady in the church? Think beyond yourself." She can sound strident, but, she tells me, she hears too many people complain about strays, complain about shelters, and then do nothing. "People don't ever see themselves as part of the problem. But if you're complaining and you're not helping, you're part of the problem. Period."

While CAIT works to educate pet owners across the state, its affiliation with the College of Veterinary Medicine permits it to reach an audience one might not think needs educating about the problem of pet overpopulation—veterinary students. In fact, I mention to Fisher that I presume anyone entering veterinary medicine would be well aware of the issue. She tells me I presume wrong. "Not all vets want to work with companion animals. Of those who do, some may be aware, some may not. But many students—even faculty—who work with large animals or those interested in herd management or livestock are not exposed to companion animal overpopulation. But when they're on a farm, where many of them will be, and they see cats and dogs, which they will, I want them to ask, 'Are those animals fixed?' I want everyone engaged and seeing the big picture."

Among the many programs CAIT runs, one in particular caught my attention, perhaps because the pet-owning population it serves is one we hear very little about. Accurate statistics are hard to come by, but the National Coalition for the Homeless estimates that between 5 and 10 percent of America's homeless keep a dog or a cat as a companion. For many, their four-legged friend composes their entire social and emotional support system. In *My Dog Always Eats First*, sociologist Leslie Irvine explores this relationship, and in so doing recounts stories of homeless pet owners who refuse housing when accepting it means giving up or separating from their best friends. Homelessness, she writes, shapes unique relationships between people and their pets, so much so that "in surveys homeless people report levels of attachment to their animals that may surpass those found among the domiciled public."

The plight of homeless pet owners and their pets caught Fisher's attention in the fall of 2005. She had learned that the city of Knoxville planned to host an all-day resource fair to connect the city's homeless to social service organizations and provide them with on-site services, like wellness checkups and legal assistance. Fisher immediately thought, "These people have pets." So CAIT offered to assist the city, and on the day of the event students and professors from the vet school gave rabies shots and vaccinations to a population of dogs and cats that rarely, if ever, see a veterinarian.

The city hosted the event for two more years, and CAIT participated, but Fisher was convinced that a more robust program was needed, one that incorporated spay/neuter. She "twisted some arms" at the vet school; persuaded companies like Purina, Novartis, and Boehringer Ingelheim to donate pet food and vaccines; and called on local veterinarians to provide spay/neuter surgeries. The result: Vets for Pets of Homeless Owners, known more simply as VPHO.

ON A WARM MONDAY EVENING in April, several pet owners hang out in an area of Knoxville known simply as "under the bridge," waiting for the VPHO team—doctors and students from the vet school—to arrive. At least one pet owner has been there for several hours. The location, tucked beneath merging interstate highways downtown, is the hub of the city's homeless community. Many homeless service organizations are nearby, and once a week Lost Sheep Ministry uses the space to serve dinner to up to 300 of the city's homeless and low-income residents. VPHO sets up its makeshift veterinary clinic here at 6:00 p.m. the second Monday of each month. Fisher tells me the woman who runs the Ministry has asked that VPHO increase the amount of pet food it distributes. "She says that pet owners are stuffing food in their pockets, and the Ministry is trying to feed them, not their animals."

Sarah—clients and vet students go by first names only—a regular, has brought her dog, Skippy, a six-year-old Maltese, and her cat, Bootsie, a four-year-old domestic shorthair. They've been waiting for two and a half hours. Sarah has been coming to VPHO's clinics for four years and always arrives early. "I don't like getting stuck at the back of the line," she tells me. Tonight she's here to have Skippy's nails trimmed and to pick up dog and cat food. Skippy will be due for his rabies shot in December. "I try to keep up on all their shots," she tells me.

Sarah's had Skippy since he was two. She saw an advertisement for a Maltese in the classified ads, and even though she didn't have the $450 that his previous owner wanted for him, she answered the ad. "An older lady had him, and she didn't take care of him. His fur was all matted. I told her I only had $50, but she wouldn't take my money. She gave me Skippy for free." I ask Sarah if it's hard to care for Skippy and Bootsie. She says it was harder when she was homeless, but she's since moved into an apartment and although she remains on public assistance, the three of them are better off.

As soon as two veterinary social work students finish setting up plastic tables where clients will check in, Sarah excuses herself to take her place at the front of the line.

Laurelei—she looks to be in her fifties and seems to be in no rush—sits cross-legged on the pavement in front of her car, a two-year-old Chihuahua nestled in her lap. Laurelei tells me that Rexy was six weeks old when she came into her life, a gift from a friend whose dog had a litter of puppies the friend couldn't afford to keep. Laurelei says she learned about VPHO from a worker at the Salvation Army, and several months ago VPHO arranged for Rexy to be spayed. "If not for this program, I don't know what I'd do," Laurelei tells me. She lives on a fixed income, and money is tight, but she absolutely loves her little dog. Tonight she's here for Rexy's monthly flea and tick treatment.

VPHO does no advertising. In order to qualify for service, a pet owner must be enrolled with a city or county organization, like the Salvation Army, that provides services to the homeless and, since VPHO expanded its eligibility, to the working poor. So it's the organizations that refer clients to VPHO. Once clients are signed in, vet students interview them to determine the needs of their pets. Beyond collars, leashes, and pet food, VPHO veterinarians provide rabies shots, vaccinations, and monthly parasite preventatives out of a mobile veterinary clinic. There is a catch, though: A pet must be spayed or neutered to receive these services. If the animal is not, a free surgery is scheduled and required if the pet is to be seen again. "I tell them because it's free, you are required to get it," Fisher says.

"We get that you're poor. We get that you have no money. We will do this for you for free. You don't have transportation; we will arrange transportation for you. And we let new folks know, we will see your animal tonight, but we will never see him again if you don't spay or neuter."

Most of the pet owners who seek out VPHO's services are thrilled to have their pets fixed, especially those with females who know caring for a litter is far beyond their means, and they return month after month to get their pets their parasite preventives or simply to say hello. They have their own sense of community, Fisher says. "They'll tell newcomers, 'You need to get in that line or that line, and she'll call your name.' And they'll tell anyone who's smoking to move away from us. They'll say, 'Don't smoke near them. They don't like the smoke.'

"And we have one guy—he just got out of prison—and he comes and visits us and tells us he cannot go back to prison because he doesn't know what would happen to his dog. He tells us this every time. 'I have to stay out of trouble, or what will happen to my dog?'"

There are a few pet owners, however, who need persuading. Often it's because they want to breed their dogs and sell the puppies at the flea market for money. Fisher quickly dissuades them of that. "I let them know that if they want to come to the shelter and help euthanize all the dogs sold at flea markets who ultimately wind up at the shelter, we can talk about not spaying their dog. I haven't had any volunteers."

Perhaps it's no surprise that Fisher hears many of the same criticisms of VPHO that Arrington hears regarding Pets for Life— that at its core, it enables society's "takers." Sometimes, Fisher says, the criticism even comes from veterinary students who go into volunteering with the perspective that if you're homeless you're lazy, or if you don't have money you don't deserve a pet.

"So I ask the student, 'Do rich people love their pets? Because

Michael Vick had a lot of money, and I don't think he loved his pets. Should he have had as many as he wanted because he had all that money?' Then I tell them that money has nothing to do with love and care. And that it takes a strong person to come to us and say, 'I need help.' And then I send the student to talk to the people, and you start to see it in the student's eyes that he gets it. And we ask students to stop stereotyping, to stop being so judgmental, and to open up their heart."

"HEY, OLD BOY," Miss Helen says as Tim Freeman places Rocky's crate on her front porch. To Chloe: "Hey, girl." As soon as Freeman frees the six pint-sized dogs from their crates, they spring forward, tails wagging. Some dash around the front yard; others jump on Miss Helen, who sits on one of several chairs scattered about the porch. Their energy belies the fact that they are hours out from their spay or neuter surgery. Miss Helen throws her head back and laughs as one of the dogs tries to kiss her lips.

Freeman sits down beside Miss Helen and puts a white paper bag filled with several bottles of medicine on a wicker table. The dogs have ear infections, he tells her, so the vet has provided eardrops. "Four drops in each ear. Swab them. Then let it sit and dry for twenty to thirty minutes." Miss Helen nods her head as she listens. "This means the world to me," she says.

Pets for Life is making phenomenal inroads in its pilot cities. According to a 2014 program analysis, the conversion rate, which measures the percentage of unaltered pets that are spayed or neutered after outreach workers establish a relationship with their owners, is 70 percent—this in communities where it is typical to find more than 90 percent of pets not fixed. This dramatic increase in spay/neuter surgeries within the community, the report suggests, provides the foundation for the start of a societal shift away from the norm that exists today, in which pet owners do not spay or neuter their pets.

To capitalize on the work being done in the pilot cities, Pets for Life and PetSmart Charities teamed up in the fall of 2012 to provide mentorship grants to ten animal welfare groups willing to implement the Pets for Life program in underserved communities in their cities. Arrington says she is seeing similar increases in spay/neuter in the "mentor cities," which stretch from Camden in New Jersey to Tacoma in Washington. "You just have to connect with people on a human level," she says.

I tell Arrington Galen's story and mention the staggering number of dogs, like Galen, who are born in the South but find homes in the North, where overall spay/neuter rates trend higher. Then I ask whether she thinks culture or demographics drive the disparity. "I think the issue is multifaceted," she answers. "As a region we can say the South is most in crisis because of sheer numbers. As an issue, I think there are communities just as much in crisis all over the country. I know from my life and my experiences that the rural white culture in the South is somewhat similar to the Midwest in terms of hunting and agriculture, and experiences as they pertain to dogs and cats are somewhat the same. Then there are urban populations that I think today are connected demographically. So that what's going on in Atlanta is similar to what's going on in Camden is similar to what's going on in Jefferson Parish. There is a lot of nuance."

But what it all comes down to for Arrington is people—people who love their pets. "It doesn't matter where you are. North, South, rural, urban. You've just got to get to the people."

Getting to the people, however, takes an extraordinary amount of time and not a little money, especially when doing things the Pets for Life way, which means embedding workers in underserved communities. Tim Freeman and Rachel Thompson have twenty square miles to cover and more than 25,000 doors to knock on. Every bag of pet food they give out, every spay/neuter surgery that gets performed, and even their salaries must be paid for. And this is just one zip code in one city. But Arrington isn't cowed. "It takes a lot of time and money to have shelters," she says. "This is a different type of work, but it's not any more expensive than what society is doing now. If we can start doing a little bit of our work as preventive instead of reactive, we could get somewhere."

In fact, the United States hasn't really been getting anywhere over the last decade when it comes to decreasing the number of shelter euthanasias nationwide, which is the only marker we have for our overpopulation problem. The number, which hovers around four million, is down markedly from where it stood in the 1970s, when it was up near twenty million, but it has since plateaued. It's almost akin to what happens when you go on a diet and those first pounds fall off relatively quickly, but then you get to where losing even one pound becomes a struggle. Arrington would say that now is the time for the animal welfare community to approach the problem differently—to embrace the model that Pets for Life is pioneering. "It works. You just have to be patient with people and be nice. We don't have to get everybody, but we can get a lot of people to spay or neuter their pets, and we can get over this hump. We'll rescue until we die. If we're going to fix the problem, we need to reach the right audience."

As Arrington sips the last of her iced green tea latte, I ask where she sees Pets for Life going in the future.

"World domination," she says, not missing a beat.

Amanda Arrington isn't kidding.

Dogs for Dollars

IT WASN'T LONG BEFORE GALEN put behind her any maternal feelings she may have had for Loki. In fact, it wasn't long before Galen decided she wanted very little to do with him.

The dogs will see each other periodically—I bring Galen to my mom's whenever we visit, and she brings our former foster with her to us. But the more time Galen spends with Loki, the less she seems to like him. It's not that she's aggressive toward him; rather, she ignores him. If a dog can give the cold shoulder, that's the tack she takes to discourage Loki from engaging her—and engage he does. Loki radiates energy—Kevin and I decided he resembles Tigger, Winnie the Pooh's bouncy orange-and-black-striped friend. Galen, on the other hand, mellowed so much post-puppyhood that her newfound serenity is a stark contrast to Loki's exuberance.

The more Loki tries to play with Galen—he usually does this by giving Galen a right paw to the side of her head or nipping at her hind legs—the more she retreats. In my mother's house, she wedges herself under the wood coffee table in the living room. In our house, she flees to her crate, which Loki quickly learned is off limits to him after Galen bared her teeth the first time he poked his head inside to check it—and her—out. Every now and then, when Galen deigns to show Loki attention, they will roughhouse, rising on hind legs, front legs thrust around each other, teeth clanking. It's a scary sight unless you know that this "fang fighting," as I've heard it called, is how dogs play. And this is clearly play because now and again they stop for a few seconds, look around as if to see if there is something more interesting to do, look back at each other, and, upon agreeing that there is, indeed, nothing more interesting, pick up where they left off. It's actually quite civilized for something that looks so savage.

I couldn't decide which dog I felt worse for: Loki, because he is such a sweet boy and because all he wants is for Galen to play with him, or Galen, because Loki keeps whacking her with his paw or, when they are in the yard, runs at her full speed, crashing into her as she stands still, stoic. Galen's one kindness toward Loki is not to get up and walk away when she is splayed out on the floor and he lies beside her, his rump nestled against hers.

Watching a puppy's canine character develop as we had with Gryffin and were now doing with Galen is one of the joys of adopting a puppy. And because dogs age so much more quickly than human children, their cognitive development—if you can call it that—and their personality evolve at warp speed. It is this joy that Tori Richards never got to experience after she adopted Charlie, a Welsh corgi–border collie mix. Richards adopted Charlie just a week after I adopted Galen. Like Galen, Charlie hailed from the South, and, like Galen, he was about two months old. But one week after Richards brought Charlie home, the reddish-gold puppy with the stripe of white fur running down the center of his forehead was diagnosed with a life-threatening virus.

ON SATURDAY, DECEMBER 4, 2010, Tori Richards made the forty-five minute drive from her Bucks County, Pennsylvania, home to a pet retailer in Central Jersey to check out a litter of border collie mixes she had seen on the website of an animal rescue group calling itself Your Furry Friend. She brought along her boyfriend, David, but not her son, Paul, then twenty-five. "I wanted to see the puppies first," Richards says. "I didn't want to get Paul's hopes up."

Tori and Paul Richards were still mourning the loss of their beloved five-year-old border collie mix, Bear, who had succumbed to colorectal cancer six weeks earlier. "Bear grew up to be one of the smartest and most loving dogs I have ever met," Paul told me in an e-mail. "He had so much love to give. He would look right into your eyes as if to say, 'I understand,' if your day wasn't going well, or he'd smile when he knew things had turned around."

Bear had been a rescue from the SPCA shelter in Lahaska, Pennsylvania, but the shelter didn't have any border collies or border collie mixes when Richards returned after Bear's death, so, like me, and like so many want-to-be dog owners, Richards turned to the Internet. She eventually found her way to the Your Furry Friend website and to photographs of its litter of border collie mixes. Now she stood inside the pet store, looking into the innocent faces of eight nine-week-old puppies, cuddling them and gauging their personalities. It wasn't easy to choose a favorite—each puppy seemed cuter than the next—but she narrowed the choice to two tiny males. Then she called Paul and asked him to meet her at the store. This dog was going to be theirs; she didn't want to make a decision without him.

While Richards waited for Paul and his girlfriend to arrive, Richards vacillated between the puppies, and she chatted with Jamie Klemper, who founded Your Furry Friend. Richards liked Klemper immediately. "She was one of the sweetest, nicest people I'd ever met," Richards told me. The two women talked about the dogs Klemper had with her that day, and they talked about the adoption fee, which Klemper said was $300. That amount sounded high to Richards, but she says Klemper told her that the fee covered all of a puppy's expenses, including fostering and veterinary care. According to Richards, Klemper also said that she didn't make any money off the dogs, that Your Furry Friend was a nonprofit organization, and that all that mattered to her was saving as many lives as she could. Finally, Richards says Klemper told her she only accepts cash because she had been cheated in the past by people who cancelled their checks as soon as they walked out the door with a dog. Now, Klemper told Richards, to protect herself from such scam artists, she runs a cash-only rescue.

Once Paul Richards arrived, it didn't take long for him to choose between the two puppies—he felt an immediate kinship to the puppy Klemper had named Storm. "[He] immediately reminded me of Bear," Paul told me. "He had the same inquisitive nature and desire to be in contact with people. I know the meeting was brief, but dogs have a way of showing their hearts."

Richards asked Klemper about Storm's health because the puppy's nose felt dry to the touch. Richards says Klemper told her that Storm might have kennel cough, and that Richards should have the puppy seen by a vet but that kennel cough is common and easily treated. Richards signed an adoption contract and persuaded a very reluctant Klemper to accept a $300 check, as neither Richards nor Paul had thought to bring cash. By this time, at least four hours had passed since Tori Richards had arrived at the pet store. But, she thought, as she prepared to leave, it was time well spent. She and her son would once again have a dog in their lives, a dog they would name Charlie.

Paul took Charlie home with him—he lived in an apartment fifteen minutes from his mother—and the two agreed that Richards would retrieve Charlie on Thursday and keep him through the weekend. In the meantime, Richards made a veterinary appointment for Charlie on Monday, December 13, at the Indian Valley Animal Hospital.

Over the course of the four days that Paul had Charlie, Paul thought the puppy seemed unusually lethargic for a nine-week-old,

Jacki Skole

especially one that is part border collie, a breed renowned for its intelligence but also for its high energy level. But every puppy is different, thought Paul, and he himself had come down with a virus that was keeping him home from work. Perhaps, he thought, he was projecting his lackluster desire to do much of anything onto the puppy. Recalling those first few days with Charlie, with the benefit of hindsight, Paul says he can't help but feel regret. "I wish I had been in better condition myself to perhaps see sooner that Charlie was starting to get really sick."

Thursday night, as Richards settled Charlie into her home, she noticed that the puppy's stool was loose and that whenever she took him outside he would sneeze as soon as the cold air hit him. So she outfitted Charlie in a tiny knit sweater in hopes it would keep him warm during their frequent trips into the backyard as she worked to housetrain him. By early Friday afternoon, Charlie seemed better; his stool, at least, had returned to normal, and he wasn't quite so listless. But by midday Saturday, he was vomiting, he had diarrhea, and he refused to leave his crate. Richards decided she could not wait until Monday for his scheduled veterinary appointment; Charlie needed to be seen immediately. She made an appointment for that afternoon at the local emergency animal hospital.

By early Saturday evening, Charlie had been placed in isolation with an admitting diagnosis of parvovirus, the highly contagious viral infection that attacks the cells lining the gastrointestinal tract, as well as a dog's white blood cells. In puppies, the virus can also strike the heart muscle, resulting in lifelong cardiac problems. Laboratory tests needed to be run for confirmation, but the on-call veterinarian said Charlie was too ill to be anywhere but at the hospital under twenty-four-hour observation.

Shocked to learn the severity of Charlie's condition, Richards returned home deeply concerned about the puppy's well-being. She immediately called Jamie Klemper to ask for her $300 back so she could put it toward Charlie's care—she knew that saving his life was not going to come cheap. Richards thought Klemper, so passionate about her dogs, would understand. But, Richards told me, she turned out to be very wrong. "Jamie refused to return the money. And she refused to believe that Charlie could have parvo. She told me I should take him out of the hospital and give him to her. She said another family had returned one of Charlie's siblings because he, too, was ill, and she was treating him with sugar water and antibiotics. She said the vet would charge me two thousand dollars to do the same thing that she could do for free."

Richards refused to remove Charlie from the animal hospital. She was scared and confused, and, if nothing else, she felt she needed to wait for the lab results to come back. "I told Jamie that if your kid is sick you take him to the doctor. So why would I bring Charlie anywhere else?"

On Sunday, Richards got the news she'd desperately hoped not to hear: Charlie had parvovirus, and he wasn't responding to treatment. His white blood cell count was falling. Richards went to the veterinary clinic to see him even though veterinary staff told her she would not be permitted to hold him, pet him, even touch him, as Charlie remained in isolation. So Richards stood behind a glass window and looked at her tiny dog lying motionless in a metal crate, a white blanket wrapped around his body, only his head peeking out. She snapped a few pictures to show Paul.

At home that night, Richards went over Charlie's adoption papers more carefully than she had previously. What she learned and what she thought she knew didn't add up. Charlie's medical records showed that he was neutered, microchipped, and vaccinated in South Carolina. The check Richards wrote to Klemper was cashed in North Carolina. And yet, during their conversation at the pet store, Richards thought she remembered Klemper saying that she lived in New Jersey. Thinking back to their conversation, Richards couldn't recall Klemper ever mentioning anything about Charlie being from the South. And then there was the adoption contract she'd signed. Section seven, under "Terms and Conditions," stated, "YFF makes no guarantees or statements regarding the dog's age, breed, health, or temperament. While YFF has made every effort to provide accurate history and assessment of the dog, YFF is not able to guarantee the dog's age, breed, medical status, behavior or disposition … Adopter accepts this dog as is with all defects, either observable or unobservable, and assumes all risk for the dog upon signing this contract."

On Monday, Charlie's white blood cell count fell further. Richards called Klemper to report on Charlie's condition and to try, once more, to recover the adoption fee. Richards says Klemper again refused to refund the money and told her that the puppy she was treating, Charlie's sibling, was doing much better, that he would likely recover. Richards would later tell New Jersey SPCA investigators that she wasn't sure whether Klemper was telling her the truth about the other puppy but that her comments did make Richards question whether she had done the right thing by bringing Charlie to the animal hospital.

Richards returned to the clinic Monday night. Charlie's breathing, vet techs told her, was erratic. He was being put on oxygen. "They said, 'We don't think you should go back there to see him because he is pretty bad now.'" But Richards went, and later that night Paul did, too. From where they stood, Charlie lay lifeless. He didn't lift his head or make even the slightest movement. It seemed he was barely breathing. I asked Paul why he visited Charlie when he knew he couldn't hold him or even be in the same room with him, that all he could do was look at the dog from behind the glass window. "Charlie was now part of our family," Paul answered. "He was already well liked by friends and family, so the decision to go see him at the vet was a given. He was in isolation at the time, but I guess we were hoping that maybe he'd pull through, and he'd have a familiar face to see when he did."

Richards says that whatever relationship she thought she'd had with Klemper deteriorated entirely in the three days Charlie was hospitalized. "The whole time Charlie was in the hospital I was in constant contact with her, calling her, e-mailing her, going back and forth about how sick he was. She said, 'I will give you another dog.' I said I didn't want another one, that she was missing the point. And the more I contacted her and pressed her for a refund, the nastier she got with me."

At 3:00 a.m. Tuesday, Richards's phone rang. It was the veterinary clinic. Charlie had died.

Ten days later, on Christmas Eve, Richards grabbed a stack of letters from her mailbox. Wedged among a host of holiday cards was a bill from the animal hospital. Tori Richards owed the clinic $1,179.50.

LIBBY WILLIAMS SAT IN HER HOME OFFICE reading an online complaint submitted just before midnight on December 13, 2010, to New Jersey Consumers Against Pet Shop Abuse (NJCAPSA). Williams founded the nonprofit in 2002 to increase public awareness about the relationship that too often exists between puppy mills and pet stores, and to inform buyers of their rights under New Jersey's pet protection law, commonly referred to as the "puppy lemon law."

But this complaint, like many Williams had begun receiving in the last several years, had nothing to do with a pet shop purchase. It was about an animal rescue. And it was strikingly similar to those that came before it: A person spends several hundred dollars to adopt a puppy from a rescue group. The puppy—in almost every case a transport from the South—becomes gravely ill within days of adoption, perhaps from heartworm, perhaps parvovirus. The puppy's owner spends several hundred, if not several thousand, dollars on treatment to no avail. The puppy dies. The adopter can't track down the rescue organization, or the organization refuses to provide a refund. Even the pleas concluding the complaints had become heartrendingly familiar. "Please help us," the one Williams was now reading said. "Please help save other families from this heartache."

The complaint was signed Tori Richards.

IN THE MID-1970S, Libby Williams was newly married and living just outside Ann Arbor, Michigan. Interested in issues of animal welfare, she began volunteering at the Humane Society of Huron Valley, a progressive organization founded in the late 1800s and one that was staffed primarily by women. "For me, this was a whirlwind relationship," Williams recalls giddily. "It was like women's lib meets Catholic schoolgirl."

The society's director, an attorney and activist, took Williams under her wing, training the inquisitive young woman to become an animal cruelty investigator and feeding Williams's growing interest in issues of animal rights. When Peter Singer's seminal work, *Animal Liberation,* hit bookstores in 1975, Williams embraced its core philosophy—that animals deserve the same protections as humans—and made it her own.

When Williams and her husband moved to Central New Jersey in the late 1990s, she decided she no longer wanted to be "a multi-issue activist." She wanted to narrow her crusade to a cause where she felt she could make a significant impact. So she targeted the pet shop industry—at the time, animal welfare groups estimated that 90 percent of puppies sold in pet stores came from puppy mills—founded NJCAPSA, and began promoting the nonprofit primarily through an online website. Almost immediately, she began receiving requests for help from people who'd had bad experiences with pet stores throughout the tri-state area, leading her to expand NJCAPSA's services to accommodate pet buyers in New York and Pennsylvania. And she took an active role trying to expose and shut down puppy mills, especially those in Pennsylvania, where commercial breeding legislation was so lax that the state had become a haven for unscrupulous breeders. (In 2008, Pennsylvania would attempt to crack down on puppy mills by toughening laws regulating commercial breeders.)

In the years following Hurricane Katrina, however, Williams noticed that the character of the complaints she received was changing, as were the questions e-mailed to NJCAPSA. "In addition to questions about pet stores, I used to get a lot of e-mails asking me about breeders. Did I know if this breeder was a good breeder or a bad breeder? But then I started getting e-mails asking me if I knew if this rescue was a good rescue or a bad rescue. And that threw me for a loop. I was surprised that bad rescues existed. But the questions kept coming. And so did the complaints. I thought: There is something going on here. I want to delve into that."

So Williams started digging, and it wasn't long before she came to a conclusion that surprised her. "I realized that rescue had become part of the pet trade and that there was a lot of selling going on for profit, and that a lot of so-called rescues were preying on the emotions of adopters. This is new ground," Williams told me. "When have we had to vet a rescue?"

In 2011, Williams dissolved NJCAPSA, rechristening the organization Pet Watch New Jersey. "I wanted to change the name to reflect all the issues of companion animals in New Jersey." And she launched Rescue-abuse.com, a repository of court filings and media stories on shady rescues.

After reading Tori Richards's complaint that December morning, Williams posted Klemper's name and the rescue's name on the NJCAPSA website and requested that anyone with information contact her. Williams doesn't launch such online fishing expeditions anymore—"I've learned that there is so much rumor, gossip, innuendo,

170

hearsay, and rescue group jealousy that I now only post someone's name once it's already public." What Williams will do—and what she did then—is comb the web for every detail she can find on a rescue and the people who run it.

Meanwhile, in North Carolina, just days after Charlie's death, Jamie Klemper was filing papers with the Secretary of State to officially change the name of her rescue.

According to the Humane Society of the United States, the estimated 10,000 privately run rescue groups at work across the United States "are not accountable to any entity or organization." That's because there are no federal rules and virtually no state regulations regarding rescues. In some states, like New York, rescues are specifically exempted from regulations that apply to pet stores and breeders. In some states, like Oregon, that have laws requiring health inspections for dogs transported into the state, the laws are not enforced; a spokesperson for the Oregon Department of Agriculture told a local television station, "We do not have the staff to do the enforcement." And in other states, like New Jersey, rescues need not be licensed.

In 2012, in response to the state's growing number of rescues, New Jersey legislators mandated that the Department of Health establish an animal rescue registry. The department did just that, but the registry, per the legislation, is voluntary, and it's not accessible to the public on the department's website. Many New Jersey rescues I talked with didn't even know of its existence, and those that did weren't sure of its purpose. I, too, had questions about the usefulness of such a registry, but the department declined to make anyone available to me to answer them. The department's spokesperson would tell me only that as of September of 2014 fifty-three rescues had applied to be listed on the registry. A Petfinder search for young dogs within

100 miles of my Hillsborough home yielded listings from more than 100 rescue groups.

In states that do license rescues, oversight can be daunting. This is primarily because most rescues are foster-based, and, just as fosters come and go, so do dogs, making enforcement challenging. A spokesperson for the animal control agency in Palm Beach, Florida, told a local news station that he believes that there are hundreds of what he calls "underground rescues"—rescues that never apply for licenses—operating throughout South Florida. Most, he said, act responsibly, but not all.

On the other hand, shelters and pet stores—the other entities from which people typically get their pets—are generally regulated by the states or municipalities in which they operate. In large part, this is because shelters and pet stores work out of brick-and-mortar buildings, allowing regulatory agencies to make regular inspections and enforce violations. This means "rogue" or "faux" rescues, as I've heard them called—also "shady," "retail," and "not real" rescues—are often exposed only after a tragedy occurs. Even then, sanctioning a rescue or proving in a court of law that it is responsible for a dog's death isn't easy. For instance, in New Jersey, the law requires adopters to show that a rescue knowingly and willfully sold a sick dog. And a ruling against a rescue isn't likely to put it out of business; in fact, evidence suggests it has little impact.

"For every good rescue that exists—and there are good ones—there is a bad one," Captain Rick Yocum of the New Jersey SPCA told me. In 2007, the organization began keeping a database of people charged with animal cruelty. Some of those people have been charged in connection to running what the NJSPCA calls "not real rescues," and that portion of the database is growing. "There are absolutely people involved in the puppy business who are in it for the money, and there is a lot of money to be made," Yocum continued. "These people don't care where the dogs come from. They don't care what the medical condition is. They just want to turn that dog for dollars."

And they are able to do so relatively easily because of the high demand for puppies in states where spay/neuter has become baked into the culture, because of a lack of regulations regarding rescues, and because oversight, even in those states where regulations do exist, traditionally has been weak. They also know, Yocum said, that few adopters will come after them if a puppy is found to be sick, especially if the condition can be treated by their local veterinarian.

Consider, Yocum said, the difference between buying a motorcycle and adopting a pet. "If I bought a motorcycle and after two or three days I found out that it was never going to run right, I would take the motorcycle back to where I bought it, I would legally demand my money back, and I would buy another motorcycle. When you throw a puppy or a kitten in as the purchase, people choose to spend thousands of dollars to treat the dog or treat the cat because in a matter of three days they fell in love. And they don't go after the person who sold it to them, and these rescues know that. Or these rescues will say, 'You can't have your money back, but you can pick another dog,' and the adopter will say, 'No, I love this dog.' And these people damn well know that, and they play on those emotions." Yocum told me that when he asks adopters why they don't return dogs to rescues, adopters often cite their concern that the dog will be turned over to a shelter and euthanized, or be dumped somewhere, and they can't bear for that to happen.

Libby Williams says some of the most egregious rescues she's come across get their dogs for free by answering ads on Craigslist. Or they place ads in newspapers asking people to turn over unwanted litters to them rather than to shelters, saying that they will find homes for the puppies. Or they buy dogs from puppy mills and advertise them as "puppy mill rescues." These "rescues" do little or no vetting of the dogs, no quarantining, no spaying or neutering, no microchipping—all considered best practices by the ASPCA and done by reputable rescue groups—and they sell the dogs for anywhere from $200 to $800. Cash only. Other shady rescues pull dogs, especially puppies, from shelters in the South, primarily those in the more rural areas and those that have high euthanasia rates. They know that overworked, often underpaid public employees in these shelters have little, if any, time to check out a rescue's background. And with the growing pressure on shelters to reduce euthanasia rates, it's in the shelter's interest—if not always in the dog's interest—to turn over dogs to any seemingly legitimate rescue that comes calling.

Bonita Fisher, who runs a small rottweiler rescue in southeast Georgia, says rescues flock to her county's shelter and to those in surrounding counties because the area is rural, dogs are rarely spayed or neutered, and euthanasia rates are high. One rescue, she says, comes all the way from Washington State to "load up on puppies and fly them to the West Coast." Most, however, transport their dogs to the Northeast.

As Fisher, now in her mid-sixties, has gotten more active in rescue, she says she's noticed a troubling trend: Rescues are transporting dogs and puppies out of state straight from the shelter. And as few rural shelters can afford to vet their dogs, this means the animals aren't being screened for parasites, infectious diseases, or even aggressive behavior; they aren't being quarantined for up to two weeks—a recommended best practice—and they don't have the Certificates of Veterinary Inspection—commonly referred to as health certificates—that are required by most states in order to transport dogs across state lines. The American Veterinary Medical Association recommends health screenings be done prior to transport, and responsible rescues routinely quarantine their dogs and get them vetted and vaccinated before they will adopt them out. But persuading rural shelters to stop releasing straight-to-transport is a hard sell, Fisher says. "The shelters are so happy to hand over the dogs because for each one that leaves through the front door, there's one less they have to kill."

Fisher has begun speaking out against rescues she perceives to be rogue—her preferred moniker—on her Facebook page because she's growing more and more disheartened and angered by what she's seeing. "Some rescue groups," she says, frustration creeping into her voice, "are puppy mills in disguise."

Fisher once volunteered at such a rescue, although she had no idea it was anything other than reputable when she was invited to join its board. She'd adopted two rotties from the organization, and because she loved her dogs and wanted to help others, she accepted—only to note certain disturbing trends later on, like the fact that the rescue often didn't have enough food to feed its dogs and that it didn't allow her access to its records.

Fisher, who lived about 160 miles from the rescue, decided to make several unannounced trips to check out the situation for herself. "It didn't take long to realize that all was not good," she told me. "On my third trip the dogs were out of food and preventives. Many needed vetting. Another volunteer and I jumped in with supplies. I also brought as many dogs as I could home to foster and tried frantically to place the existing dogs because I felt I could not leave them behind. On my fourth trip I was covered in fleas within six feet of the kennels, and I saw dogs with severe flea infestation. Their kennels hadn't been cleaned in weeks. Their water was green."

Fisher filed a complaint against the rescue with the Georgia Department of Agriculture, and that's when she learned her complaint was not the first. She also learned how challenging it can be to protect animal lovers from bad rescues; the department has just seventeen inspectors and four field officers responsible for some 4,200 facilities that include rescues, shelters, kennels, pet stores, and horse stables.

It was this experience that encouraged Fisher to start her own rescue. The timing was right—she was already fostering several dogs, and earlier in the year she'd retired from a decades-long nursing career to care for her husband, who'd been diagnosed with terminal cancer.

"This is not the way I would have chosen to spend retirement," Fisher told me, "but I've had a heart for animals my whole life, and this is something I can do from home. And my husband says the dogs help him. He says every one we save makes him better."

THE LURE TO SAVE SHELTER DOGS relegated to death row is potent—just ask anyone involved in any aspect of rescue. But unfortunately for the dogs and for the people who adopt them, good intentions can go awry. Sometimes it's due to greed. Libby Williams says rescuers have told her that they've had both transporters and volunteers strike out on their own after discovering how much money people will pay for a dog. Sometimes it's due to naiveté or incompetence. Teresa Fisher says the Companion Animal Initiative of Tennessee receives four to five complaints a week about ill-run rescues operated by people legitimately concerned about the fate of shelter dogs but who don't have any idea how to run a responsible rescue.

And sometimes, in the worst-case scenario, rescuers become hoarders. According to the ASPCA, rescues make up a quarter of the 2,000 hoarding cases reported in the United States each year. That's up from 5 percent twenty years ago, and some in animal welfare attribute this increase to the publicity surrounding the Katrina animals and the South's high shelter euthanasia rates. Others, like PETA—People for the Ethical Treatment of Animals—attribute the increase to the no-kill movement's philosophy "to avoid euthanasia at all costs." The group charges that to "save lives," rescues often take in more animals than they can handle and then warehouse the animals "in substandard, filthy, and severely crowded conditions, for weeks, months, or even years on end." The Animal Legal Defense Fund, which estimates that about 250,000 animals are the victims of hoarding each year—cats being the most common victims, followed by dogs—considers hoarding the "greatest animal cruelty crisis facing companion animals."

For rescuers who become hoarders, the slippery slope into hoarding often occurs when the number of dogs coming into a rescue exceeds the number going out, and the rescuer begins to ignore and even disregard the animals' needs. According to the ASPCA, hoarders "are often blind to the fact they are not caring for the animals and to the extreme suffering they are inflicting." Rather, they see themselves as saviors, rescuing dogs from certain death in what they frequently refer to as "high-kill" shelters.

Perhaps most disconcerting to the animal welfare community, there is no "typical hoarder." According to a diverse group of academics who came together from 1997 through 2006 to study hoarding, what many people think of as the stereotypical hoarder—a single, socioeconomically disadvantaged elderly woman who collects cats— too narrowly depicts who hoarders really are. On the Hoarding of Animals Research Consortium website hosted by Tufts University, researchers write, "Hoarding knows no age, gender, or socioeconomic boundaries." Further, they state that it is common for hoarders to live "double lives," their hoarding activity invisible to family, friends, and colleagues who are never invited into their homes.

Take the case of a woman I'll call Ellen, a New Jersey resident who the NJSPCA alleged was hoarding dogs in her South Jersey home. To friends and colleagues in animal rescue, Ellen was as committed a rescuer as there is. In addition to pulling dogs from local shelters, she would make regular trips to North Carolina to pull dogs from rural shelters. Then she would adopt them out.

I met Ellen in July of 2014. She welcomed me into her home, which is on a six-acre lot hidden from the road by a thick wall of trees. Behind her house, twenty dog kennels—six of which are large enough to hold multiple dogs—stand empty. Ellen says that several years ago she had about twelve dogs, a mix of large and small, mostly rescues from New Jersey shelters. (Unlike some New Jersey towns that limit the number of dogs a person can own, Ellen's town does not.) "I would get phone calls from people I knew who worked at area shelters the day before a dog was going to be euthanized," she told me, "and I would run in, adopt it, and bring it home." And occasionally, Ellen said, she would find dogs dumped on her property "by people for whom dogs aren't forever but for whom they're a hobby."

In 2010, her partner's cousin, who dabbled in rescue, persuaded Ellen to foster a shelter dog brought to New Jersey from North Carolina. "It started to bother the hell out of me that I couldn't do more for dogs like him," Ellen told me. "And I found I couldn't let it go. It started eating away at me. And I thought: I have to see this shelter and maybe bring home three dogs." She brought home five.

Ellen says she drove to North Carolina about eight times, bringing back puppies and dogs and advertising them in the newspaper and via flyers posted in area businesses. "A woman called on the Fourth of July and she wanted to come over that night. I thought it was odd timing, but I said okay. She wanted a puppy, but she didn't want to pay, so she left. She returned a couple of days later, and this time left with the puppy. Several days after that, the SPCA turns up saying I am selling sick dogs."

The lead SPCA investigator on Ellen's case told me that the organization had received a report that Ellen was keeping multiple dogs in unhealthy conditions. The investigator says she visited the home three times and offered to take any dogs that Ellen wanted to surrender, telling her the dogs would be vetted and placed into good homes. Ellen refused to turn over a single dog.

Unable to reach an agreement, the NJSPCA raided the home. Investigators and police removed sixty-three dogs, including six buried in a shallow backyard grave.

News accounts in the days following the seizure told of an unsightly scene: malnourished dogs living in their own waste, crates caked with excrement, piles of fresh feces on the kitchen floor, little evidence of dog food anywhere on the property, and water bowls left outdoors where what little water in them had frozen. Several dogs were found to have heartworm, others tested positive for parasites, and still others were pregnant.

The seizure, along with the public release of photographs taken during the raid and the indictment that followed, left Ellen's friends and colleagues stunned. Atlantic County Animal Shelter manager Kathy Kelsey was shocked, too. When she and her staff learned of the raid, "We went, 'Uh oh, that name sounds familiar. And sure enough, she had pulled one of our smaller dogs."

Kelsey says that what's frustrating is that based on the information Ellen provided to the shelter, she met all the criteria for adoption. The only thing the shelter didn't do—and what Kelsey says she doesn't have the staff to do—is a home visit. "And that's how the system can fail these animals."

At her trial two years after the raid, the judge found Ellen guilty of animal cruelty and selling sick dogs; she was barred from owning any animals for five years and ordered to pay $150 in restitution.

"Without the dogs here, it is an absolute hell," Ellen told me. "At first I couldn't stand even being here. They were my kids, my friends. It wasn't easy. I gained close to one hundred pounds."

In a statement following the verdict, the NJSPCA said that Ellen likely got into rescue with good intentions "but failed to recognize the fact that animals were suffering, required immediate medical care and that animals were in fact dying ... Unfortunately we see this fact pattern a great deal throughout the state of New Jersey." And, the Animal Legal Defense Fund would add, throughout the country.

So HOW ARE WANT-TO-BE PET OWNERS, who desire to do "the right thing" by forgoing breeders and pet stores to adopt a rescue dog, to know whether they are dealing with a responsible organization? The bottom line is that it is not easy. All the shelter directors with whom

I spoke, be they in the North or in the South, had stories about permitting a rescue to pull dogs only to later sever that relationship upon learning about practices the shelter considered questionable or inappropriate or downright harmful. This includes even those shelters fortunate enough to have the staff to background-check rescue groups.

When I think back to my experience adopting Galen, I realize I made no effort to determine whether Catnip Friends was the real deal; it didn't even occur to me to do so. After all, I'd found the rescue on Petfinder, which I presumed legitimized it. And while Petfinder and similar sites do have guidelines that rescues must meet to publicize their pets, Libby Williams has found that shady rescues inevitably slip through the screening process. Even at the Agway, I didn't think twice when Linda Wilferth told me she accepted only cash—I could see she was running a small operation, so it seemed reasonable that she wouldn't want the added expense of accepting credit cards or the hassle of accepting checks. And I thought nothing days later when Galen was diagnosed with kennel cough. After all, Gryffin had had it, too—it's a common shelter malady. And it never occurred to me to return Loki to Linda once I learned that he had parasitic infections. We were only fostering him, but I recall thinking that because he'd undergone the long trip from North Carolina, because he'd been present at several adoption events and been passed over, and because he was being medically treated for parasites, he had been through far too much to be sent back. I either had to find him a home or keep him. I suppose that in turning him over to my mother, I did both. I did get to wondering, though, where Catnip Friends falls on the rescue continuum. Did my experience mean that Linda was running something less than a responsible rescue? I am not convinced.

I may not have done my due diligence, but I'd argue it's perfectly reasonable to presume that those who do the grueling work of rescue— and it is grueling work—are in it to save lives, not to financially improve their own—and that the vast majority of rescuers absolutely do right by the animals. Williams confirmed to me I'm not alone in my thinking. "When people adopt from a rescue, they are caught up in saving a life. They have a reasonable expectation that all rescues are good and a reasonable expectation that they are getting a fairly healthy pet. They just don't expect that their dog is going to become critically ill in the next seventy-two hours, and when the dog does, they are furious. They say to themselves, 'I could deal with stomach upset or kennel cough.' But they don't anticipate giardia or coccidia, and certainly not distemper or parvo."

Williams and her husband share their home with two rescue dogs and several cats. Addie Mae, a beagle mix, came from One Step Closer Animal Rescue (OSCAR), an all-volunteer organization based in northern New Jersey. As rescues go, Williams says, OSCAR is one of the best. Its dogs and cats are fully quarantined, vetted, vaccinated, spayed or neutered, and microchipped prior to adoption; its fosters—there is a core group of twenty—train the dogs while in their care. Potential adopters are vetted, too—the rescue requires references, including veterinarians used in the past or being used presently if there are already pets in the home, and it does home visits, dogs in tow, to gauge how well they will fit into their new environments. And OSCAR does something I'd never heard of a rescue doing—it follows up. Williams says a representative from the rescue checked in with her once a month for three months. OSCAR also works diligently to raise money, often hosting fundraising events, because like most rescues, it is not flush with funds.

I meet Cassie Kowalchuk, OSCAR's president, at a Petco in Succasunna, New Jersey, during one of the group's adoption events. Kowalchuk doesn't have any weeks-old puppies with her, so there are none of the pens I am used to seeing when I visit Linda. Instead each dog is on a leash and paired with a handler who gives the dog treats and water and takes the dog for walks inside and outside the store. "I don't like to put the dogs in crates," Kowalchuk told me, "because it can change how they interact with people. When the dogs are on leashes they're more themselves, and people get a more accurate insight into their personalities."

Kowalchuk is in her thirties, tall, blonde, an accountant by day, who takes care of the rescue's paperwork—OSCAR is registered with both the state and the Internal Revenue Service as a nonprofit corporation. But OSCAR is not listed on the state's voluntary registry, as Kowalchuk is one of the people I spoke with who'd never heard of it.

In the last several years, Kowalchuk says, OSCAR has begun "cleaning up" after irresponsible rescues. "Some rescues won't take animals back, so they end up in our local shelters. Some of these shelters weren't euthanizing before, but now they're having to." Many of those dogs will ultimately become OSCAR's, and that's in part why OSCAR takes its application process so seriously. Once it places a dog in a home, the rescue intends for that home to be forever. That's why, Kowalchuk says, she would never adopt out a dog without doing a home visit. This also means that no dogs get adopted at OSCAR's adoption events. Rather, the events are meet-and-greets where potential adopters can window-shop a dog and kick off the application process.

Because OSCAR doesn't do same-day adoptions, some pet stores won't host the rescue. The reason seems obvious: Same-day adoptions translate into sales. New pet owners need everything from food and collars to toys and crates. If you don't walk out the door with a canine, chances are you won't walk out the door with canine accessories. When Kevin and I adopted Galen, we purchased a tiny pink collar, a leash, pet food, and her beloved stuffed hedgehog from the Agway; we didn't buy a crate, as we had Gryffin's. But when we decided to foster Loki, we needed another crate and puppy food, so we bought both right at Pet Valu.

Now that many pet stores, including the big retail chains, have stopped selling dogs in an effort to minimize the market for puppy mill dogs, their bottom lines have taken a hit—pet sales had generated about 20 percent of a store's revenue. Hosting rescues not only puts stores in a position to recoup lost sales, but it's good PR. And certainly, it's convenient for adopters. But Libby Williams says she's seen stores look the other way when shady rescues sell sick animals. For example, several years ago Williams urged a major New Jersey pet retailer to sever ties with a "rescue" it hosted for weekend adoption events after Williams received several complaints that dogs adopted out by the group were infected with everything from kennel cough to pneumonia to parvovirus. A warning about the rescue to another retailer had been enough for that store to refuse the rescue admission, but, according to Williams, this store manager had a very different response. "She said she had a profit quota to meet, and this is why she needed to have rescue groups in her store. She obviously wasn't willing to give up the rescue until she had another group to replace it with."

Williams offered to help the store find a new rescue group and also urged the community to pressure the store to ban the existing one. It wasn't until months later, after a family whose dog died took legal action, that the rescue was eventually shut down.

The only major retailer willing to discuss the issue with me was Pet Valu, a Canadian company whose presence is growing throughout the northeastern United States. A company spokesperson told me that illegitimate rescues do present a challenge. "In Canada we have had to pull away from some groups. In many cases the groups start with fantastic intentions, but for one reason or another they go astray. Could be hoarding, could be greed." But, the spokesperson said, bringing rescues into stores gives homeless dogs the direct exposure to potential adopters that they would not otherwise get, making the practice worthwhile for the dogs (and, of course, the store's bottom line).

To COMBAT ROGUE RESCUES, responsible groups are stepping up their use of social media to call out those who are skirting best practices and to issue "DNRs"—Do Not Rescues—to identify groups with which neither shelters nor potential dog owners should do business. At the same time, several states are devising legislation intended to crack down on groups that bring sick and also aggressive dogs across their borders. But this legislation, like the law passed in Connecticut in 2011, is often opposed by rescue groups that see the rules as draconian at best, cost prohibitive at worst.

In Massachusetts, rescue groups are fighting regulations proposed by the Department of Agricultural Resources that would overhaul an emergency order imposed in 2005, after a raid in a hotel parking lot exposed rescues exchanging dogs—some of whom were sick—for cash. That order requires all dogs imported into the state be quarantined for forty-eight hours and declared healthy by a licensed veterinarian. The new regulations, which would be some of the toughest in the country, would maintain the forty-eight hour quarantine and health check but add a requirement that dogs be vetted every thirty days until adopted, mandate that rescues create disclosure statements detailing existing medical and behavioral issues for each dog in a rescue, direct rescues to provide adopters with an estimate for the cost of treating any dog with a non-contagious health condition, and require state inspections of foster homes. Rescues argue that the rules would not only drive legitimate rescues out of business but would also be unenforceable and lead to animals spending longer periods of time in shelters for minor illnesses, thereby increasing disease and possibly euthanasia rates.

The Massachusetts Animal Coalition's Anne Lindsay has concerns about the proposed regulations, parts of which she believes to be governmental overreach, like the requirement that foster homes be inspected, but she's also fed up with rescues bringing sick dogs into Massachusetts, whether it's being done by so-called puppy flippers or by rescuers who simply disregard or are ignorant of best practices. "I am so disgusted," she told me when we spoke by phone. "I am constantly seeing these so-called rescuers bringing up sick dogs, hiding them, and then an entire litter of puppies ends up with parvo because these people don't know how to do it right. It makes me insane."

But Lindsay has a plan she believes will do more to alleviate the problem than will slapping more regulations on rescues. She is developing a training program for rescuers that would teach everything from "how a germ becomes a disease, why you have to quarantine, how to do behavioral evaluations, and even how to properly clean a crate. I want to have someone physically clean a crate and have the teacher say, 'You just contaminated the entire thing because of the way you did that.'"

Lindsay's program—she's calling it Shelter and Rescue 101—has promise. She's spoken with the state's veterinarian and staff at the Department of Agricultural Resources who see value in it. She has shelter veterinarians suggesting curriculum for it. And she knows rescuers are hungry for the information that will be taught in it. "I talk to a lot of people in rescue and I do a lot of workshops on compassion fatigue, and the one thing I see across the board is that these people are so hungry for knowledge and hungry to connect with others and hungry to share their stories with one another, and Shelter and Rescue 101 can be the place to do this. Right now I feel like everybody is criticizing, but there is no central place where all this information on animal health exists. It's all on the Internet and you can read it, but how do you know what's reliable? I want it all synthesized into a program that we can take around the state." And, I suggested, if it finds success in Massachusetts, around the country.

As Libby Williams scoured the web for information on Jamie Klemper, she forwarded Tori Richards's complaint to the NJSPCA and several state and county agencies that she hoped might offer Richards guidance in seeking recourse against Klemper. Following a months-long investigation, the NJSPCA charged Klemper with fifteen civil and criminal counts of animal cruelty, alleging she was running a for-profit puppy mill in the state of New Jersey. Klemper, who would go on to plead guilty to a single civil charge, was banned for five years from any interactions with animals in the state and ordered to pay Richards $1,500 in restitution.

Williams told me she has information suggesting that Klemper is still selling dogs under the guise of a nonprofit rescue and under at least one alias. But what Williams hasn't been able to confirm is whether any of the dogs are finding their way into New Jersey. One thing I know is that wherever Klemper's dogs may be going, they aren't coming out of Gaston County's shelter anymore. The rescue coordinator there told me that in early 2014 she denied an application submitted by Klemper to resume pulling dogs from the shelter.

Tori Richards says Charlie's death and the ordeal surrounding it took a toll on her and, even more so, on her son. Richards waited a year before bringing another dog into her home, and Dakota, a border collie, who Richards says lights up her life, came not from a shelter or a rescue but from "a private person I could trust." Paul, she says, remains dogless. "He'll watch Dakota if I go away," Richards says. "But we're not sharing her the way we were going to share Charlie."

Teach the Children

"Do you know left from right?"

Sharon O'Grady looks inquisitively at twenty-seven first and second graders sitting in a wide semicircle on the floor of a first-grade classroom in Marietta, Georgia. Some of the students shake their heads yes; some vocalize their answer. But they're all in agreement—they know left from right.

"Olga does, too. And that kind of freaks me out," O'Grady tells them, a big smile on her face. "Watch this." The students stare wide-eyed at Olga, a five-and-a-half-year-old black Labrador retriever.

"Olga, sit." The dog does, and O'Grady takes several steps away from the obedient Lab.

"Olga, heel." Olga walks to O'Grady's left side and sits down. "Good girl," O'Grady exclaims.

"Olga, side." Olga stands up, walks to O'Grady's right, then sits. "There we go, good girl!" she says again as she lovingly strokes Olga's head. To the students: "When you're in a wheelchair sometimes it's better for Olga to be on one side or the other, so she needs to know left from right."

O'Grady is the school nurse at Powers Ferry Elementary. She and Olga, her son's service dog, are guests at today's Homeless Pet

Club meeting. The club meets each Friday during an hour of the school day set aside for students to engage in clubs of their choice. Students may choose from among traditional clubs like art, chess, computers, and football—or the less traditional Homeless Pet Club. Second-grade teacher Kathie Taylor says the club—always one of the first to fill—teaches children "about the value of life and about responsibility. And it gives them a purpose."

Students who join the club work to find homes for dogs and cats living in shelters, many of which would be euthanized were it not for the students' efforts, and they learn about the different roles companion animals play in society. The club's purpose aligns well with the rationale for club time, which, according to Taylor, is a piece of a broader behavior management system designed to incentivize students to focus on learning and to act responsibly inside and outside the classroom. In other words, club time is the prize students earn at the end of each week so long as they haven't received citations for such things as failing to complete homework or disrupting class. And in this predominately minority school where 96 percent of students receive free or reduced-price lunch, nearly twice the state average and three times the district average, Principal Rattana Inthirathvongsy says club time gives children from economically disadvantaged homes a chance to experience activities inside the school that they don't necessarily have the opportunity to engage in outside of it.

"Now don't say this word when I spell it," O'Grady tells the students. "C-o-o-k-i-e-s. Like Girl Scout ... shh! Don't say it!" The children giggle and whisper to each other. "That's Olga's treat word. But Olga doesn't work for treats. She works for puppy paychecks, which are lots of love." O'Grady smiles at the dog. "But Olga knows Mommy always has something somewhere." O'Grady reaches into her purse and pulls out a few dog treats. She offers them to Olga, who seems to swallow them whole.

"She gobbled them up!" one boy shouts. The children laugh again.

Then O'Grady calls up a young girl with dirty-blonde hair stretching to the middle of her back; blue jeans with an oversized hole bare her knee. O'Grady sits the girl on a chair facing the other students and commands Olga to put her front paws across the girl's lap. Then O'Grady tells Olga to give kisses. Olga points her snout toward the girl's face and gives a quick lick to the girl's left cheek. An outburst of *ooh*s and *ah*s and *that is so sweet* follows, along with: *Can I go next?* and *Can I try?*

One at a time, students take their turn in the chair. Olga picks up a set of keys and drops them into a little girl's hand. Olga picks up a pencil and delivers it to a young boy. Olga shakes hands. She high-fives. But what impresses the students most is hearing Olga speak.

"Speak," O'Grady says to Olga. Olga barks once.

"Speak. Use your inside voice," O'Grady says. Olga barks quietly.

"Speak. Use your outside voice." Olga barks loudly. The room erupts in laughter and awe. How does Olga do that?

One of the goals of today's meeting is to expose students to the role service dogs play in helping people with limited abilities overcome their limits. And as at every meeting—whether or not there's a mammalian or reptilian visitor—a broader goal is to give students an appreciation of and respect for animals, and also for each other, and to begin to shape the attitudes of the country's future pet owners.

A young boy asks O'Grady if Olga can have puppies. "No," she answers. "Olga was raised for a purpose, to be someone's helper, so she can't ever have puppies."

Kathie Taylor jumps into the conversation. "But even if you have a dog as a pet, a dog that just fills your heart with love, you want to make sure it can't have puppies either, right?" The students nod their heads yes. "How do you make sure dogs can't make puppies?"

Several children shout the words *spay* and *neuter*. Taylor smiles and nods approvingly. "Exactly."

Later Taylor tells me, "Sometimes we have speakers who ask me if they can talk to the children about euthanasia and spay/neuter and I say, 'Absolutely.' We are honest with the kids. We explain that millions of dogs and cats are euthanized unnecessarily, and they get sad and quiet when they hear this, but it's a reality. But then we also give the children the opportunity to save lives, and that empowers them."

The students shoot their hands into the air. They want to tell O'Grady stories about their dogs.

"I've got a black-and-white dog."

"My grandpa wants to sell my grandma's dog."

"My dog had puppies, but my grandmother didn't sell them."

"My dog's never been to the vet."

"I feed my dog the same cookies as Olga eats."

IF IT WEREN'T FOR ELEMENTARY SCHOOL students and their stories about their pets, there might not be Homeless Pet Clubs in more than 150 schools across ten states. The clubs are the brainchild of Michael Good, a veterinarian in Cobb County, Georgia, who found himself in an elementary school auditorium in 2010 staring into the faces of about 300 first, second, and third graders.

"A client had asked me to speak to students about being a veterinarian. I said, 'Okay,' and then I forgot about it. So the day before I'm supposed to speak, my client calls and says, 'You didn't forget, Dr. Good, did you?' And, of course, I did, and I'm booked solid for the whole afternoon, but I go anyway. And I'd assumed I'm speaking to a bunch of high school students, and I'm gonna tell them how much money a vet makes and about how many years you've got to go to school, and I walk in, and I see first, second, and third graders. I am caught totally off guard, and I have ninety minutes to tell these kids what a vet does. Well, it takes less than a New York minute. I say, 'As a vet, I get your best friend well so he can go home and play with you.' And then I'm done, and I still have ninety minutes left.

Well, to the credit of this young teacher, she asks the kids if anyone has a question, and there were three hundred kids, and three hundred hands go up. And not one of them asks me a question. They tell me stories about their pets; and Grandma's pet; and their neighbor's cat having kittens; and going for a walk in the woods with their dog and it chasing a squirrel up a tree, and they can tell me every branch it climbed; and they talked with a loud voice and a big smile on their face, and they were so passionate about telling their story. And I got to thinking—what if we got millions of kids all over this country to tell stories about dogs who don't have homes, and we make shelters promise not to kill any dog whose story is being told? Then these animals are going to get great homes."

By 2010, Good was as invested in rescue work as he was in growing a small veterinary empire—he owns seven veterinary clinics in Cobb County, Georgia, just north of Atlanta. I spent a day with Good in the spring of 2013. He gave me a tour of the first clinic he opened after graduating from veterinary school in 1978 and of his newest, still under construction, in which he planned to house the Homeless Pets Foundation, the nonprofit he founded two decades later to find homes for dogs and cats in Georgia shelters. But first on Good's agenda that day was a speech to a group of Atlanta-area pet sitters on the genesis of the Homeless Pet Clubs and how the pet sitters, individually or as a group, could get involved.

Tall and gregarious, with a full head of gray hair, Good's passion for animals, combined with a gift for gab and a good-sized ego, make him an engaging speaker who rarely passes up an opportunity to tell his story and recruit people to participate in his programs. This day he's in Gwinnett County, Georgia. In a few days he jets off to Colorado. He tells everyone who will listen that "Homeless Pet Clubs are the answer to ending euthanasia for population control in America's shelters."

Good grew up in the late 1950s outside South Bend, Indiana,

with little in terms of material wealth. By the time he came into the world, his mother—the youngest of thirteen children—was a divorcée already raising two children. As he likes to say, "My mother married her high school sweetheart, and after two kids, he divorced her and married his other high school sweetheart."

Good's mother met his father in a bar, and within a few short years she was married again and added Good and his younger brother to her growing brood. But, Good says, his father brought little to the relationship, so after eight years, his mother kicked him out. Now a single mother, she raised her children and her animals—"Growing up I had horses, a goat, chickens … "—on a quarter-acre property.

Good got his first dog and, he says, his first patient, when he was nine. "I'm in the house, and I hear a gunshot. I go outside, and there's this dog crawling into our backyard, and it's bleeding, and our neighbor has got a gun, and he's going to put the dog out of his misery. I say, 'What are you doing?' and he says, 'I'm gonna kill him. He was in my chicken coop.' So I say, 'He's my dog.' Now, I'd never seen this dog before, and at the time, I'm hoping the good Lord will forgive me for saying a little white lie. But I say, 'His name is Bullet.'" This line draws a laugh from the pet sitters. "It just seemed instinctive to me to save him, to say, 'This dog is mine.' He was my first patient because we were too poor to take him to a vet. I raised him, and he was my loyal, faithful companion."

After high school came an expedited college experience—Good, who paid his way through Purdue University, says that when he learned he could take twenty-eight hours of classes for the same price as eight hours, he chose twenty-eight and graduated in two years. Good was then accepted into and graduated from the University of Georgia's veterinary school. It was quite the accomplishment for a kid whose high school guidance counselor had told him he didn't have a chance of becoming a veterinarian.

Armed with his degree and a zeal for treating animals, Good

went to work in Cobb County. Quickly he became the vet of choice for rescue groups. "People would come in and give me sob stories about how they love their pets but can't afford to pay full price, and I could relate to them, so I would cut my prices. Soon all these rescue groups started calling on me because they'd tell one another, 'Go see Dr. Good. He's a pushover.'" This was Good's introduction to rescue and to the problems plaguing Georgia's overcrowded shelters. But seeing rescues as part of his veterinary practice didn't have the effect on him that seeing dogs inside a shelter would ultimately have, and certainly not the effect that euthanizing shelter dogs would.

In the late 1990s, Southern Hope, a rescue group whose dogs and cats Good had treated in his practice, took over the Fulton County Animal Shelter. The shelter had been run for more than four decades by a nonprofit humane society in what was apparently so abhorrent a manner that the city finally fired the group. Good, upon seeing the shelter, would later tell reporters and audiences that it resembled a "Doggie Auschwitz."

In order to take over the shelter, Southern Hope needed a medical director, so they turned to Good, telling him they needed his help to turn around the shelter, to open it to the public, to bring in rescue groups. Good says he tried his best to say no—as medical director he would need to be at the shelter for three hours a day, seven days a week—and he had a busy, burgeoning practice to run. But Southern Hope's pleas won out.

On his first day as medical director, Good says, he had to euthanize between forty and fifty healthy dogs simply because the shelter was severely overcrowded and more dogs would be coming in the next day. His second day was no different, nor his third. "I would take my time, and I would talk to these dogs. I would tell them that I'm going to find a solution to this if it's the last thing I do because all these dogs I had to put to sleep were young and vibrant and healthy. So I made an oath to those dogs. I swore that I'm gonna find a way to save these animals because I'm an animal lover, and I'm a veterinarian, so I should be smart enough to do this." Tears fill his eyes. Fifteen years later, Good's sorrow remains as palpable as it did all those years ago.

Within weeks, Good began taking sick and injured dogs back to his veterinary clinic, where he and his staff would nurse them back to health and find them homes. He started with the sick and injured because legally they could be euthanized the day they entered the shelter. Thus, in 1998, the nonprofit Homeless Pets Foundation, the precursor to Homeless Pet Clubs, was born. Good launched a website and posted pictures along with stories of the dogs and cats that were in need of homes, and he encouraged animal lovers to adopt, foster, or donate money. Good himself has seven dogs—mostly German shepherds—that spend daylight hours in his large, fenced-in backyard, coming into the house in the late evening when Good returns home from work or his many speaking engagements. He also has two cats that can't be adopted out because they have FIV—feline immunodeficiency virus—also known as feline AIDS.

Finding homes for his rescued dogs in the Atlanta metropolitan area was not always possible, so Good launched the "Underhound Railroad," a service that moves dogs from Atlanta to communities in the North where they are more likely to find a home. Good was trying to find an answer to every need he perceived, and progress was being made. Within two years of being managed by Southern Hope, the Fulton County shelter's euthanasia rate had fallen to 45 percent from 98 percent, and the Homeless Pets Foundation was saving about 1,200 dogs and cats a year. But that wasn't putting even the smallest dent in the problem of homelessness, as Good estimates that the Atlanta area alone euthanizes more than 100,000 animals annually. There had to be a way to get more people, to get whole communities, involved in saving the lives of these homeless animals.

So, in 2010, when Good came up with the idea for the Homeless

Pet Clubs, he thought it brilliant in its simplicity. Teachers could sponsor Homeless Pet Clubs in elementary, middle, junior, and high schools, making the clubs accessible to children as young as five, as old as eighteen. (Good now thinks clubs can be successful with kids who attend nursery schools and pre-kindergarten programs, so long as they have an engaged teacher.) And because these would be clubs—extracurricular activities outside the mandated curriculum—there would be little, if any, need for them to go through the rigorous process of being approved by boards of education or curriculum committees.

Once a club is formed, members choose a dog or cat from a shelter that has agreed to become a Homeless Pet Club partner, thereby promising not to euthanize any animal being sponsored. The club then harnesses the power of social media and good old-fashioned word-of-mouth to tell the animal's story to members' families and friends, who, it is hoped, will then share the story with their families and friends, and so on, and so on, and so on. Once a home for the pet is found, members choose another dog or cat, and the process repeats itself over and over again.

Young students, like Kathie Taylor's second graders, also make posters and flyers to hang around the school, at their parents' places of business, at churches, at grocery stores, at restaurants. And they have parties each time one of their dogs or cats finds a home. In best-case scenarios, an adoptive family brings its new four-legged family member to the celebration to personally thank the children for saving the animal's life.

When I visited Taylor's club, the students were in the midst of a campaign to find a home for a miniature pinscher–terrier mix they'd named Taylor in honor of their teacher. The canine Taylor, who bears a striking resemblance to Loki, is believed to be about two years old and was picked up as a stray in Murray, one of Georgia's northernmost counties. Kathie Taylor tells me that choosing a pet to sponsor engages students in the arts of negotiation and compromise.

"I use the smart board to show the students pictures of dogs and cats, and I read the biographies about each animal that have been put together by shelter staff or staff at Dr. Good's veterinary clinic. Then we discuss our choices."

Good presumed correctly that teachers would have little problem filling their clubs with students, as children are naturally drawn to animals. Perhaps that's because from their youngest years, children are told stories about animals, they "read" picture books featuring animals, and they go to sleep at night snuggling the stuffed ones that share their beds. Because of this relationship, what child, Good asks, would think it is okay to kill healthy dogs and cats for population control? A 2012 AP-Petside.com poll found that more than 75 percent of American adults are against the practice. Good believes if that question were asked of children, pollsters would find 100 percent against it. "Ask a child what to do with a dog who doesn't have a home, and the child will tell you quite firmly, 'Find it one.'"

Per Good's plan, there is also a learning component to the clubs. Students need to understand why there are so many homeless pets in shelters, and so even in the earliest grades they are introduced to the concepts of spaying and neutering.

"We need to change the culture. We need to save lives. And spay/neuter is the basis for all of this," Good told me. He makes a comparison to the anti-smoking campaigns that hit public schools in the 1970s and slowly began to change attitudes toward cigarettes. "Back then, kids would go home and tell parents that smoking kills. Now I want kids to go home and talk to their parents about spay/neuter."

I vividly recall, as a child in the seventies, delivering the anti-smoking message conveyed to me in the classroom to my parents. I also remember that my father didn't heed my pleas to quit and would, at times, get angry at my frequent assertions that he was killing himself and that, with his secondhand smoke, he was also killing me and my sister. (He finally quit in 1986 after my grandfather lost a battle with emphysema, but by then the damage had been done. I lost my dad to lung cancer in 2012.) But I never smoked, nor did my sister. We, at least, learned that lesson, and therein lies one of Good's great hopes—that students in pet clubs today will internalize the call to spay and neuter the pets they may own tomorrow.

LIKE A LONG LINE OF HUMANE educators before him, Good believes that teaching children that animals are not disposable, that they are sentient beings to be treated with kindness and respect, makes children more empathetic not just to animals but to people. Such thinking can be traced to the writings of nineteenth-century philosophers who were contemplating the morality of the human-animal relationship at the same time that humane movements were getting off the ground in England—the first humane organization, the Society for the Prevention of Cruelty to Animals, was established in London in 1824—and in the United States. These were philosophers like Herbert Spencer, who in 1896 wrote, "Whoever thinks that men might have full sympathy with their fellows, while lacking all sympathy for inferior creatures, will discover his error upon looking at the facts." And before Spencer, there was Arthur Schopenhauer, who in his 1837 essay *On the Basis of Morality* famously wrote, "Compassion for animals is intimately associated with goodness of character, and it may be confidently asserted that he who is cruel to animals cannot be a good man." Beliefs like Schopenhauer's and Spencer's stand in stark contrast to those of such renowned philosophers as René Descartes and Baruch Spinoza, who, writing in the seventeenth century, espoused little regard for animals.

Descartes, for example, believed that dogs did not have the capacity to think and that they had no emotions and no feelings, even for the most intense pain. According to Patricia McConnell in *For the Love of a Dog,* "[Descartes] illustrated this principle by nailing live dogs to barn walls and eviscerating them. While the dogs writhed and screamed, he told the crowd of onlookers that their struggles were merely automatic movements of the body—no more felt by the dog than a clock feels the movement of its hands."

Unlike Descartes, Spinoza did believe that animals, like humans, are sentient beings, but he by no means advocated for their humane treatment. On the contrary, in *Ethics IV*, Spinoza writes that "the law against killing animals is based more on empty superstition and unmanly compassion than sound reason. The rational principle of seeking our own advantage teaches us the necessity of joining with men, but not with the lower animals, or with things whose nature is different than human nature ... Not that I deny the lower animals have sensations. But I do deny that we are therefore not permitted to consider our own advantage, use them at our pleasure, and treat them as is most convenient for us."

Two hundred years after Spinoza, Schopenhauer—whose pet of choice was reportedly the poodle—criticized the Dutch philosopher for his belief that animals exist to serve people. What fascinates the writer in me is that Schopenhauer didn't solely speak to the morality of how animals are to be treated and how that treatment reflects on a human's character; he went so far as to condemn animals' treatment by the English language, writing, "in English all animals are of the neuter gender and so are represented by the pronoun 'it,' just as if they were inanimate things. The effect of this artifice is quite revolting, especially in the case of primates such as dogs ... " Wow.

Schopenhauer was a supporter of the English SPCA and its successor organizations in New York and Philadelphia. And, like Schopenhauer, Henry Bergh in New York and Caroline Earle White in Philadelphia believed that one's treatment of animals correlated to one's treatment of people—and, perhaps more important, that kindness could be taught.

So Bergh and White were early promoters of bringing humane

education into the classroom. Writing for the *Journal of Education*, Bergh espoused his belief that "the children of America needed to have planted in their minds the seeds of kindness that would flower in manhood and womanhood into a broad humanitarianism." For her part, White's WPSPCA issued short books geared toward school-age children bearing such titles as *Early Lessons in Kindness* and *Take Not the Life You Cannot Give*. White also launched the Juvenile Society for the Protection of Animals, an organization for boys, whom she believed to be more prone to cruelty than girls, though she did later open it up to both genders.

But the man said to be the father of humane education, both for his belief in its utility and for his efforts to expand its reach into America's homes and schools, was lawyer, philanthropist, and founder of the Massachusetts Society for the Prevention of Cruelty to Animals, George Angell. According to a history of the movement published by the National Association for the Advancement of Humane Education (NAAHE), Angell devoted his life to the cause, believing that too many people were unaware of the plight of "domestic animals," who he believed were all too often overworked, overpunished, and underfed.

In the 1880s, Angell founded the American Humane Education Society, the first humane education organization in the United States; fought successfully to make humane education compulsory in Massachusetts schools; and brought the English-born Band of Mercy movement to America. The Bands, as conceived of in 1875, were formal groups whose mission was to teach children to be kind to animals, and they did this through stories, songs, and activities. At regularly held meetings, members would recite the Band of Mercy pledge: "I will try to be kind to all living creatures, and try to protect them from cruel usage."

Angell wanted to get Bands of Mercy inside America's schools, so he teamed up with the National Education Association to encourage teachers to bring them into their classrooms. The Bands proved to be so popular that by the early twentieth century there were more than 27,000 groups meeting inside and outside America's schools.

Support for humane education reached its pinnacle in the early 1900s. P.P. Claxton, the United States commissioner of education from 1911 to 1921, believed it to be an "inalienable right" of all children. California's superintendent of education, in an address to teachers, said it was as essential to learning as reading, writing, and arithmetic. And by 1926, twenty-three states had passed legislation providing that some type of humane education be taught.

But by the middle of the century, support for humane education began to wane. According to the NAAHE's history, this is because the mid-1900s saw a rethinking of the philosophy behind education. No more were schools championed as a "major force in the development of the moral life of a child." Rather, according to NAAHE, "Specific moral codes were not to be taught. Teachers were to present the facts and students were to make up their own minds. When moral issues did arise, they were to be handled with caution."

The result, according to a 1960s study by The George Washington University on the state of humane education and the feasibility of reintegrating it into school curricula, was that little was being done nationally to teach humane education. And where humane education was being addressed, it was often in an ad-hoc manner (primarily as it is today)—a visit to a shelter, a lesson on pet care, a film, a book. Lacking, the study found, was follow-up or any kind of approach to weave humane education into an overall K-12 curriculum.

Educators were also starting to question whether there was any evidence that humane education could shape children into kinder, more compassionate adults, and what types of long-term programs would need to be in place for that goal to be realized. Good is a believer, even if his evidence right now is primarily anecdotal. He says principals whose schools host Homeless Pet Clubs report that students in the clubs show an increase in self-esteem, improved social skills and ability to work well with others, an enthusiasm for learning new things, and even a reduction in absenteeism. Good also notes that principals cite a decrease in bullying. Among the Powers Ferry first and second graders who've participated in the clubs, Principal Inthirathvongsy told me he definitely sees a positive evolution take place once students have participated in a pet club. "The kids become more compassionate, and they believe that the situation that exists today in shelters is not okay. They also tend to be more empathetic, in tune with their classmates, and they become more helpful."

Good also believes that the lessons these students learn will last a lifetime. He bases this, in part, on the experience of legendary broadcasting executive Frank Stanton, who was named president of CBS in 1946 and went on to head up the network for nearly three decades. Stanton, Good learned, had been extraordinarily impacted by the Bands of Mercy while growing up in Ohio in the 1920s—so impacted that when he built a philanthropic organization more than half a century later, he told his staff that if they were to find a program that makes kids in schools feel about animals the way the Bands of Mercy made him feel, they needed to fund it. Stanton died in 2006. Four years later, the Stanton Foundation gave Good the first of two grants to help fund the Homeless Pet Clubs.

THE CHEROKEE COUNTY ANIMAL SHELTER, like Gaston County's shelter, is located not on the outskirts of town beside some landfill but rather next to a senior citizen center and across the street from a Boys & Girls Club. The shelter consists of two buildings. The intake building, which isn't visible from the main road, is tucked behind the structure that houses the dogs and cats up for adoption. It is nearly thirty years old, has been renovated many times, and is due to be replaced in the next year or two. The adoption building—the building that's open to the public—is about twelve years old; it's clean and spacious, with get-acquainted rooms where people can spend time determining whether a dog or cat, a puppy or kitten is right for them and whether they are right for the animal.

Shelter director Sue Garcia was the first director to offer up her shelter as a Homeless Pet Club partner after Cobb County's shelter turned down Good's entreaty. "I originally wanted to team up with Cobb," Good had told me. "It's where I work. It's where I live. But they basically said, 'It sounds like too much work.'"

So Good called on Garcia.

Northward on Interstate 575, Cherokee County begins where Cobb County ends. Communities in Cherokee closest to the border are typical suburban subdivisions but continue north, and Cherokee takes on a more rural character. It's that character, Garcia believes, that is likely why Cherokee's shelter takes in one-and-a-half times as many animals for every 100 residents as does Cobb's shelter and as do shelters in some of the other counties that ring metro-Atlanta.

From the moment Garcia got the director's job in 2007, she began trying to come up with ways to bring down the shelter's euthanasia rate, which hovered at about 80 percent. She had a Facebook page created to publicize the shelter's dogs and cats beyond what the county web page was doing. She opened up the shelter to both in-state and out-of-state rescue groups and says she puts rescues through a rigorous vetting process. "We're pretty strict about who we will work with," she tells me. "We've said no to rescues before, and they whine and cry, and they're ugly on Facebook. But we don't care. We're about the animals."

And Garcia instituted a program called Paw It Forward, in which people donate money so that the shelter can adopt out its pets for free. It works like this: People who can't or don't want to adopt a pet—perhaps they already live with one or several animals and can't take in another—pay the fee for a future adoption. "There are a lot of people out there who want to help the animals," Garcia tells me, "and if you give them a specific goal it's a lot easier to persuade them to donate than saying, 'Just write a check.'"

Once the Paw It Forward fund is full, Garcia holds free adoption days that attract people from all over the state, thanks to advertising on Facebook and stories that run in the media. During a recent event, Garcia says, the shelter adopted out seventy-one animals. The program may successfully move animals out of the shelter, but I asked Garcia: Isn't there a concern that if people can't afford the adoption fee they won't be able to afford the feeding and vetting that go along with pet ownership?

"It was a concern at first," she says. "It took a lot of convincing and a lot of study, but the ASPCA has done research on this, and the bottom line is that those people who want a pet, whether they can afford one or not, are going to get one. And they may get one of those free puppies being given away in the Walmart parking lot that aren't spayed and aren't neutered and aren't vetted. And where would I rather they get their pet from? I would rather they come and get an animal that's been vetted and spayed or neutered from our shelter than one from a parking lot. So it at least gives them a step in the right direction, and if the animal comes from the shelter then it's not going to reproduce."

Despite all that the staff at the Cherokee County Animal Shelter was doing to move dogs and cats into homes, the shelter was still having to euthanize for space. So when Good proposed a partnership, Garcia accepted. Good says his promise to Garcia was simple: "I said, I'm going to help you drive traffic into your shelter." For her part, Garcia tasked Laurie Kekel, her marketing guru, to reach out to the local school board to begin to grow the number of Cherokee County schools that have clubs.

Kekel says Good gave them the idea, and "we ran with it." As luck would have it, a longtime shelter volunteer worked in the superintendent's office, giving the shelter a direct line to the school board. Kekel also ramped up outreach to the county's public, private, and parochial schools. "We go to every school that has a fair or festival, and we man a table and give out information about the shelter and about pet clubs. And sometimes we have pet club students help us."

Kekel reached out to Girl and Boy Scout troops and to county libraries to form community groups, and to local businesses to form business groups. "We have a teacher who leads a school club whose husband is in a business club," she tells me. As of May of 2014, the shelter had more than sixty clubs working on its behalf to find homes for its homeless dogs and cats. Its euthanasia rate has fallen so sharply that the Cherokee County animal shelter no longer euthanizes for space.

The idea to create community clubs and business clubs occurred to Good as soon as he put the school club program in place. Why, he asked himself, should schoolchildren be the only ones working on behalf of homeless pets when the problem is everyone's? Community groups like Elks and fire departments and scouting troops could get involved. And so, too, could businesses; in fact, Good tells businesses that starting a pet club is good for business. "It shows the community you care about animals, and if you team with a school club, it shows the community you care about kids. It's great PR and it costs you no money."

That the pet clubs are free to join and free to run is one of Good's strongest selling points. In appealing to the Atlanta-area pet sitters, he says, "Traditionally there have been four ways you could work in animal welfare. You could adopt. You could foster. You could volunteer. You could donate. But maybe you don't want any more pets in your house. Maybe you don't have time to volunteer. Maybe you don't have money to donate. That's fine. Now there's a fifth way you can help. You can sponsor a dog or cat and tell its story."

"I DON'T WANT TO DO A SHAMELESS PLUG for Homeless Pet Clubs, but Homeless Pet Clubs is what started all this," says Chip Moore, the director of Georgia's Gwinnett County shelter. He's talking about the shelter's remarkable turnaround. "This unit was created in the nineteen seventies, and 2012 was the first year in our history that we saved more dogs and cats than we euthanized. And Homeless Pet Clubs was the trigger because when we brought the clubs into this place, the theory of 'that's just a dog' changed. They are all homeless pets. They belonged to somebody at some point in time, whether it be that brief moment when they were born—they belonged to somebody. And now we're just kind of their middle man, working to find them their new home. That was the shift in the thinking—not of the public but of our employees."

Just as all dogs have stories, all shelters do, too, and the story of the Gwinnett County shelter, while still being written, is worth taking a moment to tell.

In December of 2011, after months of increasing public pressure, the Gwinnett County Board of Commissioners formed a task force to come up with recommendations for overhauling the policies and procedures that, for years, had resulted in large numbers of dogs and cats being euthanized. Several weeks later, the board launched an internal investigation into what it described as a "culture of bigotry" at the shelter. Volunteer Susan Ruelle, who pushed for the task force, says the situation at the shelter was bad for the staff and deadly for the animals.

"Gwinnett County has a rule," Ruelle told me. "Strays must be held for five days. After that they can be put up for adoption or euthanized. The regime in place at that time chose to euthanize. They didn't care whether there was space for the animal or not. They were euthanizing just to euthanize. If an animal sneezed, if it coughed, it was gone. If its time was up, it was gone. If it looked at them cross-eyed one day, it was gone."

In the midst of the internal investigation and before the task force had issued its report, the shelter's director retired. Chip Moore, then a sergeant on the police force, got a phone call from the chief—animal control and the county's shelter is under the purview of the police department. "I was told to report to animal control on March 5, 2012. I never wanted to come here, didn't ask to come here. It was more or less: 'You are over at animal control now. Here are the keys. Here is your staff.' It was supposed to be a two-week assignment, and then it turned into two months and then six months and then: 'We don't know when you'll be done.'"

The staff was not particularly welcoming to Moore. To them, he was yet another in a line of officers placed in the top position who knew little about animal control, little about animal sheltering. Volunteers and rescue groups that wanted the shelter to be in the life-saving rather than the life-ending business weren't impressed either. Moore told me, "My first week, a rescue group had a Channel Two news truck parked across the street doing a story about how bad this place is."

None of that cowed Moore. He is a big man in both size and personality, and despite having no experience working in animal control, when he is charged with a mission, he says, he carries it out. In eighteen years on the force he'd worked "burglary, robbery, homicide, undercover dope, narcotics, and on a federal drug task force." He would figure this out.

"I got into the animal control truck, I learned how to be an animal control officer, and I rewrote the operating procedures. I came into the kennel, and I learned how to clean, how to feed, and I rewrote that procedure. I learned how the spay/neuter facility worked. I talked to every employee individually, and what I said to them was, 'You work here. I don't. What do you think needs to be changed?' And people were like, 'Whoa, he's asking me what I think.'"

Ruelle says Moore's conversations weren't just important to his education, they were empowering to a staff that had been demoralized by the previous administration. "Before Chip came in, staff would tell me their ideas, and I'd say, 'Why don't you just tell the administration what you need?' and they would say, 'It doesn't go anywhere, so it doesn't matter.' And I'd say, 'You have this great idea. It's a smart idea.' And they'd just say, 'Nope.'"

Moore says that in speaking with employees he would often ask, "Why do we do things this way?" And they would often answer, "Because that's the way we've always done it."

"I would respond, 'I may not know what we're doing, but I know that this just doesn't make any sense.' So then we'd talk about it, and we'd often have a eureka moment."

Take the intake process. "The procedure was that when people would come in, we'd ask for their ID, we'd take their animal. I thought, 'Okay, but we're not asking these people why they're giving up their pet.' So I created a questionnaire intended to pull heartstrings. It asks, 'Is your dog good with your kids? What is your dog's name? Why are you giving it up? Is it because you can't afford food? Is it because you can't afford vet care?' And we spent several months contacting rescue groups, spay/neuter clinics, food banks. So now we can tell people, 'If you can't afford food or vetting because you are down on your luck, go to these places, and they will help you so you don't have to give up your dog. Our intakes immediately decreased by thirty-five percent within the first month. Just because of that questionnaire. That's the kind of stuff where I was going, why are we not doing this?"

Another thing Moore did was to take an objective look at the shelter's interior and find it wanting. "You walked in, and it looked like an institution, a prison." That was a shame, he thought, because the exterior has great curb appeal. Set beside a pond and on several scenic acres, the shelter was built in 2007 to replace a small, outdated facility next to police headquarters. Moore set out to bring some of that exterior appeal inside.

As he walks me through the kennel space, Moore points out work done by artists, art clubs, and Girl Scouts. At one corner there's a rendering of a tree. Hanging from one of its lower branches is a boy in blue overalls, a slingshot peeking out of his right pocket. A brown-and-white dog, a long pink tongue dangling, stands in tall green grass, playfully eyeing the boy. A mother duck painted in shades of brown, yellow, and white walks with two tiny ducklings.

Surrounding the windows through which visitors can see each dog, artists and Girl Scouts painted window boxes filled with brightly colored flowers and whimsical shutters in a variety of hues. Lining a hallway the length of the kennel, green stems and leaves have been added to children's handprints, turning each print into a flower of a different color. "I want this to look and feel like a happy place," Moore tells me. "Now it's on its way."

He's also making use of a large, semicircle-shaped conference room whose wall of windows looks out over the pond. "This room will hold two hundred people, and the previous administration used it for storage. It was floor to ceiling full of junk," he tells me as we enter. "My theory is, I have the building—why not use it, even for events that aren't animal-related? Yesterday, for instance, there was a women's safety class. The event had nothing to do with animals. But after the class, guess where everybody went? Out to look at the animals. We got four adopted."

Homeless Pet Clubs also use the space for meetings. And on the third Saturday of each month, the shelter hosts Paws and Pages, an hour-long period when children can read to therapy dogs or simply sit next to a dog while Mom or Dad reads to the child. One canine regular, Crash Dog, is a shelter-graduate-turned-certified-therapy dog. Recently, Moore says, he offered the room to area veterinarians needing a location to host a continuing education lecture. "Seventy-eight vets showed up, and a majority of them said they'd never been here and that they didn't like us." Moore's tone reflects the incredulity he felt that people who had never been to the shelter could have such antipathy toward it. "There is this weird divide between animal control, rescue groups, and veterinarians that I just don't understand," he says. "But I gave them a tour of the kennel, and now all but one agreed to partner with us." I ask why one of the vets was a holdout. Moore shakes his head. "I can't answer that," he tells me.

Sue Garcia embraces that same philosophy of doing everything you can to bring people into the shelter. Get them in, and it changes for the better the way they view shelters and the animals inside them—and that leads to more adoptions. So the Cherokee County shelter uses its premises to host kids' birthday parties. It held a Girl Scout Jamboree for about 100 scouts. The girls got a lesson on bite prevention and training tips that they could use on their own pets. They ate pizza, received an animal shelter patch, and took pictures with a one-year-old pit bull named Pumpkin Pie. One staff member is trying to figure out the logistics of instituting slumber parties.

The day I'm in Gwinnett County, the shelter is hosting a fair to kick off the 2014 ASPCA Rachael Ray $100K Challenge, a contest pitting fifty shelters from around the country—each chosen by the ASPCA—against one another. The winning shelter is the one that saves more lives between June and August than it did the previous year over that same period. Bounce houses and vendors selling pet-related wares fill the parking lot. Steady streams of people stroll through the shelter. Moore wants to win because he desperately wants that $100,000 so he can purchase a mobile spay/neuter unit. He's been trying to find the money in his budget, but it's not there, not yet.

"I tell my employees all the time, we need to stop thinking inside these four walls that we see every day in this building. The problem is not inside these four walls. The problem is what's outside them." With that in mind, Moore has opened up the shelter's spay/neuter suite once a week to local pet owners. And the shelter is now partnering with the shelter medicine program at the University of Georgia's vet school. "UGA was reaching out to the counties around the school to find a shelter they could call home base, and all the shelters were turning them away. When they came to us, I was like, 'Come on in. Why not?' So now, not only do I have the experience of the vets who work with me at our spay/neuter clinic, I have all of UGA."

"Why," I ask, "would other shelters turn down what seems like a great opportunity?"

"More work. I mean, I just don't understand. To me the benefits greatly outweigh any work the partnership can create."

At one in the afternoon I walk into the shelter's lobby to meet a couple of Girl Scouts who, at ten years old, are about the same age as my daughters. In dress and mannerisms, Caitlyn Coker and Julia Razetto so resemble Lindsey and Dhani that there doesn't seem to be any geographical divide between them. Caitlyn, Julia, and several other girls are members of a Homeless Pet Club created through their Girl Scout troop. The club satisfies a twenty-hour community service requirement, but it is clear by talking to the girls and watching them scamper about the kennel that they are already dog lovers. Of course, they are also influenced by the canines each lives with, both of whom are rescues.

I ask the girls how their club decides which dogs to sponsor.

"We choose certain dogs that are hard to get adopted," Caitlyn tells me. "We wouldn't choose puppies because they are easy to get adopted. We would choose older dogs—"

"And the kind that people would think are bad," interjects Julia, referring to pit bulls. The shelter has a lot of them, and they, more than any other breed, are still euthanized for space.

"The first dog we sponsored was named Holly," Caitlin says. "She was a beagle, and one of the hard parts about getting her adopted was she had a problem with her right eye, and she was older. But she was so sweet."

Holly found a home. As did Cinnamon, Rose, Libby, Cookie,

Bailey, and Grady, all of whom were named by the girls. The shelter identifies dogs by number. "We wanted them to have names because it gives them more personality," Caitlin tells me.

During a typical club meeting, the girls would decorate their dog's window to draw visitors' attention to her. (The girls had a tendency to choose females over males, a trend they hadn't realized until our conversation.) And an animal control officer would talk to the girls about the many reasons why dogs end up in shelters. The officer would speak specifically about dogs they would see as they toured the shelter and generally about reasons for pet overpopulation. After the "work," the girls would play with the dogs in one of several get-acquainted outdoor enclosures. Several of the spaces include agility equipment built by local Boy Scout troops—just another of Moore's ideas to increase community involvement, and in this case the dogs benefit, too.

"I didn't mind doing the work," Julia tells me, "because to me, it's not fair for dogs to get abused or abandoned or hurt for no apparent reason."

"I think it's hard to understand how people can even abandon a dog," continues Caitlin. "We would go into the kennel and look at the dogs and think, 'How could someone not love them? They're too adorable and too sweet.' I think some people just think humans are much better than animals, and I want to show people that animals have souls, they have feelings … "

"They have hearts," adds Julia.

I ask the girls if they will continue with the pet club next year, as they met their community service requirement and earned their bronze award.

"I think so," says Caitlyn. "It's a way for us to help animals."

"And a way to connect with them," says Julia.

Michael Good would be proud, though I'm sure he'd tell me that he would not expect anything less from the girls' experience.

For Chip Moore, the energy that the pet clubs bring to the shelter is priceless. "My staff is still tired, and they're still burned out. But we feel like we have a mission." Like Cherokee's shelter, Gwinnett's partners with more than sixty school, community, and business clubs. In 2013, the euthanasia rate fell to a historic 13 percent.

By this point in my travels I had visited many shelters, and from a strictly physical standpoint, the Gwinnett County shelter has the benefit of being new and being located in an easily accessible location. Could such a turnaround occur in an aging, run-down shelter? I wasn't so sure, but Moore was optimistic. "I would agree to an extent that having a new shelter helps. Would we have this success and turnaround even at the old building? I believe that it is still possible. I'm working with two metro-Atlanta shelters right now to try to help them. But I'm not the grand pooh-bah, master of anything, believe me."

I ask Moore if he plans to stick around the shelter or whether his superiors have other plans for him. We're in the conference room with Susan Ruelle. The two exchange glances.

It seems one of the changes proposed by the task force—and approved by county commissioners—is that the job of shelter director should go to someone with shelter and rescue experience rather than to a police officer. Moore is a darn good officer, but other than his brief stint running the shelter, he lacks experience.

"They wouldn't hire me. They were flying in people for interviews, and they were going to send me back to uniform."

"I marched back in front of the commissioners and raised Cain," says Ruelle. "I said, you need to hire the person who is here doing the job. You know some people are religious, some people are not, but I told them, 'He's meant to be here. It was totally fate that God put him here."

Even members of the task force went before the commission asking members to cast aside the rule they'd just adopted, the rule the task force had proposed. But the commissioners refused. The job of director, they said, was going to go to a civilian.

"I wanted to keep my law enforcement credentials, but I also wanted the job. I firmly believe in what we're doing here, what we've already done," Moore says. "We've had folks fly down here from shelters in Connecticut, California, and Tennessee to see what we're doing and to take our ideas home with them. That means we, as Gwinnett County, stand the chance of potentially impacting thousands and thousands and thousands of animals that aren't even in our county. That's why I gave up a nineteen-year law enforcement career. That's why I became a civilian to keep this job."

I get the chills. "You left the force?"

"Yup. I never ever thought as a rookie cop in Norcross dodging bullets in the middle of the night that nearly two decades later I'd be dealing with bounce houses and puppies. But here I am, and I'm staying."

I'm surprised how quiet it is at the Cherokee County shelter on a Saturday afternoon. Besides my rental car, there is only one other vehicle in the parking lot. Inside the shelter I see several volunteers and a mother and son who are getting acquainted with a pug mix named Rusty, whose name aptly describes the color of his fur. But there are no other visitors, and I find that worrisome. No visitors mean no adoptions.

Before entering the kennel, I ask Laurie Kekel how many dogs are in there.

"Three," she says.

"Three?" I couldn't possibly have heard correctly.

She laughs at my stunned response. "Yes, I have more dogs in my house right now. I own five."

Kekel told me that the situation today is by no means common, and that there are about eight dogs in the intake building who are not yet ready to be placed up for adoption—they still need to be vetted and complete their period of quarantine—but that the shelter is, for now, the beneficiary of a perfect storm that swept through in 2010–2011. That's when Kekel launched the shelter's Facebook page, when she and Sue Garcia overhauled the volunteer program, and when they partnered with Homeless Pet Clubs.

In a typical summer, Garcia tells me, the shelter will take in up to 800 animals, but she's optimistic that her staff will be able to move them out fast enough that she won't need to euthanize for space. So far this year's adoptions are up over last year's numbers; it's a positive trend. "We got ahead, and we plan to stay ahead," she says.

I watch as the mother and son leave the shelter; Rusty is back in the kennel. Fiona, a brindle terrier–hound mix, and Hunter, a Lab mix, are in their runs. Later that night I go onto the Cherokee County shelter's Facebook page. Kekel has posted an update: Rusty, Fiona, and Hunter are no longer homeless. Each has been adopted. Each has a home.

Meeting Miss Daisy

I STOOD IN FRONT OF THE RESERVATIONS DESK at the Hyatt Regency in Jacksonville, Florida, scanning the faces of passersby, trying to sense who, like me, looked as if she were searching for a stranger. I checked my watch. It wasn't yet one o'clock. Good, I thought, I'm not late. One of my goals in attending the Best Friends conference was to speak with Ruth Steinberger, founder of the nonprofit organization Spay FIRST!, and to attend a presentation she was slated to give about bringing spay/neuter programs to low-population and rural areas, a cause to which she has devoted her adult life, and one she doesn't believe gets enough attention in animal welfare circles. Rather, she'd told me when we spoke by phone, too many people get caught up in rescue because it's a feel-good enterprise. "It's easy to see the animals and see them get homes, so people get waylaid into rescue." To stop canine suffering, to save lives, she says, Americans need to look beyond rescue.

Soft-spoken but opinionated, Steinberger is a native New Yorker who grew up first in Brooklyn, then in Westchester County. She attended college in Virginia but dropped out and relocated to Floyd County, in the rural southwest part of the state. In the early 1970s, the area, set on a plateau atop the Blue Ridge Mountains, was a haven for artists and members of the back-to-the-land movement. Steinberger found it a perfect fit for her progressive views and artisanal leanings.

Always an animal lover, Steinberger noticed that her new community was home to more stray dogs than she'd grown up around, and most of them weren't fixed. Utilizing the resources of the veterinary school at Virginia Tech, which was about forty-five minutes away, and with funding from a humane society in a neighboring county, she launched a small spay/neuter transport program. "I went rural road by rural road, going to any house I saw with a sign offering free puppies, or identifying any place that had a female dog with male dogs chasing her around." Steinberger's approach to Floyd County's dog problem heralded the approach that Amanda Arrington would take with Pets for Life some thirty years later.

"It was time consuming, it sure was," she told me. "But I could make a huge difference for less energy by transporting a dog to surgery than I could by taking the litters, getting them fixed, and finding them homes. Unplanned puppies are a challenge as soon as they are born, and they are the most likely dogs to be neglected, to be abused, to become homeless." Prevention, Steinberger decided, was the solution—not just to shelter overpopulation but to the entirety of the pet overpopulation problem and to the suffering it engenders.

Today Steinberger runs Spay FIRST! from her home in Oklahoma. She hadn't intended to leave Virginia, she told me, but sometimes a single event—hers occurred in 1999—leaves a person feeling she has little choice but to act. "I was on a camping trip with the intent to wind up in West Texas. I had a horse with me and all my art supplies and two dogs. I got into southern Oklahoma, and I stopped to get diesel fuel, and a stray dog came up to the truck, and then a second stray dog. So I grabbed emergency dog biscuits from behind the driver's seat, and a third dog comes up. Now, I'm from the East, where you don't see packs of dogs, and finally there are eight, nine, ten dogs, and there's this girl watching me as I'm handing out biscuits.

She's probably fourteen years old, very pregnant, literally barefoot. We start talking, and I ask, 'Do you know whose dogs these are?' And she says, 'Well, they're yours, ain't they?' And I am now really afraid I'm going to end up with all these dogs, and it's going to end my trip, and I'm miserable. I say, 'No, I'm serious. Do you know whose these are?' And she says, 'My mom owns this place, and we throw food scraps out for them at night, and they hang around.' I said, 'Has anybody helped you with getting them spayed or neutered?' And she said the closest humane society—she knew where it was, and this is what was sad; she and her mom knew they needed to get the dogs fixed—but she says, 'They don't help people like us.' Meaning they were poor. They were Okie. And I knew right then I was going back to Virginia, selling my place, and moving to Oklahoma. What went through my mind was, 'This is the worst place I've ever seen. I'm moving here.' I had one of those feelings where you know you cannot turn your back. And I moved. And my intention was to start a little two-county program similar to what I had in Virginia, but it's grown."

In 2010, Steinberger founded Spay FIRST! after more than two decades spent working with animal welfare groups, veterinarians, and local officials to develop cost-effective programs to bring education about the benefits of spay/neuter and the surgery to some of the country's most economically challenged rural areas. Such programs include "in-clinic clinics"—in which humane groups and private veterinary practices serve low-income pet owners by collaborating to turn the private clinic into a low-cost, high-volume clinic for a few hours a week or one day a month—as well as "spay pods," which are high-volume mini-clinics in low-human-population areas that have an overpopulation of pets. Spay pods are open just a few days a month to keep overhead costs down, and they are financially self-sustaining—overall costs are balanced against the fees charged for surgery. This balance is achieved by utilizing free or low-rent space, using only veterinarians trained in high-volume spay/neuter, opening only on days the appointment schedule is full, and keeping the cost of surgery to no more than $45.

In 2003, Steinberger began bringing spay/neuter—in the form of high-volume surgical clinics called MASH clinics—to the impoverished Rosebud Sioux Reservation in South Dakota, where addressing canine overpopulation had, for years, meant a tribal policy of rounding up and shooting stray dogs. According to a report issued by the tribe, the policy, not to mention the situation, was untenable. "Homeless dogs, often seriously affected by mange and parasites, froze and starved to death each year, and packs of stray dogs sometimes survived by cannibalism. The number of dog bites was over twenty times the national average. The tragedies traumatized animals and people throughout the reservation, including those who hired the people to shoot the dogs." In 2002, committed to finding a humane way of dealing with its canine population problem, a tribal health official reached out to Steinberger for help.

Incredibly, after just two years of hosting annual clinics, Steinberger says, the overall condition of the dogs brought in for surgery had improved. Curious as to whether this was due to a decrease in competition for food or to dogs receiving improved care, Steinberger says she got the idea to conduct "a wholly unscientific" but worthwhile poll. In 2005, she called two grocery stores and inquired about sales of pet food. What she learned heartened her: As the number of dogs on the reservation decreased, pet food sales increased. Years later in England, attending an international conference sponsored by the World Health Organization on managing dog populations, Steinberger would tell conference-goers that her findings showed "that when people can finally afford to care, they usually do."

Further, a 2010 report by the tribe's animal control officer and Steinberger revealed that after seven years of annual and then tri-annual spay/neuter clinics, "nearly seven thousand animals have been removed from reproductive circulation," most via surgery, with some having been adopted into communities outside the reservation. Dog bites were down 50 percent, animal cruelty complaints had fallen 75 percent, and school officials reported that there were no longer packs of dogs searching for food in schoolyard Dumpsters and terrorizing children.

All of this experience preventing unwanted litters has thrust Steinberger to the forefront of a growing spay/neuter advocacy movement that believes that both mandatory spay/neuter laws and a public spay/neuter infrastructure that makes the surgery accessible and affordable to pet owners at every income level are the only way to control the country's pet population and thereby curb the killing.

To Steinberger, accessibility and affordability have distinct meanings in the spay/neuter realm. Access, she argues, means having a veterinary clinic, a spay/neuter facility, or a transport program like the one run by the Humane Alliance in Asheville, North Carolina, or the one she ran in Virginia, within fifty miles of a pet owner's home. Affordability means the cost of the surgery is less than what a low-wage or minimum-wage worker makes in a day, which is about $50. To Steinberger's count, fewer than ten states can claim to have accessible and affordable spay/neuter services available to resident pet owners. And that, Steinberger believes, is not only a travesty, but it reflects a failure of both public officials and the animal welfare community.

"I really feel the biggest roadblock to ending animal suffering is that we in animal welfare haven't even begun to demand that spay/neuter be our primary response to pet overpopulation. We have not normalized spay/neuter. We have normalized collection and dispersal as the publicly supported model nationwide. But I think it is fairly simple. If you have a shelter that collects, you need to have spay/neuter access."

To this end, Steinberger would like to see pet overpopulation framed as both a public health issue and as a taxpayer issue. "We as taxpayers fund shelters, we fund collection models, we fund euthanasia, killing. But we're not funding prevention, and spay/neuter equipment costs less than cremation equipment. There's no humane logic to this."

Steinberger would also like to see those in animal welfare—from shelter employees to rescue workers to the large animal welfare agencies—take a more active role lobbying state legislatures and town and county councils. "I think about Mothers Against Drunk Driving. They became local. They became advocacy-oriented. They demanded. We don't go to our council meetings. I doubt that most of the people at this conference know who their city and state and federal representatives are. We have not taken the steps that Mothers Against Drunk Driving took. We have not created local advocacy."

Few, if any, in animal welfare would disagree that making spay/neuter surgery accessible and affordable to all pet owners, no matter their income, would go a long way toward stopping the killing that takes place inside and outside of shelters. And while most people in animal welfare would agree that there is a role for local and state governments to play, what that role should be is in no way universally agreed upon. And of course, there are people in and out of public office who don't believe that government has any role to play in subsidizing spay/neuter programs, be they through an animal population control program like New Jersey has or through the types of licensing programs instituted in counties like Duval in Florida and Gaston in North Carolina—the type of program the Smoky Mountain Animal Care Foundation's Chris Protzman would like to see operating in Blount County, Tennessee.

But the issue that sparks the most debate is the push for mandatory spay/neuter laws. For Steinberger, making spay/neuter affordable and accessible is not enough to stem pet overpopulation. Until fixing pets is as much a part of caring for them as feeding and sheltering them, she says, mandatory spay/neuter laws, like other public health and safety laws, are essential. "Seat-belt laws faced a host of objections when they were being debated. Opponents said, 'They're dangerous for small kids, so let's all not use seat belts.' People can nitpick anything to make any public health and safety issue unpalatable. The fact is you have to have statutes to make people wear seat belts and to make people use child safety seats. If people need urging to travel with their kid in the safest way, they probably need some urging to do the best thing for their dog and for their community. And that we in animal welfare are still balking at mandatory spay/neuter to me is unconscionable."

One animal advocate who thinks quite differently than Steinberger on this issue is Peter Marsh, an attorney and activist in New Hampshire. "If you don't have an affordable and accessible spay/neuter program and the sanction for not having your pet spayed or neutered is forfeiture, then you put pet owners in a terrible bind," he told me. "They run the risk of losing their pet. They might abandon it. And if a community has an affordable and accessible spay/neuter program, then I believe you don't need a mandatory spay/neuter law."

Just as Steinberger draws her conclusion about the necessity for mandatory laws from experience, so, too, does Marsh, who in the early 1990s began orchestrating a plan that would ultimately do what most people thought impossible: Dispel the widely held beliefs that shelter overpopulation is inevitable and that ending the shelter euthanasia of healthy dogs and cats is impossible.

PETER MARSH JOGGED up the steps of the state capitol building in Concord, New Hampshire; took the podium; and adjusted a microphone. It was August of 1992, and the organization that Marsh had co-founded a year earlier, Solutions to Overpopulation of Pets (STOP), had organized a candlelight vigil in memory of all the healthy dogs and cats euthanized in New Hampshire's crowded shelters during the first seven months of the year. The vigil's purpose was twofold—to publicize the plight of homeless companion animals and to put pressure on the legislature to pass a bill creating a state-funded, low-cost spay/neuter program similar to the one New Jersey established in 1983. A prior attempt to push through the legislation had passed the state Senate but stalled in the House. STOP didn't want that to happen again.

To showcase the staggering number of adoptable dogs and cats that had already lost their lives that year, staff from shelters throughout the state had created paper collars with descriptions of each euthanized animal—its breed, its age, its name if it had one, its date of death—and laid them out on the lawn in front of the capitol building. "The chain of collars," Marsh told the vigil's attendees, "is a way to try to get to understand that this is not an abstract tragedy, that animals die one by one, each animal with its own identity, its own personality, and its own history." (See the vigil online at www.shelteroverpopulation.org.) Looped together, Marsh would later write in *Getting to Zero*, his book about ending shelter overpopulation, the chain of collars stretched for nearly a mile.

One by one, shelter workers walked to the podium and read the collars—to bear witness, Marsh would say, and to tell stories, sometimes through tears, about a dog or cat who'd touched them deeply but whom they'd had to euthanize. A young man, twentysomething, told the story of a six-month-old shepherd mix surrendered by a family that said they couldn't handle the dog's rambunctious personality. The family had adopted the dog from the shelter just a few weeks prior and had assured staff they understood perfectly well what to expect from a puppy. A soft-spoken middle-aged shelter employee talked of a stray cat who loved kittens so much she would try to lick them clean whenever she was let out of her cage and who would become visibly distressed if she heard a kitten's cry. Another shelter worker, a young blonde, cried as she spoke of her disappointment in her fellow citizens. "I hadn't originally planned to come up here and speak," she told those gathered before her, "but I wanted my voice to be heard. Just yesterday the girls and I shared in a celebration—my first year as a kennel worker. It was a celebration for me because I had made a difference in these animals' lives. We at the Laconia Humane Society are the last people to show these animals they are loved before they are humanely put to sleep. And I want society to know that we are angry that we have to bear this burden for their irresponsibility to their animals. We are called murderers because we care enough to take these animals off the street where they are abused, neglected, and just dumped like trash. I want society to take responsibility for these lives." Then she read from three collars she held in her hand. "A German shepherd, a pedigreed dog. Five two-week-old kittens. Two three-month-old kittens who spent much of their life in the shelter. It wasn't much of a life."

The vigil was the launch of what would become an all-out campaign to get the spay/neuter bill passed. For Marsh, making the surgery affordable was the foundation of what STOP called its Millennium Plan—a strategy designed "to end the killing of cats and dogs in our state's shelters for treatable illnesses or to make space for incoming animals by the year 2000." It had become clear to Marsh and his colleagues that without a state-subsidized spay/neuter fund, pet owners who lived in poverty would not be able to afford the surgery. The state did have private organizations working to bring down the cost—several nonprofits provided vouchers that cut the cost of surgery by half—but that was still not enough to bring it within the financial reach of the state's poorest pet owners. And it was those owners who were turning in the majority of dogs and cats to shelters, even though they made up a minority of the population. To bring the cost of spay/neuter surgery down to $10, STOP needed elected officials to create a state-subsidized fund and needed veterinarians to participate in a low-cost program, as there were no high-volume clinics in the state. As Marsh said to me, "The only service delivery system we had at the time was private veterinarians."

Marsh says that to get the veterinary community on board, STOP turned to New Hampshire's veterinary medical association. "This is something we thought about a lot. We intentionally didn't want to limit the program to a few private vets, so we negotiated through the medical association even though we knew we would have to pay more to get broad participation." According to Marsh, to reach a deal, STOP agreed to pay "a fairly steep price": Veterinarians who participated in the spay/neuter program would be reimbursed 80 percent of the retail cost of the surgery.

Selling the idea to the state's predominately Republican House and Senate, along with its Republican governor, was the bigger challenge, Marsh told me. "Our opponents said, 'You guys are just dreamers, bleeding hearts. You can make spay/neuter affordable for these people, and they could care less. They're not going to get their animals spayed or neutered. The reason they don't is the same reason why they are poor. They are irresponsible.'"

To make the bill politically more palatable to legislators, STOP lobbied for a shelter adoption provision that would allow citizens at any income level to pay a flat $25 fee for the spaying or neutering of a pet adopted from a state shelter. It also agreed to a sunset provision that would automatically repeal the bill in three years unless the legislature voted to renew it. Ultimately, Marsh says, "we got enough people to support us, including the veterinary medical association and the Department of Agriculture, that we got the bill passed."

STOP had been prescient in its thinking. Although it and other animal welfare groups had been running public awareness campaigns about the benefits of spaying and neutering pets—benefits to both companion animals and to society—it wasn't until the Animal Population Control Program (APCP) took effect in the summer of 1994 that shelter intake and euthanasia began to drop—sharply and quickly. Within a year, STOP was heralding the results. "It was like hitting one number after another on your Powerball card," Marsh writes in *Getting to Zero*. "Shelter after shelter reported the same thing. After a decade in which intake and euthanasia rates had not changed very much, now they had fallen off a cliff! … Every one of the eight open admission shelters in the state saw a drop in euthanasias of between 15% and 58% compared to the year before!"

In terms of operating the program, the biggest challenge was keeping it flush with funds so surgeries didn't have to be delayed, as every delay meant the potential for another litter. As set up by the legislature, the program's funding is derived from a $2 surcharge tacked onto the licensing fee already paid by dog owners. According to a 2003 case study of the APCP by Sharon Secovich, the program did run out of money its first three years, although in 1995 the shortfall was attributed to the state, which "removed $60,000 from the APCP budget for use in other programs." Since 1998, however, the program has remained in the black. "Often the problem with spay/neuter programs isn't getting people to participate," Marsh told me. "It is getting the funding to pay for all the surgeries. Not having sufficient funding is where most programs fail."

But Marsh makes clear that STOP did not foresee an affordable and accessible spay/neuter program as anything more than the Millennium Plan's foundation—an essential piece but not at all its entirety. "You really need a comprehensive set of programs," he told me. "It's like a pyramid to get to zero." So the Millennium Plan approached the problem from two directions. It developed a series of self-financed programs to decrease the number of pets entering shelters and a series of programs to increase the number adopted out of them, but the emphasis was on intake.

Decreasing intake is essential, Marsh told me, because studies consistently show that euthanasia rates "follow intake rates like a shadow." Marsh points to nearly three decades of data from California shelters showing that euthanasias rise and fall as intake rises and falls. Further, researchers in California found no relationship between euthanasias and adoption rates, which remained relatively constant over the years. As other states, like Delaware, Michigan, Virginia, and Utah, have started collecting and analyzing their shelter data, their findings have mirrored California's. In fact, across the country, shelter adoption rates tend to be similar, but intake rates can vary widely, and euthanasia rates have followed their trajectories.

So STOP developed programs focused on keeping dogs and cats out of shelters. That, of course, meant increasing spay/neuter rates, both to reduce the puppy population and because, as Marsh points out in *Getting to Zero,* intact dogs show up in shelters three times more frequently than their fixed counterparts. "Hormone-driven pets can do several things that strain the relationship with their caretakers," he writes, "such as destroying household furnishings, soiling the house, or attacking other animals or people ... All this makes it much more likely that a caretaker will eventually have had enough and bring an intact pet to a shelter."

The state-funded spay/neuter program made it possible for low-income pet owners to fix their pets, but STOP also needed shelters to implement pre-release spay/neuter programs, and it needed to target those people who could afford the surgery. It also needed to dispel a popular myth—that female dogs and cats are healthier when spayed after delivering their first litter, a practice Marsh calls "spay delay." Studies in both Massachusetts in the 1990s and Tennessee in the 2000s found that more than four out of five litters come from dogs who are sterilized—often at private veterinary clinics with pet owners paying full price—after they have had at least one litter.

So STOP stepped up its public information campaign, distributing brochures and posters about the benefits of "timely pet sterilization" to veterinary hospitals, human-services agencies, welfare offices, and community groups. It ran public service announcements on cable television stations. And it set up a toll-free hotline to refer pet owners to the best spay/neuter program for them and followed up with pet owners two months later, offering assistance if they had not gotten their pets fixed.

STOP also aided shelters in their efforts to get dogs and cats adopted into their communities by supporting shelter-sponsored adoption-related events and promotions. And STOP established a program made possible by what today seems like a relic of modern technology: the fax machine. But in the mid-1990s—before the widespread use of e-mail—STOP used fax machines to send information almost immediately to link the state's open-admission shelters into a single network it called "Pet Net." In *Getting to Zero,* Marsh writes, "Every Tuesday, each shelter would fax us a list of all the cats and dogs they had available for adoption with information about each one, such as size, breed, and color and whether they could be safely placed in homes with other dogs or cats or young children. We would then make up a complete list of the dogs and cats available for adoption in all of the shelters and fax it back to shelters, veterinary hospitals, and rescue groups the next morning."

Doing their part, shelters would keep a list of the breeds that adopters in their area were looking for, notifying potential adopters when an animal that fit their description showed up on the Pet Net listing. If an adopter could not get to the shelter that housed the animal, the adopter's local shelter would have the dog or cat transferred to it. STOP also maintained a hotline for prospective pet owners who could request that STOP track down the shelter pet of their choice. Because STOP, too, kept a list of desired dogs and cats, it would contact people when an animal like the one they were looking for entered a shelter. It was a work-intensive system, but it successfully moved dogs and cats out of shelters and into homes.

Through STOP's many efforts to engage the whole of the state's animal welfare community, from shelters to rescues to veterinarians,

227

and through adequate funding from public and private sources, New Hampshire ceased the practice of killing adoptable dogs and cats in the state's open-admission shelters in 1999, one year ahead of the goal laid out in STOP's Millennium Plan. And it did so, according to a 2001 report by the International City/County Management Association (ICMA), at a significant savings to taxpayers. The ICMA found that in the program's first six years, shelters took in nearly 31,000 fewer animals than they did in the six years preceding its launch, at a savings of about $3.2 million in unpaid impoundment and shelter costs. Factoring in the expense of running the program, which the ICMA reported to be $1 million, "the state saved more than $2.2 million in the program's first six years." New Hampshire has also maintained this status quo; thus, according to the ASPCA, for more than a decade the Granite State has had the lowest shelter euthanasia rate in the nation.

To be sure, New Hampshire isn't North Carolina, or Georgia, or Tennessee, or any other Southern state. It has a comparatively small population—it ranks forty-second in the nation. It is small territorially—it ranks forty-sixth. And, according to a 2012 U.S. Census Bureau study, it has one of the lowest poverty rates in the country. The Southern states, the study found, have the highest.

But in the eighties and early nineties, New Hampshire's euthanasia rate stood at 62 percent, higher than four of the other five New England states, according to the New England Federation of Humane Societies. And the state had long had to contend with the influx of Southern dogs, as some rescue groups started bringing in dogs from the South even before Hurricane Katrina. New Hampshire faced other challenges, too, Marsh says, as many of the resources available to communities today didn't exist in the early nineties. "Specialized high-volume clinics, mobile surgical suites, and MASH-type programs were just being developed. Pediatric spay/neuter was not widely practiced, and sterilization-at-adoption programs were in their infancy. There was little precedent for publicly funded spay/

neuter programs. And the survey data and research findings that could help inform programs were few and far between."

Perhaps most important, there were no models. "No one knew how to stop the killing or even if it could be stopped."

In the wake of New Hampshire's success, Marsh has been advising humane organizations, rescue groups, shelters, and animal control agencies across the country on how to establish effective shelter overpopulation programs in their communities—for instance, he's been working closely with First Coast No More Homeless Pets in Jacksonville and its coalition of animal welfare partners to make strides in North Florida.

Speaking with Marsh, it is hard not to share his optimism that canine overpopulation is a problem for which there are solutions. After all, it's not that we haven't made progress; it's that we've hit that plateau after watching America's shelter population plummet throughout the 1980s and 90s as spay/neuter became more widely available. Marsh argues that this initial progress coincided with national public education campaigns like the "Be a P.A.L. — Prevent a Litter" campaign launched by the Humane Society of the United States in 1988. "You look at progress from the late seventies to 2000, and it was not driven by publicly funded spay/neuter programs or the no-kill movement; it was all due to education."

And today, education does not seem to be a focus of the nation's largest animal welfare organizations, although it should be, Marsh says. "It's a puzzle to me. I don't know why we're not seeing national campaigns, not that I haven't been lobbying about it to the ASPCA, to Best Friends. I think public campaigns are absolutely critical."

Education. Legislation. Sterilization. This is the triad that Marsh argues can transform a community that euthanizes healthy, adoptable dogs to one that does not. It's the triad that guided his work in New Hampshire. And it's the triad, he says, that every community—big or small, rural or urban, southern or northern—can use as its guide. "You have to sort out the barriers because every community is different," Marsh told me. "But it can be done. It just takes the will to do it."

Marsh's confidence is contagious—at least while in conversation with him. But later, thinking back on our discussion, I couldn't help but wonder: Do we Americans have the will?

I PLUGGED THE ADDRESS INTO THE GPS; I knew it would show me the way, as it had in Georgia, in Tennessee, on multiple trips to North Carolina. And I knew that while I wasn't sure whether what I was about to do was right, I was going to do it anyway. I had come too far in my journey to uncover Galen's roots to turn back now. I started the car and breathed deeply.

Ruth Steinberger has written that the single greatest predictor of whether a dog will end up in a shelter is being born in an unplanned litter. The dogs are sometimes surrendered to the shelter as puppies; other times, the puppies are given away to "any willing taker," only to be surrendered by their new owners because these adoptions, Steinberger writes, "are more fragile than if the pet is obtained following a deliberate decision to spend money and purchase a dog."

I knew Galen had been surrendered to the Gaston County shelter by her owner—Sue King had told me that. But I was still curious; I wanted to know *why* she was surrendered. Perhaps I would soon have my answer.

The address ... if not for Galen's stubborn opposition to taking walks, it is unlikely I would have come upon it. Even though Galen had agreed to take those short walks with me around the horseshoe-shaped development across from our house, she revoked her consent several weeks later. I'd leash her up, and we'd get fewer than 100 feet from home when she would sit down. If I tugged the leash to coax her along, she would lie down. No amount of tugging, sweet talk, or American cheese could get her going. However, if I said, "Let's go home," she would pop up and prance home.

One afternoon when Kevin wasn't in the mood to argue—he could sometimes get Galen to walk around the block, whereas my efforts routinely failed—the two returned home, and while still in the driveway he unhooked the leash from her collar. Instead of following him into the backyard to play ball, as was her custom, she took a few steps toward the street. Then she looked back at Kevin. Then she looked toward the street.

"It was like she was telling me she wanted to go for a walk, but she didn't want to be on the leash," Kevin told me later. Galen, like Gryffin before her, had tasted the freedom of walking without a leash during hikes in the Sourland Mountains. There, she blazes the trail, stopping every few feet to turn around and make sure we are following her. In his day, Gryffin would charge ahead and lose sight of us, and we of him, every few yards. Sure enough, Galen completed the walk, unleashed, by Kevin's side. She did so again the next day and the day after that. We don't live in a high-traffic area, but I can't say I was thrilled with her newfound lust for independence.

One of the walks I enjoyed with Gryffin—and expected to take with Galen—took us two miles along a narrow, windy road to a series of paddocks, where we would watch horses graze and, if we were lucky, frolic. But it requires a dog to be leashed because when the rare car does pass, it's often moving at upwards of forty miles per hour. I used to do some of my better thinking during those strolls, yet Galen refuses to take that walk with me. I could go by myself, but going for a walk without a dog when you live with a perfectly healthy one sucks all the joy right out of the experience.

The walks with Gryffin were particularly therapeutic during periods of stress or writer's block—both of which occur more often than I'd like—so with Galen, I had to seek therapy elsewhere. I found it in mindless household chores. I'd throw a load of laundry into the washing machine, vacuum the hardwoods—Galen sheds incessantly—or clean out a closet or cabinet. One morning I focused my efforts on a kitchen cabinet where I keep dog supplies, barbecue tools, and random items that don't have a logical home elsewhere in the kitchen. My purpose was twofold—wipe down the interior but also pull out Gryffin's medical file, which was wedged under a container of dog food and a box of heartworm pills. In addition to his veterinary records, the file included paperwork I'd received from the Georgia shelter from which I'd adopted him. I'm not sure why I'd kept the documents all these years, but I was glad I did—I had started a blog and wanted that information for a post.

As I sat on the floor, flipping through the file, my heartbeat quickened. Before my eyes was a sheet of paper with the words *Gaston County Police, Animal Control Section* across the top. When Kevin and I adopted Galen, I'd stuffed her paperwork in with Gryffin's without reading it, figuring it would be there if I ever needed it. But I was sure, or so I thought, that I'd pulled it all out when I decided to contact Linda Wilferth. Now I held in my hand a copy of Galen's intake report, what the shelter refers to as an "Animal Entry Sheet."

The document noted Galen's age when she entered the shelter (six weeks old), her coloring (black/gray/white), her breed (Lab mix), the date she was surrendered (November 15, 2010), and the time (11:51). As to whether she was "vicious," a "fighter," or whether she'd bitten anyone in the past ten days, the answer to each was no. Then, in the center of the page, in all capitals, I read the words that saved her life: EUTHANIZE HOLD. I presume the hold was put on once Linda informed the shelter that she intended to rescue the litter. Immediately underneath was an address that someone had used black pen to cross out.

I examined the address. Despite the effort to conceal it, I could read it easily.

THE GPS ESTIMATED THAT THE TRIP from Terry Kenny's law office on Main Street in Gastonia to the address on Galen's paperwork would take twenty-one minutes. It wasn't yet four o'clock, so I figured I had at least three hours before the late-summer sun set. I pulled the white Ford Focus onto Main Street and irrationally cursed the car rental company at the Charlotte airport for giving me a car with New Jersey license plates.

Heading south, Gastonia quickly shed its urban identity for a more rural one. For much of the drive, mine was the only car on the road. I tried to get a sense of the socioeconomics of this part of the city, but it was difficult, as I saw few houses, and those I did see ran the gamut from aging and run-down to newly constructed. As for businesses, I passed a horse farm—mother and foal were trotting side-by-side inside a gated pasture—and about a mile later, a dairy farm advertising grass-fed beef. I also passed a handwritten sign by the side of the road that read LAB PUPPIES FOR SALE. What struck me most was the verdant landscape. Back home, my house was sitting on two acres of dry, sunburned lawn. Perhaps not surprisingly, I later learned from Gastonia census data that its key economic indicators are similar to those of the community Pets for Life targets in Atlanta. What differs are the size and racial makeup of the population, Gastonia's population being both smaller and significantly whiter.

I stuck to the speed limit, but my mind raced. Would I find the house? Would anyone be home? What would I say, showing up as I was about to do, completely unannounced? I didn't want to come across as an elitist Northerner. I had purposely dressed nicely—but not too nicely. My black cotton sundress was sleeveless, knee-length, understated—how many times had my daughters, even my female students, commented on the lack of color in my wardrobe? I wore silver hoops in my ears, flip-flops on my feet. (Later, I would take off my wedding band and engagement ring and leave them in the car, shedding the one sign of material wealth I had on me.) I just wanted to find out how Galen and her litter ended up in Gaston County's animal shelter. Did the person who surrendered the puppies know their odds for survival were slim, that they were more likely to be killed than adopted? Was there even a way to ask these questions without offending?

The sign startled me: WELCOME TO SOUTH CAROLINA. The document from the shelter clearly stated that Galen was surrendered by someone with a Gastonia, North Carolina, address. Since I'd begun my journey, I had put my full faith in my GPS, and it had yet to misdirect me. I thought about turning around, but I had come this far, and, according to the GPS, I was minutes from my destination.

Two left turns later, I crossed back into North Carolina. From the aged and weathered look of the few houses I passed, it was apparent I'd arrived in one of the poorer parts of the city. A right turn took me down an unpaved road past a cluster of metal mailboxes into a development of mobile homes. Bumping along at about ten miles per hour over dirt, rocks, and rather large ditches, the Focus felt poorly built for this terrain. Why hadn't the city, the county, paved these roads?

I again questioned my decision to press forward. Who was I to think I could simply show up at a stranger's home to ask questions about a dog given up years ago? And why hadn't I asked for a rental car with North Carolina license plates? I recognized I was being ridiculous, but here I was, a lone female in a car with Jersey plates, driving along the North Carolina/South Carolina border in a neighborhood so far from the heart of Gastonia that lawmakers hadn't bothered to pave the roads, about to drop in on people I'd never met, to ask if they'd surrendered puppies to a shelter that until recently euthanized more dogs and cats than it released. Reason aside, I had come too far to turn back.

The GPS proved unhelpful when it came to finding the house itself, announcing that I had reached my destination when I arrived at a three-way stop with houses set on one- to two-acre plots to the left, to the right, and ahead of me. Making matters more difficult, none of the properties or any others in the neighborhood had numbers, at least not anywhere that I could see. So I drove around the block a couple of times trying to figure out exactly which house the GPS was directing me to.

Finally, I pulled in front of what I thought might be the correct one. Glass and plastic bottles, cylindrical metal canisters, cigarette boxes, and household garbage lay scattered amid a tangle of overgrown grass and weeds. I got out of the car and stepped onto the edge of the property. There was no pathway to the house, which stood several yards from the curb. A series of steps leading to the front door looked as if it, like the grass and the weeds, had grown out of the earth. Five very large cats occupied the steps, some prone, some seated. I didn't see any dogs. The cats stared at me; I stared back, not at all happy. I'm not a cat person. I was scratched by a neighbor's cat when I was about five years old, and since then I've had an irrational fear of them. There was no way I could bring myself to approach the house, and I certainly could not climb the steps to knock on the door. Fortunately, the air was warm and the humidity low, so the windows were opened wide. From my vantage point, I could make out someone sitting at a table smoking a cigarette; I could hear muffled talking.

I took another breath and looked around. Standing there, absorbing my surroundings, I found myself hoping I was at the wrong house. Then, keeping my eyes trained on the cats, I called out, "Excuse me!"

A man, fiftyish perhaps, in jeans and an untucked, rumpled yellow button-down came to the door, cigarette in hand. He gave me a quick once-over before stepping outside, onto the landing.

I spoke first. "Hi. I know this may sound like an odd question, but did you, by chance, turn a litter of puppies over to Gaston County's animal shelter about two years ago?"

He shook his head. "Don't got a dog."

"I'm looking for house number three-fourteen. Would you know which property it might be?"

He shook his head again.

Silence.

Then he pointed over his shoulder, gesturing behind him. "I think a house over that way has dogs."

I thanked him, and moments later I was back in the car, bumping along the unpaved road. Do I try another house? I wondered. And if it's not the right one, how many more do I try? I also hadn't told Kevin about my plan to show up unannounced at Galen's previous owner's home, probably because he would have advised against it—at a minimum he would have suggested I not show up alone. And while his concern would, of course, have been for me and my safety, I think he would have been even more concerned for Galen's previous owner, whose privacy I would be invading to further this journalistic pursuit of mine.

I pulled in front of another house—this one gray, with five cars crowding the driveway—and looked through my passenger window, into the yard, for any sign of canine inhabitants.

That's when I saw them—two of them—a dark brown shepherd-looking dog tethered to a tree several hundred yards to the left of the house and a black Lab-like dog tethered to a small shed at the rear of the property.

I turned off the car and took another deep breath. Then I grabbed my notebook and a pen and stepped out of the car.

The black dog erupted, barking and straining forward on his tether. The brown dog barked a few times but seemed less bothered by my presence. I could hear a third dog inside the house. Shifting my gaze to the front door, I saw what looked like a Chihuahua standing on its hind legs, scratching wildly at the bottom of the screen door.

I had barely stepped onto the driveway when a woman came outside. As she did, several cats I hadn't noticed scampered off in different directions. The woman had blonde hair, secured in a low ponytail, and a slight frame. She looked to be in her late forties, early fifties. She walked toward me, and we met near the top of the driveway.

"I'm sorry to bother you," I said, "but did you by chance surrender a litter of puppies to the Gaston County animal shelter in November of 2010?"

She looked at me for a moment, her face expressionless. Then, slowly, as though debating whether such a question deserved an answer, she said in a soft, low voice, "Yes, I did."

My heart skipped a beat. I told her that I lived in New Jersey and that I had one of the puppies—that my husband and I had named her Galen, and that we'd adopted her from a rescue group that had transported the dogs north. I spoke quickly, feeling an urgent need to explain my presence. Then I told her Galen was as adorable as she was quirky.

"Her mama's quirky, too," said the woman, with a hint of a smile and a strong Southern accent. She told me her name was Laurie Baker and that she was "born and bred" in North Carolina.

Baker pointed to the dog tethered to the tree. "That's Daisy," she told me, "the mama." I turned my attention to the brown dog. She was lying in the grass, facing us, but seemingly uninterested. Daisy is an Aussie-Lab mix, like Galen, but the two don't share any resemblance. Whereas Galen looks like a small Lab with an Aussie's gray merle coat highlighted by patches of bronze on her ears and behind her legs, Daisy looks like an Aussie with a Lab's solid coat, which on her is dark chocolate.

Baker told me she took in Daisy when the dog was just seven weeks old. That's when a friend of Baker's learned that Daisy's owner was surrendering Daisy and her littermates to animal control. The friend knew that Baker's family would provide a loving home, so she offered Daisy to them; Baker accepted.

"She's beautiful," I said, explaining that Galen looks nothing like her mother.

"Daisy also has beautiful eyes," Baker told me. "One is blue, the other is brown." I asked if I could pet Daisy and take a picture of her, but Baker said that wouldn't be a good idea, adding, "She is very moody."

I asked Baker why she surrendered Daisy's litter to the shelter. She said that she couldn't afford to care for seven more dogs, nor could she find them homes. The thing is, she told me, she never intended for Daisy to get pregnant: It just happened, but it's only happened once. Galen's father, Baker said, is a neighbor's yellow Lab.

My thoughts immediately turned to the situation Daisy must have found herself in. The property isn't fenced, nor were there any dog runs that I could see. So the chances are good that Daisy was tied to the tree when she was in heat. The neighbor's dog presumably sensed it—males can sense females in heat from more than a mile away—and came by and impregnated her. Tied up as she is now, she would not have been able to stop his advance—that is, if she had even wanted to. I didn't ask, so I'll never know the real situation surrounding Daisy's pregnancy, and I knew that I was anthropomorphizing, but still, I felt my heart go out to her.

Baker told me she hated having to take the puppies to the shelter, but she felt she had no other choice. She hoped that if she turned them in someone might adopt them. "The shelter is an hour away, and I was so upset that I had to take my son with me," she told me. "I knew the puppies could be killed, and that's what worried me. I even called the shelter the next day to check on them."

What she'd learned gave Baker hope that the puppies would be fine. "All they said was that all seven had been adopted. I asked if they went at one time, to one person, and the lady on the phone said, 'Yes, ma'am.' My heart just fell, I was so glad."

I asked Baker whether she'd ever considered spaying Daisy. She would have liked to, she said, but she couldn't afford it then or now. Spike, the black dog, wasn't fixed either. The Chihuahua, who was still in the house and still barking, was already spayed when Baker got her. As for the Animal League's low-cost clinic, Baker had not heard of it.

I thanked Baker for her time, and we turned our backs to each other—she to walk toward her house, me to walk toward the car. As soon as we split apart, Spike resumed barking. I glanced at Daisy. She was lying comfortably in the grass, seemingly far less interested in me than I was in her.

I opened the car door and eased myself into the front seat. Galen, I thought, could be a poster child—or perhaps I should say poster dog—for a primary cause of the country's dog problem: those all-too-common unintended litters. I glanced through the window at Daisy and felt that familiar angst I sometimes feel when overwhelmed.

There are solutions to America's dog problem. Spay/neuter programs and adoption programs save lives every day, and new programs are being tried and tested and refined all the time. It's just that too often the disparate members of the animal welfare movement work in isolation, unengaged with one another, competing with and even undermining one another, and doing so at every stage of the process. And those of us outside the movement are often blind to the role we play in perpetuating the status quo. We adopt a rescue dog or a shelter dog and pat ourselves on the back, but we do nothing to address the underlying problem. And then there are the questions of money and will.

I looked at my watch. Kevin, the girls, and Galen were at my in-laws' home on the Jersey shore. Galen would have gone to the dog beach at some point in the day—it's a narrow stretch of sand relegated to dogs because there are more scenic, larger beaches for people. Galen would have run along the sand; she would have jumped through the waves; she may or may not have fetched a stick or played with other dogs—she's fickle like that. Galen has webbed paws and took to the water more gracefully than Gryffin, who splashed mightily as a puppy until he mastered his technique. I put the key in the ignition and pulled away from the curb, glancing at the dogs one last time. Spike had settled down and now, nose to the earth, was sniffing whatever it is that dogs sniff. Daisy had yet to even shift her position.

Days later, I e-mailed Baker and offered to pay to have Daisy and Spike fixed at the Animal League's low-cost spay/neuter clinic. I was feeling guilty that I had returned to New Jersey leaving dogs capable of reproducing with a family that I knew couldn't afford to care for any future litters. During my conversation with Baker, I had briefly considered making the offer, but I had thought it would be presumptuous of me to do so. Now I wished I had because Baker didn't e-mail me back. She never accepted my offer.

Afterword

THE THUNDER ROARED more loudly than I'd heard in years. Then it roared again and again with intermittent flashes of lightning. "She's shaking!" Dhani shouted from the family room.

Galen had never before shown any fear in the face of thunder, no matter how loud the clap. It was something Kevin and I noticed immediately because Gryffin hated storms. The only time he'd shed his independence to nestle up against one of us was during a thunderstorm. Sometimes we'd laugh at the irony: Our handsome boy, who lived his life as our stalwart protector, cowered before this one act of Mother Nature and nothing else. Our little girl, who seemed to be scared of her own shadow, didn't flinch; often she'd go about her business, outside, in the rain, seemingly oblivious to the rumbling. But this was a powerful storm. Even I found myself startled at the suddenness and explosiveness of some of the booms.

Lindsey, Dhani, and Galen huddled together on the small landing leading to the second floor. The girls petted Galen and hugged her and told her she was going to be all right. I loved seeing Dhani take the lead. That Lindsey would embrace a new dog was never an issue, certainly not she of "Lindsey is not Lindsey without a dog." But Dhani had seemed to tolerate Gryffin—and dogs in general, for that matter—more than she loved him, though I'm not sure she would admit to that. But now Dhani will tell you she's a dog person, and she attributes that entirely to Galen, despite Galen's rough entry into our lives.

Back when Galen was creating havoc herding the girls, a trainer told me that much of an Australian shepherd's high energy level is due to evolution and the breed's history as a working dog. I decided that a working dog needed a job, so I found one for Galen. Now she wakes the girls each morning. All I say is, "Galen, let's wake the girls," and she hurries out of her crate—still her favorite hangout—runs up the stairs, enters Dhani's room, and jumps onto the bed, where she digs Dhani out from under her covers. When Dhani is sufficiently awake, Galen jumps down, uses her nose to push open Lindsey's door, and repeats the process. The best part about our morning routine is that the girls wake happy, as it's hard to be grouchy when fifty-eight pounds of tail-wagging canine stands over you, face in yours, wet nose and whiskers tickling your cheek. On mornings when Kevin takes Galen to day care and the two leave before the girls need to get up, I hear groans of "where's the dog?"—never a sunny "good morning, Mommy."

Galen's also given herself the job of welcoming the girls home from school. The girls' bus stop is at the end of our driveway, so when Galen hears the bus pull up, she runs to the door. I watch from the window as the girls drop their backpacks and themselves onto the driveway to get eye-to-eye with Galen. Lindsey pets her; Dhani tends to kiss her and let Galen put her paws on her shoulders to make like they're dancing. If the window is open I can sometimes hear Galen whine and whinny like a horse, making the high-pitched sounds she makes whenever she says hello to someone. The more she likes you, the louder and more expressive the whine, which coincides with a more full-throttled wagging of her entire backside, not merely her tail.

As I write this, Galen is about to turn four. She's as quirky as ever.

She still refuses to walk on the hardwoods or enter the kitchen. She still slinks about the house as though she is guilty of something, but of what we know not. And when she's not in her crate, she lies on the living room floor with her head tucked underneath the couch. She's also quite mellow—people who meet her always comment on that and also on how well behaved she is. I'd like to say Kevin and I can take credit for her good behavior, but I think it's more her personality than anything we've done. We did teach her the basics—sit, lie down, come—but that's been the extent of our training. That she can walk without a leash and hang out in our friends' unfenced backyards without our fear of her running away has less to do with training than a complete lack of wanderlust on her part. I've often said that we couldn't lose Galen if we tried—she rarely lets us out of her sight. In that way she is also like Gryffin, though I think he kept us in sight to protect us; she does it so that we can protect her.

Four years after Gryffin's sudden death, I'm amazed at how often I think about him, how often Kevin and I still comment to each other about him. It's as though having Galen in our family keeps Gryffin's memory from growing old. I especially miss Gryffin when I want to take a walk and our little homebody won't walk with me. She also won't play ball with me. Any activity Galen considers play she reserves for Kevin. I can throw her favorite purple ball, and she will stand idly and watch it roll by. There have been times she and Kevin were playing in the yard when I came out, grabbed the ball, and threw it, only to watch Galen refuse to fetch it. And it's clearly a choice she makes because when Kevin picks up the ball, the game's back on. Initially I was offended at Galen's dissing of me, but I've come to accept it as just another of her quirks. And of course, the bright side is she never pesters me to play with her.

Rather, Galen is entirely a daddy's girl. When she's got excess energy to expend, she stalks Kevin around the house, taps him repeatedly on the leg with her paw, and stares him down; she's very persistent. On many a Sunday morning, as he's sitting in his favorite chair with a cup of coffee and the *New York Times*, Galen will try his patience so much that it's not unusual for me to hear him say, "Okay, dog, you win," and then see her prancing behind him as he heads to the laundry room to put on sneakers. "You chose her," I will often remind him.

"She's still shaking," I heard Dhani say. I was in the kitchen preparing dinner. I walked over to the landing and rested my open palm against Galen's side. She was trembling—and shedding. A vet to whom I'd taken Gryffin told me that dogs shed when they're nervous or stressed. I'd been petting Gryffin while he stood on the examination table and his fur was flying, some in clumps. Now Galen's was doing the same.

Lindsey leaned forward and kissed Galen's snout. "Galen's becoming Gryffin," she said. In many ways Galen was. Kevin and I liked to draw contrasts between the two dogs, but in their physical characteristics, save for their coloring, and in their basic temperament they are quite similar. We often wonder whether we have shaped their personalities: How much of who Galen is and who Gryffin was is due to nature, and how much is nurture? It's a hard enough question to answer with human kids, let alone canine ones.

Looking at my three girls crowded together on the small landing, the humans giggling, the canine shaking, the thunder cracking every minute or so, I couldn't help but smile. Dhani and Lindsey had each been in her own room, doing her own thing, but they dropped everything to comfort their scared pooch. Watching the scene before me, I thought of a quote I came across while reporting this book: "Dogs are not our whole life, but they make our lives whole." Amen.

Appendix I
Rescue 101: Tips for finding a reputable rescue

Rescue organizations work tirelessly to find good homes for the homeless dogs and cats in their care. Unfortunately, not all rescues are reputable. The following guidelines, courtesy of Libby Williams, can help you determine whether you are dealing with a legitimate rescue group. Among the signs you may be dealing with a less-than-reputable rescue are:

- Cash-only transactions coupled with on-the-spot adoptions
- High volume of puppies for adoption
- High volume of purebred or "designer breed" puppies
- Charging more for purebreds than mixes
- No health records and, if crossing state lines, no inter-state health certificates
- No health guarantee for the animal, even for 48–72 hours
- No actual persons' names or phone numbers listed on rescue websites or Petfinder pages
- Delivers dogs to adopters in public places, like parking lots and parks or homes of friends
- Uses different names (aliases) to sell/adopt dogs
- Uses different phone numbers to avoid detection
- Switches towns or locations, especially if the towns are in close proximity to one another or in the same region

Interested in starting a rescue or ensuring yours is utilizing best practices? *Road to Rescue: Dog Rescue Best Practices Manual* by Kyla Duffy is a worthwhile resource. The manual is available at <u>www.upforpups.org</u>.

Appendix II
Pay It Forward

The programs profiled in *Dogland* are not-for-profits that survive and thrive on donations.

Animal League of Gaston County
Low-Cost Spay/Neuter Clinic
www.gastonspayneuter.com
972 E. Franklin Blvd.
Gastonia, NC 28054

Blount County Animal Center
www.blounttn.org/animal
233 Currie Avenue
Maryville, TN 37803

Coalition to Unchain Dogs
www.unchaindogs.net

Companion Animal Initiative of Tennessee
The University of Tennessee
College of Veterinary Medicine
www.vet.utk.edu/cait

Dog Days of Charlotte
www.dogdaysofcharlotte.org

First Coast No More Homeless Pets
www.fcnmhp.org
6817 Norwood Avenue
Jacksonville, FL 32208

Homeless Pet Clubs
www.homelesspetclubs.org

Libby Williams/Pet Watch NJ
www.pwnj.org

Massachusetts Animal Coalition
www.massanimalcoalition.com

One Step Closer Animal Rescue (OSCAR)
www.oscaranimalrescue.org

Pets for Life
Humane Society of the United States
www.humanesociety.org/about/departments/pets-for-life

Solutions to Pet Overpopulation
www.shelteroverpopulation.org

Spay FIRST!
www.spayfirst.org

St. Hubert's Animal Welfare Center
www.sthuberts.org
575 Woodland Avenue
Madison, NJ 07940

Stokes County Humane Society
www.stokescountyhumanesociety.com

Acknowledgments

I would like to thank all the people who welcomed me into their homes, permitted me into their shelters, talked with me on the telephone, and otherwise offered up their time and expertise to educate me on the work they are doing to seek solutions to a crisis that need not be: In the United States, we need not euthanize healthy, adoptable dogs in our nation's shelters.

A special thank you to Shannon Johnstone, who graciously permitted me to use a photograph from her *Landfill Dog* series on *Dogland's* cover. Please visit www.landfilldogs.com to see more of her important and compelling photography and to donate to organizations that better the lives of dogs and cats living at the Wake County Animal Center.

I would also be remiss if I did not thank the people whose support and whose faith in my ability to tell this story kept me reporting and writing when I could easily have put down my pen, shut down my laptop.

Jane Calfee, whom I've never met in person, but whom I believe I can call "friend." Jane contacted me early in my reporting, and while I never did figure out who put her in touch with me, I'm thankful we connected. From our first conversation about Southerners and their dogs, Jane affirmed for me that I had a story that needed to be told.

Daphne Bargman, Shari Bell, and Lisa Satterfield—three wonderful journalists (and amazing women)—whose feedback and suggestions always reflected their storytelling expertise, and whose belief in my ability to write this book was often stronger than my own.

Midge Raymond and John Yunker, co-founders of Ashland Creek Press, who took a chance on a first-time author because they believed in the message I was peddling.

Ashley Shelby—journalist, editor, author—whose insider knowledge of the publishing industry and whose editorial acumen helped me turn my reporting into a story worthy of publication.

Karen Irlando—my mom—for packing school lunches, chauffeuring her granddaughters to and from daily dance classes, and helping to keep my household running smoothly when I was on one of my many out-of-town reporting trips.

Lindsey and Dhani, who always believed their mom's book would be published.

And to Kevin, I thank you for everything, including accepting a quirky little gray puppy into our lives before you were ready.

About the Author

Jacki Skole is a journalist and adjunct professor of communication. She launched her journalism career at CNN, where she was part of a team that produced several award-winning documentaries. Jacki has also produced series and specials for *Animal Planet* and *HGTV*. Following the birth of her first child, Jacki took a hiatus from doing journalism and began teaching it at La Salle University. She's since taught several writing and media-related courses at Rider University and Raritan Valley Community College.

Jacki and her husband live in New Jersey with their three daughters— two human, one canine. Perhaps not surprisingly, it is the canine daughter who served as the inspiration for *Dogland*.

About the Dogs

Gryffin, our first child. I find it amazing that nary a day goes by that I don't think about him—still.

Galen, the quirkiest little girl. She is submissive, she is stubborn, and she has my family wrapped around her little gray paw.

Loki, a sweeter boy you will never meet. One moment he is Tigger—bursting with energy. The next, he is curled beside you on the couch, head and paw resting on your chest.

Ice Frosting, *Dogland*'s cover dog. The two-year-old male pit bull spent thirty-one days in the Wake County, North Carolina, animal shelter before being pulled by a Pennsylvania-based animal rescue. Two weeks into his impoundment, Shannon Johnstone photographed Ice Frosting for her *Landfill Dogs* series.

Ashland Creek Press is an independent publisher of books with a world view. Our mission is to publish a range of books that foster an appreciation for worlds outside our own, for nature and the animal kingdom, for the creative process, and for the ways in which we all connect. To keep up-to-date on new and forthcoming works, subscribe to our free newsletter by visiting www.AshlandCreekPress.com.

CPSIA information can be obtained
at www.ICGtesting.com
Printed in the USA
FSOW01n0843051115
12960FS